Essentials of Psy

Everything you need to know to administer, sc

MW00584237

I'd like to order the following *Essentials of Psychological Assessment:*

- ❏ WAIS®-IV Assessment (w/CD-ROM) / 978-0-471-73846-6 • $48.95
- ❏ WJ III™ Cognitive Abilities Assessment, Second Edition / 978-0-470-56664-0 • $38.95
- ❏ Cross-Battery Assessment, Second Edition (w/CD-ROM) / 978-0-471-75771-9 • $48.95
- ❏ Nonverbal Assessment / 978-0-471-38318-5 • $38.95
- ❏ PAI® Assessment / 978-0-471-08463-1 • $38.95
- ❏ CAS Assessment / 978-0-471-29015-5 • $38.95
- ❏ MMPI®-2 Assessment, Second Edition / 978-0-470-92323-8 • $38.95
- ❏ Myers-Briggs Type Indicator® Assessment, Second Edition / 978-0-470-34390-6 • $38.95
- ❏ Rorschach® Assessment / 978-0-471-33146-9 • $38.95
- ❏ Millon™ Inventories Assessment, Third Edition / 978-0-470-16862-2 • $38.95
- ❏ TAT and Other Storytelling Assessments, Second Edition / 978-0-470-28192-5 • $38.95
- ❏ MMPI-A™ Assessment / 978-0-471-39815-8 • $38.95
- ❏ NEPSY®-II Assessment / 978-0-470-43691-2 • $38.95
- ❏ Neuropsychological Assessment, Second Edition / 978-0-470-43747-6 • $38.95
- ❏ WJ III™ Tests of Achievement Assessment / 978-0-471-33059-2 • $38.95
- ❏ Evidence-Based Academic Interventions / 978-0-470-20632-4 • $38.95
- ❏ WRAML2 and TOMAL-2 Assessment / 978-0-470-17911-6 • $38.95
- ❏ WMS®-IV Assessment / 978-0-470-62196-7 • $38.95
- ❏ Behavioral Assessment / 978-0-471-35367-6 • $38.95
- ❏ Forensic Psychological Assessment, Second Edition / 978-0-470-55168-4 • $38.95
- ❏ Bayley Scales of Infant Development II Assessment / 978-0-471-32651-9 • $38.95
- ❏ Career Interest Assessment / 978-0-471-35365-2 • $38.95
- ❏ WPPSI™-III Assessment / 978-0-471-28895-4 • $38.95
- ❏ 16PF® Assessment / 978-0-471-23424-1 • $38.95
- ❏ Assessment Report Writing / 978-0-471-39487-7 • $38.95
- ❏ Stanford-Binet Intelligence Scales (SB5) Assessment / 978-0-471-22404-4 • $38.95
- ❏ WISC®-IV Assessment, Second Edition (w/CD-ROM) / 978-0-470-18915-3 • $48.95
- ❏ KABC-II Assessment / 978-0-471-66733-9 • $38.95
- ❏ WIAT®-III and KTEA-II Assessment (w/CD-ROM) / 978-0-470-55169-1 • $48.95
- ❏ Processing Assessment / 978-0-471-71925-0 • $38.95
- ❏ School Neuropsychological Assessment / 978-0-471-78372-5 • $38.95
- ❏ Cognitive Assessment with KAIT & Other Kaufman Measures / 978-0-471-38317-8 • $38.95
- ❏ Assessment with Brief Intelligence Tests / 978-0-471-26412-5 • $38.95
- ❏ Creativity Assessment / 978-0-470-13742-0 • $38.95
- ❏ WNV™ Assessment / 978-0-470-28467-4 • $38.95
- ❏ DAS-II® Assessment (w/CD-ROM) / 978-0-470-22520-2 • $48.95
- ❏ Executive Function Assessment (w/CD-ROM) / 978-0-470-42202-1 • $48.95
- ❏ Conners Behavior Assessments™ / 978-0-470-34633-4 • $38.95
- ❏ Temperament Assessment / 978-0-470-44447-4 • $38.95
- ❏ Response to Intervention / 978-0-470-56663-3 • $38.95
- ❏ Specific Learning Disability Identification / 978-0-470-58760-7 • $38.95
- ❏ IDEA for Assessment Professionals (w/CD-ROM) / 978-0-470-87392-2 • $48.95
- ❏ Dyslexia Assessment and Intervention / 978-0-470-92760-1 • $38.95
- ❏ Autism Spectrum Disorders Evaluation and Assessment / 978-0-470-62194-3 • $38.95

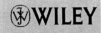

Essentials

of **Psychological Assessment** Series

ORDER FORM

Please send this order form with your payment (credit card or check) to:
John Wiley & Sons, Attn: J. Knott, 111 River Street, Hoboken, NJ 07030-5774

QUANTITY	TITLE	ISBN	PRICE
_____	_____	_____	_____
_____	_____	_____	_____
_____	_____	_____	_____
_____	_____	_____	_____
_____	_____	_____	_____

Shipping Charges:	**Surface**	**2-Day**	**1-Day**
First item	$5.00	$10.50	$17.50
Each additional item	$3.00	$3.00	$4.00

For orders greater than 15 items,
please contact Customer Care at 1-877-762-2974.

ORDER AMOUNT _____

SHIPPING CHARGES _____

SALES TAX _____

TOTAL ENCLOSED _____

NAME_____

AFFILIATION_____

ADDRESS_____

CITY/STATE/ZIP _____

TELEPHONE _____

EMAIL_____

❏ Please add me to your e-mailing list

PAYMENT METHOD:

❏ Check/Money Order   ❏ Visa   ❏ Mastercard   ❏ AmEx

Card Number _____ Exp. Date _____

Cardholder Name *(Please print)* _____

Signature _____

*Make checks payable to **John Wiley & Sons**. Credit card orders invalid if not signed.*
All orders subject to credit approval. • Prices subject to change.

To order by phone, call toll free 1-877-762-2974
To order online: www.wiley.com/essentials

Essentials of PAI® Assessment

Essentials of Psychological Assessment Series

Series Editors, Alan S. Kaufman and Nadeen L. Kaufman

Essentials

of PAI® Assessment

Leslie C. Morey

 John Wiley & Sons, Inc.

Library of Congress Cataloging-in-Publication Data

Morey, Leslie Charles, 1956–
    Essentials of PAI assessment / Leslie C. Morey.
      p. cm. — (Essentials of psychological assessment series)
    Includes bibliographical references and index.
    ISBN 978-0-471-08463-1 (pbk)
      1. Personality Assessment Inventory.   I. Title.   II. Series.

RC473.P56 M667 2003
155.2'8—dc21

                                                    2002032434

Dedicated to my mother,
for providing that European influence
that helped add an intuitive spark to empiricism.

CONTENTS

SERIES PREFACE

I n the *Essentials of Psychological Assessment* series, we have attempted to provide the reader with books that will deliver key practical information in the most efficient and accessible style. The series features instruments in a variety of domains, such as cognition, personality, education, and neuropsychology. For the experienced clinician, books in the series will offer a concise, yet thorough way to master utilization of the continuously evolving supply of new and revised instruments, as well as a convenient method for keeping up to date on the tried-and-true measures. The novice will find here a prioritized assembly of all the information and techniques that must be at one's fingertips to begin the complicated process of individual psychological diagnosis.

Wherever feasible, visual shortcuts to highlight key points are utilized alongside systematic, step-by-step guidelines. Chapters are focused and succinct. Topics are targeted for an easy understanding of the essentials of administration, scoring, interpretation, and clinical application. Theory and research are continually woven into the fabric of each book, but always to enhance clinical inference, never to sidetrack or overwhelm. We have long been advocates of "intelligent" testing—the notion that a profile of test scores is meaningless unless it is brought to life by the clinical observations and astute detective work of knowledgeable examiners. Test profiles must be used to make a difference in the child's or adult's life, or why bother to test? We want this series to help our readers become the best intelligent testers they can be.

In *Essentials of PAI® Assessment,* Dr. Leslie Morey presents a basic foundation for the use and interpretation of the test that he developed and first published in 1991. The text also provides an update on the developing body of research on the PAI that can help experienced users of the instrument refine their interpretive strategies. The book reflects an integration of the theoretical foundation of the test with the research database that has evolved since its introduction, as well as the clinical insights gained by the author in his applied use of the instrument for nearly 15 years. The goal of the volume is to provide the reader with the fundamentals of administration and interpretation for the PAI while also offering the more advanced user some tips for combining the different types of information provided by the test.

Alan S. Kaufman, PhD, and Nadeen L. Kaufman, EdD, Series Editors
Yale University School of Medicine

Essentials of PAI® Assessment

One

The *Personality Assessment Inventory* (PAI; Morey, 1991) is a self-administered, objective test of personality and psychopathology designed to provide information on critical client variables in professional settings. The PAI consists of four sets of scales: 4 validity scales, 11 clinical scales covering major categories of pathology corresponding to the *Diagnostic and Statistical Manual of Mental Disorders (DSM)* nosology, 5 treatment scales measuring constructs related to treatment and case management, and 2 interpersonal scales. When the PAI was first introduced, it was described as "a substantial improvement from a psychometric perspective over the existing standard in the area" (Helmes, 1993, p. 417) and as "one of the most exciting new personality tests" (Schlosser, 1992, p. 12). Since this introduction, it has gained rapidly in popularity as a clinical and research tool. In a recent survey, Piotrowski and Belter (1999) reported that the PAI was ranked fourth by directors of internship training in terms of personality tests employed by interns. Similarly, Belter and Piotrowski (2001) found that the PAI ranked fourth in terms of objective tests in graduate testing course work in training programs approved by the American Psychological Association (APA), and Boccaccini and Brodsky (1999) reported that the PAI was among the most widely used measures relied upon in legal cases involving emotional injury.

HISTORY AND DEVELOPMENT

The development of the PAI was prompted by the limited number of alternative instruments that adhered to the tenets of the construct validation framework while providing measures of clinically important constructs. Developed between the years 1987 and 1991, the PAI sought to incorporate major theoretical and empirical knowledge surrounding important constructs and to use this knowledge as a conceptual road map in the development of a self-report instrument. The PAI instrument and test manual were published in 1991 by Psychological Assessment Resources (PAR), along with personal computer-based software that would score and provide an interpretive report for the instrument. As research on the instrument continued to accumulate, the interpretive software continued to be revised, with a major recent revision (Morey, 2000) representing an interactive program that would allow examiners to explore various aspects of the test results in real time. In 1997, a screening version of the PAI was published, entitled the *Personality Assessment Screener* (PAS; Morey, 1997). The PAS provided a screening mechanism for users to make triage decisions about the need to administer the full PAI, and its use in a computerized assessment allowed a certain measure of adaptive testing to occur that could facilitate the efficiency of testing.

FOUNDATIONS OF THE PAI: THEORY AND RESEARCH

The first step involved in using the PAI effectively is to understand how the instrument was developed and why it has the characteristics that it has. The development of the PAI was based upon a construct validation framework that emphasized a rational as well as quantitative method of scale development. This framework, guided by the model of construct validation described in classic works by Cronbach and Meehl (1955), Loevinger (1957), and Jackson (1971), placed a strong emphasis on a theoretically informed approach to the development and selection of items as well as on the assessment of their stability and correlates.

The constructs assessed by the PAI were selected on the basis of two criteria: the stability of their importance within the conceptualization and nosology of mental disorder and their significance in contemporary clinical practice. These criteria were assessed through a review of the historical and contemporary literature and eventually resulted in the inclusion of 18 substantive construct scales supplemented by four validity scales. These scales are briefly summarized in Rapid Reference 1.1. In generating items for these syndromes, the literature on each construct was examined to identify the components that were most central to the definition of the concept, and items were written with the goal of providing an assessment of these components. The theoretical articulation of the constructs to be measured was assumed to

≡ *Rapid Reference 1.1*

PAI Full Scales and Abbreviations

Validity Scales

Inconsistency (ICN): Determines whether the client is answering consistently throughout the inventory. Each pair consists of highly (positively or negatively) correlated items.

Infrequency (INF): Determines whether the client is responding carelessly, randomly, or idiosyncratically. Items are neutral with respect to psychopathology and have extremely high or low endorsement rates.

Negative Impression (NIM): Suggests an exaggerated unfavorable impression or malingering.

Positive Impression (PIM): Suggests the presentation of a very favorable impression or reluctance to admit minor flaws.

Clinical Scales

Somatic Complaints (SOM): Focuses on preoccupation with health matters and somatic complaints associated with somatization or conversion disorders.

Anxiety (ANX): Focuses on phenomenology and observable signs of anxiety, with an emphasis on assessment across different response modalities.

Anxiety-Related Disorders (ARD): Focuses on symptoms and behaviors related to specific anxiety disorders—particularly phobias, traumatic stress, and obsessive-compulsive symptoms.

Depression (DEP): Focuses on symptoms and phenomenology of depressive disorders.

Mania (MAN): Focuses on affective, cognitive, and behavioral symptoms of mania and hypomania.

Paranoia (PAR): Focuses on symptoms of paranoid disorders and on more enduring characteristics of the paranoid personality.

Schizophrenia (SCZ): Focuses on symptoms relevant to the broad spectrum of schizophrenic disorders.

Borderline Features (BOR): Focuses on attributes indicative of a borderline level of personality functioning, including unstable and fluctuating interpersonal relations, impulsivity, affective lability and instability, and uncontrolled anger.

Antisocial Features (ANT): Focuses on history of illegal acts and authority problems, egocentrism, lack of empathy and loyalty, instability, and excitement-seeking.

(continued)

Alcohol Problems (ALC): Focuses on problematic consequences of alcohol use and features of alcohol dependence.

Drug Problems (DRG): Focuses on problematic consequences of drug use (both prescription and illicit) and features of drug dependence.

Treatment Scales

Aggression (AGG): Focuses on characteristics and attitudes related to anger, assertiveness, hostility, and aggression.

Suicidal Ideation (SUI): Focuses on suicidal ideation, ranging from hopelessness to thoughts and plans for the suicidal act.

Stress (STR): Measures the impact of recent stressors in major life areas.

Nonsupport (NON): Measures a lack of perceived social support, considering both the level and quality of available support.

Treatment Rejection (RXR): Focuses on attributes and attitudes indicating a lack of interest and motivation in making personal changes of a psychological or emotional nature.

Interpersonal Scales

Dominance (DOM): Assesses the extent to which a person is controlling and independent in personal relationships. This scale reflects a bipolar dimension, with a dominant style at the high end and a submissive style at the low end.

Warmth (WRM): Assesses the extent to which a person is interested in supportive and empathic personal relationships. This scale reflects a bipolar dimension, with a warm, outgoing style at the high end and a cold, rejecting style at the low end.

be critical because this articulation had to serve as a guide to the content of information sampled and to the subsequent assessment of content validity. To understand how the PAI operates, it is important to distinguish between this approach and one that is more purely empirical, such as a criterion-keying approach or a factor analytic approach to item selection. From this perspective, the validation of an instrument is a complex process that cannot be reduced to a single coefficient or a single discrimination. Assessment techniques instead must be evaluated within the context of a theoretically informed network that makes explicit hypotheses about interrelationships among indicators of various constructs. The key point to understand is that on instruments developed according to these principles, the scales are designed to measure particular constructs that are represented by the names of the individual scales. This structure contrasts with that of instruments in which scale names are task descriptions (e.g., the subscales on the Wechsler intelligence scales), factor names (e.g., the 16 Personality Factor Questionnaire [16PF]), or even numerals (e.g., the Minnesota Multiphasic Personality Inventory [MMPI]).

In the development of the PAI, both the conceptual nature and empirical adequacy of the items played an important role in their inclusion in the final version of the inventory. The goal was to include items that struck a balance between different desirable item parameters, including content coverage as well as empirical characteristics, so that the scales could be useful across a number of different applications. Of paramount importance in the development of the test was the assumption that no single quantitative item parameter should be used as the sole criterion for item selection. An overreliance on a single parameter in item selection typically leads to a scale with one desirable psychometric property and numerous undesirable ones. Thus, the construct validation approach intends to avoid the pitfalls associated with so-called naive empiricism in test construction. (See Rapid Reference 1.2.)

≡ Rapid Reference 1.2

Personality Assessment Inventory (PAI)

Author: Leslie C. Morey

Publication date: 1991

Copyright holder: Psychological Assessment Resources

What the test measures: Mental health and personality functioning

Age range: 18 years and above

Administration time: 50–60 minutes

Qualifications of examiners: Graduate-level training in psychodiagnostic assessment. Purchase of PAI materials requires (a) an advanced professional degree that provides appropriate training in the administration and interpretation of psychological tests or (b) license or certification from an agency that requires appropriate training and experience in the ethical and competent use of psychological tests.

Publisher: Psychological Assessment Resources (PAR)
16204 N. Florida Avenue
Lutz, FL 33549
(800) 331-8378

There are two facets of construct validity that played a particularly important role in the development of the PAI: *content validity* and *discriminant validity*. To understand the conceptual rationale for the instrument, it is worth reviewing the importance of these two elements of construct validity and their implications for the interpretation of a psychological test. The following paragraphs summarize the influence of these aspects upon the development of the PAI.

Content Validity

The content validity of a measure involves the adequacy of sampling of content across the construct being measured. This concept is sometimes confused with *face validity,* which refers to whether the instrument appears to be measuring what it is intended to measure, particularly as it appears to a lay audience. These terms are not synonymous; a test for depression that consists of a single item such as *I am unhappy* may appear to be highly related to depression (i.e., high face validity) but provides a very narrow sampling of the content domain of depression (i.e., low content validity). The construction of the PAI sought to develop scales that provided a balanced sampling of the most important elements of the constructs being measured. This content coverage was designed to include both a consideration of breadth as well as depth of the construct. The *breadth* of content coverage refers to the diversity of elements subsumed within a construct. For example, in measuring depression it is important to inquire about physiological and cognitive signs of depression as well as features of affect. Any depression scale that focuses exclusively on one of these elements at the expense of the others will have limited content validity, with limited coverage of the breadth of the depression construct. The PAI sought to ensure breadth of content coverage through the use of subscales representing the major elements of the measured constructs, as indicated by the theoretical and empirical literature on the construct. Thus, in interpreting the PAI scales and their structural composition, it is useful to consult the relevant literature that provides the basis for this structure, such as the importance of cognitive features in depression, the distinction between positive and negative symptoms of schizophrenia, or the differential contribution of behavior and personality in the diagnosis of antisocial personality disorder. Useful references for these structures are provided in the *Professional*

Manual (Morey, 1991) and in the *Interpretive Guide* (Morey, 1996).

The *depth* of content coverage refers to the need to sample phenomenology across the range of severity of a particular element of a construct. To assure adequate depth of coverage, the scales were designed to include items that addressed the full range of severity of

the construct, including both its milder and its most severe forms. One aspect of the instrument that resulted from this consideration was the item response scaling; the test items are answered on a four-alternative scale, with the anchors *totally false, slightly true, mainly true,* and *very true.* Each response is weighted according to the intensity of the feature that the different alternatives represent; thus, a client who answers *very true* to the item *Sometimes I think I'm worthless* adds 3 points to his or her raw score on the Depression scale, whereas a client who responds *slightly true* to the same item adds only 1 point. As a result, each item can capture differences in the severity of the manifestation of a feature of a particular disorder. The use of this four-alternative scaling is further justified psychometrically in that it allows a scale to capture more true variance per item, meaning that even scales of modest length can achieve satisfactory reliability. It is also justified clinically because sometimes even a *slightly true* response to some constructs (such as suicidal ideation) may merit clinical attention. Furthermore, clients themselves often express dissatisfaction with forced-choice alternatives, expressing the belief that the true state of affairs lies somewhere in the middle when two extremes are presented.

In addition to differences in depth of severity reflected in response options, the items themselves were constructed to tap different levels of severity in the manifestation of a problem. For example, cognitive elements of depression can vary in severity from mild pessimism to severe feelings of hopelessness, helplessness, and despair. Through examining the item characteristic curves of potential items, the final items were selected to provide information across the full range of construct severity. The nature of the severity continuum varies across the constructs. For example, for the Suicidal Ideation (SUI) scale, this continuum involves the imminence of the suicidal threat. Thus, items on this scale vary from vague and ill-articulated thoughts about suicide to immediate plans for self-harm.

Discriminant Validity

A test is said to have *discriminant validity* if it provides a measure of a construct that is specific to that construct; in other words, the measurement is free from the influence of other constructs. Although discriminant validity has been long recognized as an important facet of construct validity, it traditionally has not played a major role in the construction of psychological tests. This state of affairs is unfortunate because discriminant validity represents one of the largest challenges in the assessment of psychological constructs.

There are a variety of threats to validity in which discriminability plays a vital role. One such area of great importance involves *test bias*. Simply put, a test that is intended to measure a psychological construct should not be measuring a demographic variable, such as gender, age, or race. This does not mean that items on psychological tests should never be correlated with age, or gender, or race. However, the magnitude of any such correlations should not exceed the theoretical overlap of the demographic feature with the construct. For example, nearly every indicator of antisocial behavior suggests that it is more common in men than in women; thus, it would be expected that an assessment of antisocial behavior would yield average scores for men that are higher than those for women. However, the instrument should demonstrate a considerably greater correlation with other indicators of antisocial behavior than it does with gender; otherwise, it may be measuring gender rather than measuring the construct it was designed to assess.

In the PAI, a number of steps were taken to minimize the likelihood of test bias. First, every item on the PAI was reviewed by a bias panel (consisting of lay and professional individuals, both men and women, of diverse racial and ethnic backgrounds) to identify items that—although they were written to identify emotional or behavioral problems—might instead reflect other factors, such as sociocultural background. This panel represented a conceptually based approach to this particular aspect of discriminant validity. A second, empirical strategy for eliminating test bias involved the examination of item psychometric properties as a function of demography. The intent of this approach was to eliminate items that had different meanings for different demographic groups; for example, if an item inquiring about crying seemed to be related to other indicators of depression in women but not in men, then that item was eliminated because interpretation of the item would vary as a function of gender. Note that this strategy will not eliminate mean demographic differences in scale scores; for example, an item inquiring about stealing may have a similar meaning for identifying antisocial personality for both men and women yet still be more common among men. In this example, the resulting gender difference is not a function of test bias; rather, it is an accurate reflection of gender differences in the disorder. Demographic differences are not necessarily a sign of bias; conversely, a test with no such differences can nevertheless be biased.

The issue of test bias is one that is particularly salient in light of past abuses of testing and current legislation designed to prevent such abuses. However, such bias is just one form of potential problems with discriminant validity. It is particularly common in the field of clinical assessment to find that a measure that supposedly measures one construct (e.g., anxiety or schizophrenia) is in fact highly related to many constructs. It is this tendency that makes many instruments difficult to interpret. How does the clinician evaluate an elevated score on a scale measuring schizophrenia if that scale is also a measure of alienation, indecisiveness, family problems, and depression? At each stage of the development of the PAI, items were selected that had maximal associations with indicators of the pertinent construct and minimal associations with the other constructs measured by the test. By emphasizing the importance of both convergent and discriminant validity in selecting items for inclusion on the PAI, the interpretation of the resulting scales is straightforward because they are relatively pure measures of the constructs in question.

ESSENTIAL REFERENCES FOR THE PAI

The *Personality Assessment Inventory Professional Manual* (Morey, 1991) is the essential technical reference for the instrument because it contains detailed information about the

DON'T FORGET

The PAI does not use separate norms for men and women. Instead, items were selected to have the same meaning regardless of gender. Average scores for men and women are primarily different on ANT and ALC, on which men tend to score roughly 5 *t* points higher than do women.

test's development and basic psychometric information. The most comprehensive guide to interpretation of the test is the *Interpretive Guide to the Personality Assessment Inventory* (Morey, 1996), which summarizes the interpretive implications of research conducted in the initial years of the test's publication. A separate manual, *Personality Assessment Screener: Professional Manual* (Morey, 1997), is provided for a screening instrument (described in more detail in chapter 9) derived from a small subset of PAI items that can be useful for a number of applications, either as a stand-alone instrument or in combination with the full PAI. Finally, a number of review articles and book chapters are helpful for focused topics, such as forensic applications (Edens, Cruise, & Buffington, & Vollum, 2001; Morey & Quigley, 2002) or treatment planning (Morey, 1999).

🐾 TEST YOURSELF 🐾

1. **The PAI was developed using**
   (a) contrasted empirical groups.
   (b) orthogonal factor analysis.
   (c) construct validation approach.
   (d) forced-choice methods.
2. **The PAI was first developed and published in the late 1970s.** True or False?
3. **The PAI attempted to assure content validity by**
   (a) providing balanced coverage of all major facets of constructs.
   (b) including items that lay respondents could recognize as important.
   (c) including items that sampled experiences at different ranges of severity.
   (d) both a and c.
4. **Procedures to minimize test bias in the PAI included**
   (a) equating item means across different demographic groups.
   (b) having a bias panel review all items.
   (c) using separate norms for men and women.
   (d) using only items with subtle content meaning.
5. **The scale names have no particular significance on the PAI, and only scale number should be used.** True or False?
6. **All PAI items involve choosing between two response alternatives.** True or False?

7. At what point were PAI subscales developed?

   (a) during the conceptual design of the test

   (b) by factor analyses of the final item pool

   (c) in clinical judgment studies after the test was published

8. What empirical criterion was used to select PAI items?

Answers: 1. c; 2. False; 3. d; 4. b; 5. False; 6. False; 7. a; 8. There were several, and no single criterion was emphasized.

Two

ADMINISTRATION

The PAI was developed for use with adults who are 18 or older. In some instances, the test can be informative with older adolescents, particularly those who are no longer in school or who live outside the parental home. However, in such instances, caution in interpretation is particularly warranted because the resulting scores will be of limited comparability to the adult scale norms. Readers should consult the PAI manual to obtain a clear understanding of the age influences on particular scores, which contains age correlates for scales as well as norms for specific groups (e.g., college students) that might provide greater comparability.

The test can be administered individually, in groups using a paper-and-pencil questionnaire form, or on a personal computer using software available from the publisher. Generally, research has found minimal differences between these two methods of questionnaire administration (Finger & Ones, 1999), and under normal circumstances the results should be considered interchangeable. Under either method, administration time is typically 1 hour or less. As a self-report instrument, the PAI does not require special instructions for administration because the directions presented to the respondent on the test form are sufficient to permit most clients to complete the test accurately. However, one important aspect of the testing situation involves the development and maintenance of rapport between the clinician and the examinee, and it is important to review the standard administration situation in light of this issue.

ESTABLISHING RAPPORT

Because the PAI is a self-report instrument whose success hinges upon its ability to accurately capture the experiences of the respondent, it is critical that the clinician and the respondent form an alliance to work toward meeting the purposes of the assessment. To the extent that this alliance can be established prior to the completion of the PAI, the likelihood of a candid and accurate representation of the respondent's concerns and behaviors will be greatly enhanced. One particularly useful approach to facilitating this alliance is the notion of therapeutic assessment, which views the assessment as a method of intervention rather than as a specific means of information gathering (Finn & Tonsager, 1997; Fischer, 1994). This approach attempts to involve clients as integral collaborators in the assessment process rather than as passive participants. One central component of the approach involves encouraging clients to generate their own, individualized assessment goals. Clients thus become actively involved in the therapeutic process by defining questions about themselves and the concerns that they would like the assessment to address, thereby moving toward considering the assessment as something that is being done for them rather than to them.

INFORMED CONSENT

The importance of candid responding in the assessment situation is not limited to the respondent; part of the formation of the alliance depends on an accurate disclosure by the clinician of the nature and purpose of the assessment. Some of this disclosure involves informing the client about the parameters of the assessment itself, whereas other aspects involve the manner in which the information obtained will be used. With respect to the former, the clinician should explain the components of the assessment, the time and location of testing and subsequent feedback, the estimated time required to complete the assessment, and any arrangements concerning billing or fees. With respect to the latter aspects of testing, clients should be told how information obtained from the test will be used, the circumstances under which such information would be shared with others, and who the recipient of such information would be. If the assessment is being conducted on behalf of a third party (such as is often encountered in legal cases), the nature of this relationship should be explained to the client. In forensic applications of the PAI, it is particularly important for clinicians to describe their obligations to respondents with respect to the confidentiality and privileged nature of any results and to explain the limits of such confidentiality.

INTRODUCING THE PAI

As part of the overview of the procedures involved in the assessment, the respondent should be given some information about the PAI. It is useful to convey that the test is used for a variety of different purposes and is used in many different countries; this framing of the multiple uses of the test may reduce clients' resistance to some questions that they believe are not applicable to themselves. As part of the description, it should be mentioned that some questions deal with some sensitive emotional issues, whereas other questions are more aimed at understanding how their personality is similar to and different from those of other people. It should be emphasized that regardless of the application, there are no correct answers; clients should be encouraged to simply give an accurate description of their experiences so that the results can help them understand themselves better. Some mention of the standardized nature of the instrument can also help the respondent understand that their answers will be compared to those provided by people in general as well as compared to those of other people in similar circumstances (i.e., treatment settings or preemployment screenings).

ASSESSING SUITABILITY FOR SELF-REPORT ADMINISTRATION

The valid administration of the PAI assumes that the respondent is physically and emotionally capable of meeting the demands associated with completing a self-report instrument. Care should be taken in testing clients who—by the nature of their disorder—may be confused, disoriented, highly distractible, or manifesting extreme psychomotor retardation or agitation. Individuals whose cognitive abilities may be compromised by the effects of drug or alcohol intoxication or withdrawal or by disorientation stemming from neurological deficit or disease should be tested with caution; clients with the latter types of problems are easily fatigued, and

DON'T FORGET

While introducing the test and obtaining informed consent, the examiner should be alert to factors that can distort test findings, such as educational background, language fluency, sensorimotor limitations, disorientation, or intoxication.

their progress should be monitored closely. Administrators should also be sensitive to physical or sensorimotor deficits, such as lack of visual acuity or motor weakness in the client's dominant hand, that might affect his or her ability to complete the test in a valid manner.

Valid completion of the PAI also requires that the respondent be able to read and understand the PAI instructions and items. Reading-level analyses of the PAI item booklet instructions and test items indicate that reading ability at the fourth-grade level is needed to complete the test. Although this reading level is elementary and compares favorably to that of other multiscale inventories (Schinka & Borum, 1993), it should be noted that years of completed education is not a reliable indicator of reading level. Typically, measured reading comprehension falls substantially below achieved level of education. In cases in which it is questionable whether the requisite fourth-grade level is met, it may be necessary to first administer a brief test of reading comprehension. When such a test is not available, a crude screening of reading ability can be accomplished by having the client read the test instructions and the first few test questions aloud to the examiner. In such instances the examiner should determine whether this information is fully understood before leaving the client alone to complete the remainder of the test.

Under exceptional circumstances, an oral administration of the test may be necessary when the client is simply incapable of reading the test booklet or marking the test answer sheet. An audiotape is commercially available from the test publisher that includes verbal renderings of the test instructions and test items read at a comfortable pace; the client indicates his or her responses on a separate answer sheet. This type of administration is preferable to an in-person reading of the same material by a live examiner because the latter situation places the test into a context of direct social communication, such as that represented by a clinical interview. Some research evidence suggests that clients may be more likely to reveal problems in self-report format than in interview presentations of similar material (Domken, Scott, & Kelly, 1994; Rush, Hiser, & Giles, 1987), particularly when clients provide verbal responses directly to the clinician. As such, use of the more impersonal audiotape may more closely parallel the original questionnaire method as it was standardized, and clients should provide their responses in written rather than oral form if at all possible. Because any of these departures from standard administration may have unforeseen effects upon the test, the resulting

CAUTION

If oral administration of the PAI is necessary, respondents should still provide answers in written form on an answer sheet rather than as verbal replies to the examiner.

scores should be interpreted with caution.

Particular caution should be exercised in testing clients whose native language is not English; for such clients, educational attainment and even apparent spoken English fluency may bear little relationship to reading level. Although PAI items were screened during construction in an effort to avoid idiomatic phrases that might limit cross-cultural applications, distortion can still result if the respondent's ability to read English is limited. A Spanish translation of the PAI is commercially available from the publisher; data gathered from this translated version indicates reasonable convergent validity with diagnostic indicators (Fantoni-Salvador & Rogers, 1997), although the internal consistency of the treatment consideration scales seemed to be lower in the Spanish-speaking sample than in the test standardization sample (Rogers, Flores, Ustad, & Sewell, 1995). There are also authorized translations of the instrument into a variety of different languages, including French, Danish, Korean, and Hebrew.

In summary, valid completion of a self-report instrument involves a complex combination of motivational, cognitive, and emotional factors. Although the PAI includes validity scales that are designed to assist in determining whether the profile validly represents client experience, clinicians must not rely solely on these scales to make such determinations. Determining that an individual is capable of responding to a self-report instrument is itself a professional decision—one that should be considered carefully in the contact with the client leading up to the actual administration of the test.

SOLICITING QUESTIONS AND GOALS

After the nature of the assessment has been discussed with the client, the examiner should encourage the client to raise any questions that he or she might have, either about the circumstances of assessment or about the procedures themselves. Every effort should be made to address these questions as completely as possible, although for some types of questions it might be preferable to defer answers until testing has been completed or until the testing feedback is given. As part of this phase of the administration, the model of therapeutic assessment (e.g., Finn, 1996) can be adapted to encourage the client to formulate his or her own goals for information to be obtained from the assessment. This approach is centered around questions that

DON'T FORGET

Soliciting goals for the assessment from the client can facilitate a positive attitude toward test taking and result in a more candid and accurate self-description.

originate in the client's subjective experience. As the examiner gains an understanding of these issues, he or she and the client work together to develop an individualized set of assessment questions that the client wishes to address as part of the evaluation process. Part of the framing process is to narrow questions that are posed so that they can serve as guides to the assessment processes. Thus, part of the goal of soliciting client questions is to have client and examiner work together to formulate expectations for the assessment. This participation can make the assessment itself a therapeutic process that can confirm, challenge, and change how clients think, act, and feel about themselves.

ADMINISTRATION CONSIDERATIONS

The standard administration of the PAI can involve either individual or group testing situations; in either situation, the testing environment should protect the confidentiality of the client's item responses. For this reason and for purposes of test security, testing should be done under the direct supervision of the examiner (e.g., the test should not be taken home to be completed), and the client should be discouraged from interacting with anyone other than the examiner during the testing session. The testing situation should provide adequate lighting, writing surface, and pencils; it should also be free from distractions such as noise or pedestrian traffic. Clients should be shown where facilities such as water fountains or toilets are available, and they also should be shown where the examiner will be situated if he or she is needed—it is recommended that the examiner be accessible but not physically present while the test is completed. If circumstances require that an audiotaped administration of the test be completed, the client should be shown how to operate the tape recorder to pause and rewind the tape as needed.

As a self-report questionnaire, most clients can complete the 344 questions within 1 hour, although clients with concentration problems or psychomotor retardation might take as long as 90 min. In some instances, clients may ask questions about the test items, such as definitions or clarifications of certain concepts. In the rare instances in which a client is unfamiliar with the definition of a word, use of a dictionary definition is advisable. More typically encountered are requests to clarify qualifiers in the test items such as *frequently* or *slightly;* here, the examiner should encourage respondents to use their own interpretation of the meaning of these qualifiers.

TEST FEEDBACK

Clinicians have an obligation to provide clients with some feedback regarding the results of the assessment; this feedback is particularly critical in clinical applications of the test. A growing number of studies have suggested that providing assessment feedback can have therapeutic effects for the client (e.g., Finn & Tonsager, 1992; Newman & Greenway, 1997). In one study that examined the PAI as part of this feedback process, Ackerman, Hilsenroth, Baity, and Blagys (2000) examined the interaction between early-treatment psychological assessment and the development of the working alliance in subsequent therapy. Results indicated that 13% of the individuals who participated in a collaborative model of therapeutic assessment terminated psychotherapy within the first 4 patient contacts, as compared to 33% of the individuals who participated in the more traditional assessment model. Additionally, participants' experience of the assessment process and the therapeutic alliance was more positive within the collaborative assessment group, and this appraisal carried into the psychotherapy sessions.

In a typical feedback session, the clinician should review the nature of the test itself (e.g., concepts such as test norms) and then address the test results. The feedback provided should focus on the assessment questions developed in the first session; this strategy places the emphasis of the session on the primary concerns of the client and also allows a more focused and circumscribed discussion. Finn (1996) recommends a set order for such discussion, beginning both with findings that are generally positive in nature and with findings that the client is most likely to acknowledge. Subsequently, questions into which clients may have less insight are discussed, but this discussion should take place only after clients have had the opportunity to elaborate on earlier findings. Efforts are made to maintain the collaborative character of the relationship developed in the first session by encouraging input from the client to verify, modify, or reject test findings. The goal of the feedback is to present recurring themes that appear in the assess-

> **DON'T FORGET**
> ....
> In presenting test feedback, it is often helpful to begin with positive aspects of the results (such as personal strengths) and with problems of which the client is already aware. This practice can facilitate later discussions of issues into which the client may have less insight.

ment data and tie these themes to the client's goals for the assessment and for treatment. The session typically ends with the client's summarizing his or her interpretation of the feedback and describing his or her subjective impressions of the session.

The nature of the assessment may necessitate some departure from this strategy; in all circumstances, sound clinical judgment should be used in determining the timing of any feedback to patients and in deciding what information will be helpful. In most instances, it is not advisable to simply let the client read an automated report. Some statements might not be applicable, the technical language might not be understood, or the language may seem too pathologized and cause undue concern. However, descriptions of high scores can be provided, using language that the patient can understand. Words such as *normal* and *abnormal* should probably be avoided, and results are better framed as being above or below what the average person reports. Scores that indicate therapeutic targets or problems should be discussed as areas to work on rather than what is wrong with the patient. The PAI profile is a fairly straightforward reflection of what the patient has reported, and in our experience patients readily recognize themselves and report little discrepancy when given feedback.

🪶 TEST YOURSELF 🪶

1. **Computer administration of the PAI is likely to yield results comparable to those from a paper-and-pencil administration.** True or False?

2. **A respondent providing verbal answers to a verbal administration of the PAI is likely to yield results comparable to those from a paper-and-pencil administration.** True or False?

3. **What is the estimated reading level of the PAI items?**

4. **Standard administration time for the PAI is**
   (a) 1 hour or less.
   (b) 2 hours.
   (c) 3 hours.
   (d) 4 hours or more.

5. **The PAI should only be administered in English because there are no authorized translations of the instrument.** True or False?

6. **Providing clients with test feedback is generally not recommended because the material is typically anxiety arousing.** True or False?

7. **When providing test feedback, it is often useful to begin with**
   (a) the most severe problem.
   (b) issues about which the client seems unaware.
   (c) apparent personal strengths or assets.

8. **When using the Spanish translation of the PAI, particular care should be taken in interpreting which scales?**

Answers: 1. True; 2. False; 3. fourth-grade level; 4. a; 5. False; 6. False; 7. c; 8. treatment consideration scales

Three

HOW TO SCORE THE PAI

Like most structured personality tests, the PAI is very simple to score. Scoring the instrument is a completely objective process; although each item receives a different weighting, this weight is determined entirely by the response of the client, not by the test author and not by the evaluating clinician. These responses are then mechanically compared to the responses of 1,000 individuals selected to match the characteristics of the community at large, resulting in a *t* score that constitutes an objective comparison to the average scores in this population.

The first step in scoring the PAI is to examine the answer sheet and determine the number (if any) of unanswered items. If 18 or more items (i.e., more than 5% of the questions on the test) were left unanswered, the client should be asked to review and complete these items if possible. Even fewer items left unanswered can compromise the interpretation of particular scales; in general, scores on a scale or subscale should not be interpreted if more than 20% of the items on that scale were left unanswered. Thus, if two items on the eight-item DEP-C subscale were left blank, that subscale should not be interpreted. However, if the remaining 22 items on the 24-item full DEP scale *were* completed, then an interpretation of the DEP can be made with appropriate caution in consideration of the missing items.

PAI SCORING

The hand-scored answer sheet for the PAI is self-contained in that it includes the item keys necessary for obtaining the raw scores for each of the PAI scales and subscales. These materials allow the test to be scored without the use of any separate hand-scoring templates or answer keys. This scoring is accomplished through the use of an answer sheet that is a carbonless two-part form

DON'T FORGET

....

Do not attempt to interpret the PAI if 18 or more items on the test were left unanswered. Also, do not interpret individual scales if 20% of items on that scale were left unanswered.

on which marks made by the client on the top side of the form produce a mark on an attached underlying form. After testing has been completed, the test scorer tears the perforation at the top of the answer sheet and peels away the upper page. The bottom (carboned) page provides the item scores for each of the 344 items on the test. Each response receives an item score of either 0, 1, 2, or 3, depending on the alternative endorsed by the client; these item scores are indicated directly on the answer sheet next to the marks produced by the client. Shaded boxes mark the items that belong to the different PAI scales and subscales; in general, the items that constitute a scale reside in the same row of the answer sheet. Because the client answers the test in columns of answers, the 40 rows of the answer sheet mean that items for a scale are typically 40 items apart. Thus, the NON scale includes Items 1, 41, 81, 121, 161, 201, 241, and 281. To obtain the raw score for NON, the scorer would sum the item scores for each of these eight items, and this number would be entered in the appropriate space on the separate profile form. For scales that include subscales, the raw score for the full scale is simply the sum of the raw scores for its subscales.

The most complicated PAI raw score to calculate is that for the Inconsistency (ICN) scale. This scale is computed by comparing responses to 10 pairs of items that have similar content; if the responses appear to reflect discrepant content, the test items appear to have been answered inconsistently. Calculating the ICN raw score must be done carefully to ensure accuracy. A box similar to that presented in Rapid Reference 3.1 is located on the PAI profile form. In this box there are spaces for entering the item scores for the 10 pairs of items—20 items in all. The item scores to be compared are adjoining; thus, the score for Item 75 is compared to that for Item 115, Items 4 and 44 are compared, and so on. For the first 8 pairs of these items, consistent responding would result in item scores that are similar. Thus, the absolute value of any difference between the scores of the item pair adds to the raw score of the ICN scale. For example, if the item score for Item 75 is 1, and the item score for Item 115 is 2, then this difference of 1 point contributes to the total score of ICN.

≡Rapid Reference 3.1

Scoring the ICN Scale

1. Compute the absolute difference in item scores for the following item pairs:

		Score		**Score**	**Difference**
Pair 1.	Item 75	_____	Item 115	_____	= _____
Pair 2.	Item 4	_____	Item 44	_____	= _____
Pair 3.	Item 60	_____	Item 100	_____	= _____
Pair 4.	Item 145	_____	Item 185	_____	= _____
Pair 5.	Item 65	_____	Item 246	_____	= _____
Pair 6.	Item 102	_____	Item 103	_____	= _____
Pair 7.	Item 22	_____	Item 142	_____	= _____
Pair 8.	Item 301	_____	Item 140	_____	= _____

2. Reverse the scoring for items 270 and 190 by subtracting their scores from 3:

$$3 - \text{Item } 270 \ \_\_\_\_\_ = \_\_\_\_\_ \ \text{Reverse } 270$$
$$3 - \text{Item } 90 \ \_\_\_\_\_ = \_\_\_\_\_ \ \text{Reverse } 190$$

3. Compute differences in scores for last two item pairs:

		Score		**Score**	**Difference**
Pair 9.	Reverse 270	_____	Item 53	_____	= _____
Pair 10.	Reverse 190	_____	Item 13	_____	= _____

4. Add the difference scores for Pairs 1 through 10 to obtain the ICN raw score.

For the last two item pairs listed in the box, consistent responding should lead the item scores to be *opposite* for the items in the pair. Thus, for the pair of Items 270 and 53, if the score for one of these items is 3, the score for the other item should be 0 if the person answered these items consistently. Thus, to reflect this reversal, the item score for one of the items in the pair is first subtracted from 3 to place these item pairs on the same scale as the first eight pairs. For example, if the item score for Item 270 is 1 and the item score for Item 53 is 2, the contribution to ICN is calculated as follows:

$$\text{Item pair score} = (3 - \text{Item } 270) - \text{Item } 53$$
$$\text{Item pair score} = (3 - 1) - 2$$
$$= 0$$

Thus, in this example the item scores for items 270 and 53 represent consistent responding, and that item pair contributed nothing (0 points) toward the total raw score of ICN.

The values obtained by these calculations for each of the 10 pairs of items are then summed to obtain a raw score for the ICN scale. This raw score is then entered in the appropriate space on the separate profile form.

After all the scale and subscale raw scores have been calculated, t scores are then determined by locating the corresponding tic mark for each scale (located on the front side) and subscale (back side) on the separate test profile form. For each score, the elevation of this tic mark on the profile form corresponds to a t score that provides a standardization of that raw score against a census-matched normative sample of 1,000 community-dwelling adults. These t scores provide a simple linear transformation of the raw scores so that each scale has a mean of $50t$ and a standard deviation of $10t$ in the community, with percentile equivalents corresponding roughly to those expected in a normal distribution, as shown in Rapid Reference 3.2. Lines on the profile form indicate $50t$ (the average score in the standardization sample) and $70t$ (the score corresponding roughly to the 96th percentile in this sample).

Scoring of the PAI is also available through the use of computer software available from the test publisher that provides, for a one-time cost, unlimited scoring and interpretations of the instrument. Many clinicians prefer computer scoring because it is less susceptible to transcription or calculation errors. In addition, the computer software automatically scores a variety of supplemental indexes that are described throughout this volume, many of which would be cumbersome to score by hand.

Rapid Reference 3.2

Approximate Community Percentile Equivalents for PAI t scores

t score	Percentile
$40t$	16th
$50t$	50th
$60t$	83rd
$70t$	96th
$80t$	99th

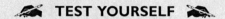

TEST YOURSELF

1. **Standard scores for the PAI are obtained using**
   (a) linear *t* scores.
   (b) uniform *t* scores.
   (c) normalized *t* scores.
   (d) log transform *t* scores.

2. **The score for each individual PAI item is determined by**
   (a) regression weights determined during test development.
   (b) conversion of responses to a present-absent discrimination.
   (c) the response indicated by the client.
   (d) a rating made by the evaluating clinician.

3. **If five or more items are left blank on the 24-item SOM scale, that scale should not be scored and interpreted.** True or False?

4. **On the ICN scale, the items in all of the item pairs should receive the same item score.** True or False?

5. **The PAI uses a standard score known as a t score that**
   (a) has a mean of 100 and a standard deviation of 15 in the community.
   (b) has a mean of 50 and a standard deviation of 10 in the community.
   (c) has a mean of 100 and a standard deviation of 15 in clinical settings.
   (d) has a mean of 50 and a standard deviation of 10 in clinical settings.

6. **How many participants were included in the PAI community normative sample?**

7. **A total of 22 scoring templates are required to hand-score the PAI.** True or False?

8. **What is the maximum number of items that can be left blank on the PAI that will still allow some interpretation?**

Answers: 1. a; 2. c; 3. True; 4. False; 5. b; 6. 1,000; 7. False; 8. 17 items

Four

INTRODUCTION TO INTERPRETATION

Interpreting the results of the PAI requires a solid understanding of important concepts in personality and mental disorder, a firm grasp of psychometric theory, and a familiarity with the standard PAI scales and supplemental interpretive indexes. The optimal strategy for interpretation often varies as a function of the context of the assessment—for example, the interpretation of a protocol from an applicant for a position as a police officer might involve emphases different from those for one obtained from an inpatient in a psychiatric hospital. As Meehl and Rosen pointed out in their famous 1955 article, the contextual expectancies of assessment can lead the interpreter to draw different conclusions from the exact same profile when those profiles were obtained in dramatically different contexts.

One useful way that PAI interpretation can attempt to make use of a contextually based approach is through the use of a set sequence of decisions. Each decision provides a context for decisions made later in the sequence. For example, one of the first decisions to make in profile interpretation is to decide whether a profile appears to reflect some distortion in responding. Thus, if the interpreter decides that a test protocol appeared to be answered in a more or less random fashion or perhaps in an exaggerated fashion, the subsequent interpretation of items indicating suicidal ideation will be much different from the interpretation that would be made if such distortion did not appear to be present.

This interpretive sequence can be broken down into four steps. In the first step, a decision is made about the extent to which a profile is free from potential response distortions. This process is often referred to as determining the validity of the profile. In the second stage, the interpreter considers the appropriate reference comparison for the profile under consideration; in some instances, this comparison will be shaped by the decisions made in the first step of the sequence. In the third step of interpretation, the individual scales and their component parts are examined. Finally, the fourth stage involves a consideration of the impact of particular combinations or configurations of scales. Although these aspects of interpretation receive considerable description in later chapters, the following sections provide a brief overview of how these steps can fit together in an interpretive sequence.

STEP 1: ASSESSMENT OF POTENTIAL PROFILE DISTORTION

Generally, the beginning point in the interpretation of self-report measures is a determination of whether the results provide an accurate reflection of the experience of the respondent or (alternatively) whether the results may be distorted in some way. This process begins even before the PAI is administered; factors such as the nature of the referral for assessment, the intended use of the results, and the ultimate recipients of the test information all provide a context that can dramatically affect the likelihood that test results will be distorted. Various procedures for identifying such distortion are presented in detail in chapter 5.

STEP 2: DETERMINATION OF APPROPRIATE REFERENCE COMPARISON

After a decision has been reached concerning profile distortion, the next phase involves a consideration of the appropriate frame of reference against which to evaluate the profile. This frame of reference can vary as a function of a number of different aspects of the assessment. Three particularly important reference contexts to consider involve community versus clinical comparisons, distorted versus nondistorted comparisons, and comparisons in specific referral contexts. These considerations are described in the following sections.

Community Versus Clinical Norms

The PAI *t* scores are referenced against a sample representative of adults living in the community

DON'T FORGET

The first step in PAI interpretation is determining the likelihood of profile distortion. All subsequent interpretive decisions are based on this determination.

C A U T I O N

The PAI profile skyline provides a reference point for scores that are unusual in a clinical setting. It serves primarily to illustrate differences in scores in clinical and community settings and does not constitute a cutting score for any decisions about clinical scale elevations.

within the United States. As a result, the *t* scores are central in interpreting whether a particular pattern of responses is normative in the sense of being typical of average adults. For example, nearly everyone has periods when they feel somewhat down—the test interpreter must then determine the extent to which this is normal or whether it reflects a statistically unusual degree of depression. The answer to this question is found in the *t* scores for the different scales. A score of 60*t* represents a person who lies roughly at the 84th percentile in terms of experiencing symptoms and problems of a particular type, whereas a score of 70*t* represents a score lying roughly at the 96th percentile for most scales (Morey, 1991). Thus, a score of 70*t*, indicated by a reference line on the PAI profile form as shown in Figure 4.1, represents a degree of problems and symptoms that is very unusual in the general population, thus most likely indicating a problem of clinical significance.

After a problem that merits clinical attention has been identified (i.e., one of the 11 clinical scales, AGG, or SUI falling at or above 70*t*), the contextual reference point needs to shift to a clinical focus. Expectations for scale scores in clinical populations different in many respects from those expected in the general population. There are a variety of means to accomplish this reference comparison—the test manual (Morey, 1991) includes an appendix that presents standard scores based on the clinical standardization sample; the interpretive software presents similar standard scores as part of the Interpretive Explorer module (Morey, 2000), and the hand-scoring profile form includes a reference line that represents a point that lies 2 standard deviations above the mean of the clinical standardization sample. An example of this profile can be seen in Figure 4.1; the skyline on this profile form is the aforementioned reference line.

Contrasting the various peaks and valleys of this skyline with the 70*t* community reference line illustrates the different expectancies found in clinical and community settings. Perhaps the best example of this phenomenon is found on the RXR (Treatment Rejection) scale; for this scale, the profile

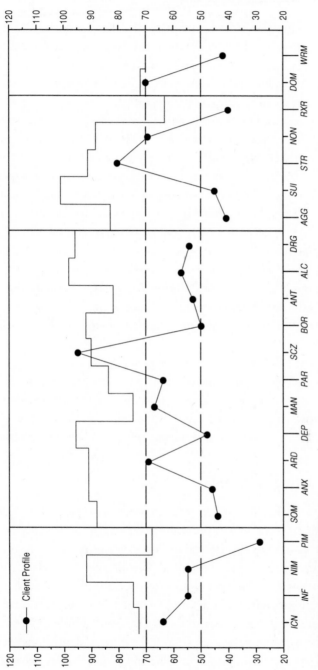

Figure 4.1 The PAI profile form

skyline falls below the 70t line, whereas for nearly all other scales the clinical skyline lies well above the 70t reference line. This result indicates that scores on the RXR scale will tend to be lower in clinical settings than in community settings. Such a finding makes sense because individuals in clinical settings are typically in those settings because they *are* interested in treatment, whereas individuals in the community are generally not in psychological treatment and would most likely reject such treatment if it were offered to them. Contextual information greatly affects the interpretation of an RXR score of 50t, which would be average in person selected randomly from the community but considerably above average for a person presenting for treatment in the community. Thus, the context provided by the rest of the profile information becomes critical in evaluating the RXR score. When no clinical scale falls above 60t, for example, an RXR score of 50t is not surprising because the person is reporting no clinical difficulties that seem to require treatment. However, the same score in a person with one or more clinical scales elevated above 70t (at which point the respondent more resembles individuals in treatment settings than people in the community) may indicate an interpretively significant lack of interest in treatment.

In summary, when there appear to be profile elevations that suggest problems of clinical significance, the interpreter should also evaluate the profile against the context of a clinical population. When such problems do not appear to be present, the initial comparison to the community norms will be more informative for interpreting the person's personality characteristics.

Response-Style-Specific Norms

A second set of decisions about normative reference points involves an appraisal of the response style of the examinee. This step entails a determination of how the respondent approached the test—was he or she more or less candid in disclosing faults than the typical person in the normative sample? If there appears to be some operation of a systematic response style, it can be useful to shift the frame of reference to how the respondent compares to other individuals who approached the test in a similar fashion. For example, if a person appears to have completed the test in a defensive manner, comparing this profile to other similarly defensive profiles allows the interpreter to take into account the typical effects of defensive responding on the profile.

Deviations from the anticipated effects of these influences can provide a variety of hypotheses about the profile under consideration.

To facilitate these comparisons, the Interpretive Explorer component of the PAI scoring and interpretation software (Morey, 2000) provides a response-style-specific standardization of the profile whenever either the NIM or the PIM validity scales is in a range that suggests significant distortion as a result of response style. This standardization was accomplished using as a normative context the profiles of individuals who scored within two specific bands of distortion (moderate and marked distortion) on these two validity scales. Results are presented as standard scores referenced against the appropriate sample. Thus, a person who presents with a moderately elevated PIM score is then compared against other individuals obtaining PIM scores in that range. The restandardized profile can then be examined to determine where the profile deviates from expectations given the response style. When PIM is elevated, suggesting defensiveness in the profile, those scores that fall below the PIM-specific norm may represent content areas about which the respondent is particularly defensive. Conversely, scores that fall above this PIM-specific norm may constitute an estimate of problem areas that would be particularly prominent if the profile were less defensive. When NIM is elevated, suggesting exaggeration in the profile, scores that fall above the NIM-specific norm may represent particularly central difficulties or difficulties that the respondent is particularly interested in emphasizing. Scores below this norm may identify content areas that—although they are still elevated by comparison to general population norms—are a less prominent part of the reported clinical picture.

Norms for Specific Contexts

A third example of alternative contextual referents involves the use of local norms that involve a standardization based upon data gathered in a specific context. One example of such a specific context is the personnel selection process. In this context, the PAI is being used as one factor in determining who gets hired for a specific job. This situation presents a general context in which individuals are typically trying to put their best foot forward, and in general these profiles often resemble those found in positive impression management groups. However, to an extent the specific expectancies for profile elevations may differ as a function of the precise nature of the job because applicants may view some personality attributes as particularly desirable (or undesirable) for a given position. The types of personality characteristics associated with success as a police officer, for example, may differ substantially from those required of an airline pilot or nuclear plant operator.

Perhaps the most well-developed contextual norms are those collected by Roberts, Thompson, and Johnson (2000) for assessing law enforcement, corrections, and public safety applicants. Individuals applying for public safety positions present for assessment in a particular context in which they anticipate that certain personality characteristics are likely to be desired by those involved in the hiring decision. Roberts et al. (2000) gathered data from 17,757 individuals completing the test in this particular context and devised an assessment procedure based on comparing a particular applicant to other applicants in this specific context. This data set also includes normative information for individuals who successfully completed probationary periods in specific job subtypes, such as police officers, firefighters, corrections officers, and communication dispatchers. When these context-specific norms are used as a reference point, the overall effects of the assessment context are removed from interpretation, and differences between individuals presenting in this context can be highlighted.

As data accumulate, a variety of different normative databases from different assessment contexts will probably become available. Although such information will help professionals who interpret results in these contexts, it will at the same time be important not to lose sight of the baseline information provided by the PAI standardization samples. For example, gathering PAI norms in substance abuse treatment settings may yield contextual norms in which the average score on DRG or ALC is high. If using such norms, a patient in such a setting might obtain a score that is below average on these contextual norms but well above average with reference to the community. Although the contextual norms can

> # CAUTION
>
> Although norms gathered for specific populations (such as job applicants or psychiatric inpatients) may help sharpen distinctions between different respondents in specific settings, community norms should be used to determine whether a scale score reflects a level of problems that is likely to be of clinical significance.

help sharpen relative distinctions among individuals assessed in a specific context, the norms from the PAI standardization sample will still be the more useful referent for determining the absolute level of difficulties.

STEP 3: INTERPRETATION OF INDIVIDUAL SCALES

Following the determination of profile validity and the selection of the relevant contextual referents, interpretation proceeds with an examination of the individual PAI scales. Each scale on the test was designed to measure the major facets of different clinical constructs, as determined by current theoretical and empirical work on those constructs. Interpretation of the data from a scale generally proceeds from an examination of (a) the full-scale score (or scores, if comparisons to different normative contexts are appropriate); (b) the subscale scores, if the scale includes subscales; and finally, (c) the individual scale items.

Assuming little or no profile distortion, the initial focus of interpretation should be on those full scales that obtain scores of 70*t* or greater. Such scores on the full scales represent a coherent pattern of difficulties that probably merit clinical attention. Given that any such scores suggest significant clinical issues, the standardized scores for these scales against the clinical standardization sample should also be determined, using information provided in the test manual or the scoring software. These clinically referenced standard scores will be of particular use in determining which elevations appear most central in the interpretation of the profile. For example, using community norms a DEP scale elevation of 80*t* appears more striking than a MAN score of 75*t*, but the former would be much more commonly encountered in clinical settings.

After the most prominent scale elevations have been identified, the next step in scale interpretation involves the evaluation of the subscales. Ten of the PAI scales have conceptually derived subscales that were constructed as an aid in isolating the core elements of the different clinical constructs that the test measures. These subscales can serve to clarify the meaning of full-scale elevations and may be used configurally in diagnostic decision making. For example, many patients typically come to clinical settings with marked distress and dysphoria, often leading to elevations on most unidimensional depression scales; however, unless other manifestations of the syndrome are pres-

DON'T FORGET

Ten of the PAI scales were constructed to have conceptual subscales. The interpretation of any of these PAI full-scale scores can vary substantially, depending on the configuration of the subscales.

ent, this does not necessarily indicate that major depression is the likely diagnosis. In the absence of features such as vegetative signs, lowered self-esteem, and negative expectancies, the diagnosis may not be warranted even if the client obtained a prominent elevation on a depression scale. On the PAI, such a pattern would lead to an elevation on DEP-A, representing the dysphoria and distress, but it would not lead to elevations on DEP-P (the vegetative signs) or DEP-C (the cognitive signs). As a result, an overall elevation on DEP in this instance would not be interpreted as diagnostic of major depression because of the lack of supporting data from the subscale configuration.

The most detailed information from the scales involves an examination of responses to individual items. Examining individual item responses is consistent with the construction and development philosophy of the test, wherein it was assumed that the content of an item would be a critical determinant of its utility to assess clinical problems. For example, each item was reviewed by a panel of experts to ensure that its content was directly relevant to the clinical construct in question. As a result, a review of item content can provide useful specific information about the nature of difficulties experienced by the respondent. The examination of the items may also remedy any mistaken assumptions about the interpretation of a particular scale score. As an example, the subscale on the PAI that assesses phobias (ARD-P) includes items that tap feared objects and situations that are commonly a focus of clinical concern. However, unless the specific items are examined, the interpreter may not realize that the scale includes many questions directed at the assessment of social phobia, or marked social anxiety in certain public situations. An inexperienced interpreter might assume that an ARD-P elevation indicates a fear of snakes or spiders—fears that are stereotypical phobias but are rarely a focus of clinical concern—and miss the social dysfunction that contributed to the elevation. In addition to item-based interpretations of scale scores, 27 PAI items were identified as critical items based on the importance of their content as an indicator of potential crisis situations and on their very low endorsement rates in normal individuals. These items were selected from diverse content areas across many different scales. Endorsement of these items can be followed by more detailed questioning that can clarify the nature and severity of these concerns.

Although item-level interpretation can be useful, it should be recognized that the reliability of individual items is limited and that greater caution must be exercised in such efforts than would be required in interpreting full-scale scores.

STEP 4: INTERPRETING PROFILE CONFIGURATION

The profile configuration represents the highest interpretive level of the instrument. Traditionally, the premise behind multidimensional inventories such as the PAI has been that the *combination* of information provided by the multiple scales is greater than any of its parts. The configural approach thus attempts to combine the information from the individual scales into a patterned whole that provides answers to important questions about (for example) the diagnosis and treatment of the respondent.

As shown in Rapid Reference 4.1, configural approaches to PAI interpretation can take four different forms: (a) profile code types, (b) mean profile comparisons, (c) conceptual indexes, and (d) actuarial decision rules. The logic behind each of these approaches and their strengths and weaknesses are described briefly in the following sections.

Profile Code Types

The simplest method for describing a profile configuration involves classifying it by its two-point code, which represents the two highest clinical scale

≡Rapid Reference 4.1

Strategies for Interpreting Profile Configuration

Strategy	Description
Two-point codes	Consider two most elevated clinical scales.
Mean profiles	Determine profile similarity to established groups.
Conceptual indexes	Look for indicator pattern suggested by theory.
Actuarial rules	Apply multivariate functions to combine scale scores.

scores for the profile. The implications of the configurations represented by each of these code types are described in chapter 7. Although the use of two-point codes in profile interpretation is somewhat of a tradition in the assessment field, it must be recognized that such a code provides a limited description of the profile configuration. First, using only the two highest scales essentially ignores the information provided by the other scales on the test. Second, because most of the PAI clinical scales are organized around conceptual subscales, meaningful differences can be observed between persons with identical codes as a function of the subscale configuration of the two highest scales. Finally, the small differences that can determine a two-point code on any psychological instrument are often of questionable reliability. As such, the profile code type provides a rough starting point for the configural interpretation of the PAI profile, but it should be supplemented by the approaches described elsewhere in this chapter.

Mean Profile Comparisons

This approach to understanding profile configuration involves a comparison of the PAI profile under consideration to those of individuals who share some particular similarity—for example, a diagnosis or a symptom. For example, the PAI manual presents the average profiles derived from numerous different groups isolated on the basis of a particular diagnosis (e.g., major depression) or symptom (e.g., self-mutilating behavior), and additional mean profiles have been described in the literature. The PAI scoring software provides an empirical comparison of the respondent's profile to each of these mean profiles through the use of an inverse correlation that provides a measure of configural similarity. Thus, for example, a respondent may yield a PAI profile that correlates .80 with the mean profile for borderline personality disorder as compared to .20 with the mean profile for schizophrenia.

Although this approach can yield interesting hypotheses about a case, the information provided tends to be limited in many respects. Such profiles do not represent a prototypical profile for a diagnosis; rather, they present the lowest common denominator for the diagnosis. Because of the extensive comorbidity among emotional disorders and because of variations in diagnostic practice among clinicians, the resulting mean profile for a given diagnosis may not fully capture the elements of the PAI that most reflect that disorder. Thus, the mean profile is only a beginning point in understanding the profile configuration.

Conceptual Indexes

A variety of PAI configural rules have been developed and studied. These represent various rules or strategies based on theory-driven hypotheses or on clinical observations. For example, within the realm of profile distortion considerations are the Malingering and Defensiveness indexes (Morey, 1996), which are described in detail in chapter 5. These indexes represent observations of unusual profile configurations that were obtained in simulation studies of distorted responding. In the realm of clinical decision making are configural indexes such as the Violence Potential index, Suicide Potential index, and Treatment Process index (Morey, 1996), each of which is described in chapter 9. These indexes were based either on theoretical formulations of specific issues or on an instantiation of previous empirical research on a topic. Although these indexes have begun to receive some attention in the research literature, there is clearly a need for cross-validation research. Nonetheless, when used in combination with other configural strategies, these theory-based indicators can be a useful guide to interpreting profile configuration.

Actuarial Decision Rules

A number of multivariate analyses have been described in the literature to identify actuarial formulas for various sorts of decisions. For example, within the realm of profile distortion considerations, discriminant function strategies have been developed and studies for identifying defensiveness (Cashel, Rogers, Sewell, & Martin-Cannici, 1995), malingering (Rogers, Sewell, Morey, & Ustad, 1996), and substance abuse denial (Fals-Stewart, 1996). In another example of such efforts, LOGIT analyses were used to construct models of diagnostic decisions provided by clinicians on patients who completed the PAI (Morey, 1996). The advantage of such approaches is that they provide objective and empirically based decision rules that can be constructed to make particular discriminations (e.g., distinguishing bona fide schizophrenia from simulated schizophrenia). However, the approach requires fairly large sample sizes to construct the multivariate actuarial functions; thus, only a limited number of such functions have been developed. Also, the calculations involved in these functions can be daunting, so their use tends to be limited to the computer-based scoring of the instrument. Finally, any such functions require cross-validation to assess their generalizability to new samples, and these efforts have been mixed, with some functions holding up well upon cross-validation (e.g., Morey & Lanier, 1998) and others demonstrating limited cross-validation (Falls-Stewart & Lucente, 1997). Nonetheless, the development of such functions has been an important addition to the strategies available to the interpreter for configural profile interpretation.

SUMMARY

There are a number of steps involved in the interpretation of the PAI profile, and for each step there are different strategies that the interpreter can use in evaluating the available information. The following chapters provide a more detailed discussion of the strategies available for conducting this process.

🐊 TEST YOURSELF 🐊

1. **Typically the first step in PAI profile interpretation is assessing the presence or degree of profile distortion.** True or False?

2. **A score on any clinical scale that is average in clinical settings should be ignored in profile interpretation because these scores are commonly seen in such settings.** True or False?

3. **To determine whether a scale score reflects a level of problems likely to be of clinical significance, the interpreter should use what comparison group as reference point?**
   (a) community norms
   (b) clinical norms
   (c) context-specific norms
   (d) response-style-specific norms

4. **Interpretation of individual items is unlikely to yield useful information and should generally not be done.** True or False?

5. **One weakness of comparing a PAI profile to the mean profile configuration of a known diagnostic group involves**

   (a) failure to consider any but the two highest scale scores.

   (b) lack of ability to measure the degree of similarity in these profiles.

   (c) the heterogeneity of individuals in diagnostic groups.

   (d) the unreliability of profile configurations.

6. **Scores are not likely to be clinically significant unless they exceed the clinical skyline on the profile form.** True or False?

7. **How can one determine whether a particular score is unusual in defensive individuals?**

8. **Normative data for the PAI are available on more than 17,000 applicants for public safety positions.** True or False?

Answers: 1. True; 2. False; 3. a; 4. False; 5. c; 6. False; 7. Use response-style specific norms; 8. True

Five

ASSESSING PROFILE VALIDITY

One of the difficulties that has beset the field of psychological assessment since its inception concerns the accuracy of self-reported information as an indication of psychological status. The reasons offered as to why self-reports may be distorted are myriad. One source of distortion may arise from an intention to deceive the recipient of the information; such examinees may attempt to distort their responses to appear either better adjusted or more poorly adjusted than is actually the case. A second source of distortion may arise from limited insight or self-deception. These examinees may genuinely believe that they are doing well or poorly, but this belief might be at odds with the impression of objective observers. A third source of distortion can also arise from confusion, carelessness, or indifference in taking a test; examinees who answer questions with little reflection (or even randomly) may yield results that do not accurately mirror their experiences.

Such concerns have led many test developers to create scales that provide measures of these sources of distortion. The PAI offers four validity scales that are designed to provide an assessment of factors that could distort the results of a self-report questionnaire and offers indexes and interpretive procedures constructed to supplement these scales. Elevated scores on any of these scales suggest that other profile information should be viewed with caution and that any interpretation of results should be tentative. In general, if a respondent obtains a score that is more than 2 standard deviations above the mean of the representative *clinical* sample on any of these validity scales or indexes, the profile is likely to be seriously distorted by some test-taking response style. This result casts serious doubt on all other information derived from the test, and under such conditions the necessity of considering the PAI protocol in light of information derived from other sources becomes particularly critical.

In this section, the specific distortions to be considered involve three different types of distortions: those arising from test protocols that were completed carelessly, randomly, or idiosyncratically by the respondent; those that might lead the interpreter to draw a more negative conclusion from the data than might otherwise be warranted; and those that might reflect a more positive clinical picture than is warranted.

DETECTING CARELESS OR IDIOSYNCRATIC RESPONDING

When clinical scales are elevated on a self-report test, several reasons for this elevation must be considered. One possibility involves a pattern of responding in which the person answers the items more or less randomly because of confusion, disinterest, resistance, or clerical errors in test taking or scoring. Because many items on the PAI reflect severe psychopathology and have low endorsement rates, such people will obtain marked elevations because many of these items will be endorsed. Two of the PAI validity scales, ICN and INF, were designed to identify this source of distortion.

ICN: Inconsistency

The ICN scale is an empirically derived scale that reflects the consistency with which the respondent completed items with similar content. The scale is comprised of 10 pairs of items with related content; five of these pairs should be answered similarly and five of the pairs are psychologically opposite. The items on ICN were the pairs that were found to be the most similar empirically during the development of the PAI. Although each pair of items is similar in content, the pairs differ from one another so that the scale does not reflect any particular construct other than response consistency.

Because ICN is intended to re-

> **DON'T FORGET**
>
> Although ICN and INF can elevate from a carelessly completed questionnaire, such scores can also arise from reading or language problems, confusion, or clerical scoring errors.

DON'T FORGET

A common cause of ICN elevations is reading comprehension problems, typically resulting in some confusion with items involving negations such as *I have no trouble falling asleep.*

flect measurement error (which is theoretically random and hence uncorrelated with any substantive construct), it tends to have low correlations with most other measures. The scale's largest correlation appears to be with the Marlowe-Crowne Social Desirability Scale (Crowne & Marlowe, 1960), a correlation of –.24. Although this correlation is low, it is informative because it suggests that people who tend to answer in a socially desirable direction also tend to answer questions consistently. Thus, if social desirability is considered to have any sort of an impression management component, a person trying to manage his or her self-presentation appears to do so with some care. This suggests that ICN elevations are probably not the result of efforts at impression management, although sometimes such scales are interpreted in this manner (i.e., people who tell an inconsistent story are not telling the truth). However, if someone is consciously trying to distort in a given direction, ICN often does not elevate at all. Rather, ICN is more likely to reflect carelessness or confusion in responding.

One commonly observed problem that can cause elevations on ICN is a failure to attend to negated items (i.e., items that have the word *not* in the statement). Although there are relatively few such items on the PAI, these items are overrepresented on ICN to examine how such items were interpreted. Subjects not attending closely may misinterpret the question that read *I have no trouble falling asleep* and instead may read the item as *I have trouble falling asleep.* This pattern alerts the interpreter that the respondent may not have been reading items carefully while completing the inventory. Another (often related) source of ICN elevations involves reading comprehension problems. An elevation may suggest that the respondent was not capable of reading the test at the required fourth-grade level. This result can be seen with some frequency in individuals for whom English is a second language; in such persons, spoken verbal fluency can sometimes provide a misleading estimate of their ability to understand written material.

The distribution of ICN is fairly similar for both normal and clinical individuals although clinical subjects tend to score slightly higher (i.e., respond slightly less consistently) than do normally functioning individuals. The distributions from clinical and normal subjects differ markedly from those derived by simulating random responding. Generally, low scores on ICN (below 64*t*) suggest that the respondent did respond consistently and probably attended appropriately to item content in responding to the PAI items. Moderate elevations (between 64*t* and 73*t*) indicate some inconsistency in responses to similar items; such inconsistency could arise from a variety of sources, ranging from carelessness or confusion to attempts at impression management. Interpretive hypotheses based on other PAI scales should be reviewed with caution if ICN is in this range.

High scores on ICN (at or above 73*t*) suggest that the respondent did not attend consistently or appropriately to item content in responding to the PAI items; a completely random completion of the PAI would result in an average ICN score of approximately 73*t*. There are several potential reasons for scores in this range, including carelessness, reading difficulties, confusion, language problems, errors in scoring, or failure to follow the test instructions. Regardless of the cause, however, the test results are best assumed to be invalid, and no clinical interpretation of the PAI is recommended when ICN scores are in this range.

INF: Infrequency

The INF scale is useful in the identification of people who complete the PAI in an atypical way because of carelessness, confusion, reading difficulties, or other sources of random responding. The scale consists of items that were designed to be answered similarly by all respondents regardless of clinical status; half of the items are expected to be answered *false* (e.g., *My favorite poet is Raymond Kertezc*), whereas the other half should be answered *very true* (e.g., *Most people would rather win than lose.*). The INF items are placed evenly throughout the PAI to identify potentially problematic responding at any point in test taking. There is no thematic connection between the content of different items on the scale. The items were selected on the basis of very low endorsement frequencies in both normal and clinical subjects; this contrasts with scales such as the MMPI's F scale, on which items were selected on the basis of infrequency in the normative sample. Such scales often yield elevations in clinical samples because the item content is confounded with psychopathological symptoms that are infrequent in normative samples but may reflect valid responding in a clinical respondent.

INF scale items were written to provide item content that would be infrequent yet not bizarre-sounding (bizarre items would include those such as *I have never seen a building*). For example, one question asks whether the respondent's two favorite hobbies are archery and stamp collecting. Interest in these hobbies is inversely related, and there are therefore few people for whom both of these hobbies are primary interests. Yet the combination is not implausible—it is merely uncommon. Because each individual item on the scale is uncommon, an individual who endorses more than a few of the items is a unique individual indeed.

The Infrequency scale is primarily a measure of carelessness in responding. However, there is another potential element underlying INF elevations, reflecting a tendency to answer the PAI items in a very idiosyncratic way. A quick inquiry about INF items can easily distinguish between these two sources of elevation. Subjects responding idiosyncratically to the inventory will have an explanation for their endorsement, albeit an explanation that suggests that the test items may have been interpreted in an unusual way. However, if a person makes idiosyncratic inferences about items that do not reflect the actual content of the item or begins to respond to items figuratively rather than literally, the results will not be interpretable in any straightforward way. Because such people are not approaching the test in the way that most people do, the results of the self-report test should not be interpreted as if they were.

The distribution of INF is similar for both normal and clinical subjects; both distributions are very different from that derived by simulating random responding. Generally, low scores (below 60*t*) suggest that the respondent did attend appropriately to item content in responding to the PAI items. Moderate elevations (between 60*t* and 75*t*) indicate some unusual responses to INF items, and at the higher end of this range one should consider potential sources such as reading difficulties, random responding, confusion, errors in scoring, idiosyncratic item interpretation, or failure to follow the test instructions. Any interpretive hypotheses based on the PAI should be reviewed with caution if INF is in this range, and some inquiry about INF responses would be useful before clinical scale results are interpreted.

High scores on INF (at or above 75t) suggest that the respondent did not attend appropriately to item content in responding to the PAI items. Completely random completion of the PAI results in an average INF score of 86t. There are several potential reasons for scores in this range, including reading or language difficulties, random responding, confusion, errors in scoring, or failure to follow the test instructions. Regardless of the cause, the test results are best assumed to be invalid and no clinical interpretation of the PAI is recommended, although an examination of specific INF items may yield useful information. For example, if the endorsed INF items are all from the second half of the test, the examinee may have completed the initial half of the instrument appropriately but began responding haphazardly at a later point. In this instance, score estimates for most PAI scales may be extrapolated from the responses to the first 160 items, as described in chapter 11 of the test manual (Morey, 1991).

Random Responding: Scale Configuration

The most prominent characteristic of a profile that consists of random responses to the PAI is that both INF and ICN fall above the thresholds for profile validity described in previous sections. This result is rare in actual protocols; only 0.2% of participants in both the community and clinical normative samples had both INF and ICN above the recommended cutoffs. The NIM scale also elevates in such profiles, although not to the extent that occurs in malingering simulation samples. In general, if both INF and NIM are elevated and the scores are comparable (e.g., within 10t of one another), then random responding is suggested. Malingered protocols tend to lead to profiles in which NIM greatly exceeds INF, typically by 20t or more.

Because random responding will include many positive responses to unusual items, the overall profile is elevated. However, these elevations are not as marked as the elevations that tend to be seen in malingered protocols; for example, fewer than half of the subscales are elevated above 70t in the random response profile. Another feature of the random profile that is noteworthy is the lack of differentiation among the clinical scales, with most falling in the range from 65t to 75t. Because of the emphasis on discriminant validity in the construction of the PAI, a relatively flat profile in the elevated range tends to be unusual because it involves clinical features that are not commonly seen in the same person (such as anxiety and antisocial features or depression and increased self-esteem). In general, malingered profiles tend to be more elevated than random profiles because responses are consistently pathological rather than randomly either pathological or healthy. The malingered profile also tends to have sharper differentiations, with some scales (such as SCZ) likely to elevate markedly and others (such as MAN) influenced less consistently when pathology is simulated.

SUBSTANTIVE SOURCES OF PROFILE DISTORTION

Unlike the random sources of profile distortion described earlier, there can also be systematic sources that can hamper interpretation of self-reported data. Such sources of distortion are probably both more common and also more difficult to identify; thus, they represent particular challenges in personality assessment. However, because these sources of distortion tend to be systematic rather than random, their effects are more predictable, and this predictability offers some hope for understanding the nature of the distortion and perhaps providing some strategies for compensating for these effects. These systematic sources can serve to have the test protocol overreport the level of problems in the respondent, or (alternatively) the distortion may lead to the underreporting of difficulties. It is important to understand that there can be both explicit distortion, in which a respondent is effortfully attempting to manipulate the clinical presentation, or implicit distortion, in which an individual is engaging in largely automatic cognitive or perceptual processes that distort self-perceptions but lie outside of awareness. It must be understood that these processes are not mutually exclusive and that explicit and implicit types of distortion can occur in the same individual. Furthermore, the direction of distortion can also vary in the same individual, such that a respondent may present a profile with stylistically inflated scores in certain areas but may suppress scores in other areas. Such complexities render this area perhaps the greatest challenge in the interpretation of self-reported clinical assessments.

The following sections describe various procedures for detecting and interpreting factors that might influence the overreporting or underreporting of problems and symptoms. In reviewing these indicators, it is important to remember that such distortions are a matter of degree—in other words, decision making needs to be informed by *how much* distortion is present rather than simply by whether the profile is invalid. Also, although some sources of distortion may color the profile in opposing pathological or healthy directions, they are not necessarily mutually exclusive; thus, any particular profile may have multiple sources of distortion operating simultaneously.

Detecting Negative Profile Distortion

As the term is used here, *negative profile distortion* refers to influences that serve to make the PAI profile appear more pathological than would be objectively warranted. One of the most dramatic examples of such distortion is malingering, which involves the effortful production of false or greatly exaggerated symptoms with the motivation of achieving some secondary gain. In some instances, these efforts appear to involve achieving attention from caregivers and sustaining the patient role rather than attaining some external incentive; this pattern can be diagnosed as factitious disorder. In either instance, the self-reported symptomatology from the PAI is likely to be markedly discrepant from objective clinical findings. In the presence of marked distortion of this sort, the PAI profile tends to more directly reflect what the respondent wishes the clinician to see, rather than to objectively reflect the patient's experience.

However, there are also sources of negative profile distortion that are not effortful—that indeed are part and parcel of psychopathology. Included here are characteristic perceptual and cognitive features that can lead to negative response styles. Several different forms of mental disorders lead individuals to perceive themselves, other people, or situations in a manner that is more negative than what might be warranted in the eyes of an objective observer. A depressed patient may view him- or herself as incompetent and inadequate, although others view him or her as able and highly effective. A situation that may appear to be of minor significance to the clinician may be viewed as an insurmountable crisis by a patient with borderline personality disorder. In each of these instances, the patient may portray his or her problems and circumstances in a manner that is more negative than it appears to the objective observer. These individuals are not malingering, however; in fact, they do have significant and perhaps severe forms of mental disorder. In interpreting the PAI profile, the clinician must be cognizant of the influence of these perceptual styles on the pattern of responses that is obtained.

The indicators described in this section appear to be influenced by these differing overreporting distortions to different degrees. Thus, they are of some use in disentangling the relative contributions of effortful as opposed to noneffortful sources of negative distortion. Three of these indicators—the NIM scale, the Malingering index, and the Rogers discriminant function—were developed explicitly to detect negative distortion. A fourth, the Cashel discriminant function, may have some use in this regard as well; however, because this measure was developed to identify positive profile distortion, it is discussed in a later section.

NIM: Negative Impression

Generally, the starting point in the evaluation of negative distortion is the NIM scale. It must be emphasized that NIM is not a malingering scale per se. The scale was designed to alert the interpreter to the possibility that the results of the test may portray an impression of the individual that is more negative than what might otherwise be merited. To put it another way, the self-report of a high scorer on NIM is probably more pathological than an objective observer would report when describing the respondent. The items were selected on the basis of low endorsement frequencies in both normal and clinical subjects, although NIM items are clearly endorsed with greater frequency in clinical patients than in normal adults. Individuals with clear-cut and severe emotional problems can and will get elevated scores on NIM, and more disturbed populations obtain higher scores than do those who are less impaired. For example, the mean of outpatient mental health patients in the PAI clinical normative sample on NIM was 59t (nearly 1 standard deviation above the mean of the community sample), whereas the corresponding value for inpatients was 65t (1.5 standard deviations above the community mean).

If NIM is a measure of a response style rather than of psychopathology, why should there be this relationship between psychopathology and NIM elevations? The answer lies in the association between certain forms of mental disorder and characteristic perceptual and cognitive features that can lead to negative response styles. Several different types of mental disorders lead individuals to perceive themselves, other people, or situations in a manner that is more negative than what might be warranted in the eyes of an objective observer. A depressed patient with a self-view of inadequacy may be viewed by others as able and highly effective. Interpersonal relationships that appear solid to others may be suspect in the mind of the paranoid individual. A situation that may appear to the clinician as relatively benign may be perceived as insurmountable by the borderline patient. Although these distortions clearly reflect psychopathology, the clinician must be cognizant of the influence of these perceptual styles in interpreting the PAI profile.

The NIM scale includes two types of items; some present an exaggerated or distorted impression of the self and present circumstances, and some represent extremely bizarre and unlikely symptoms. Each of these tendencies may cause distortion of self-reports in a negative direction. Individuals who tend to exaggerate the negative aspects of their lives can provide self-reports that appear very pathological. As noted earlier in this chapter, this response style can actually represent a prominent component of many psychopathological syndromes, but the NIM scale can enhance discriminant validity, revealing the degree to which distortion may be resulting from this perceptual style. At times, there may be so much distortion as to render the test results of dubious interpretability—this interpretation, however, does not mean that the person was malingering. Rather, the test is invalid in the sense that there are serious distortions, and extreme caution must be exercised in interpreting the test results at face value. Nonetheless, the result may accurately depict the way such persons feel about themselves and their circumstances.

It is true, however, that patient groups tend to score considerably lower on NIM than do research subjects instructed to simulate the responses of a mentally disordered patient, and the scale therefore serves as a useful beginning point in the detection of malingering; this is because another element of NIM items is more closely related to malingering. These items were written to sound as if they represented pathological symptoms, but they are in fact extremely rare or nonexistent in clini-

> ## CAUTION
>
> Research suggests that the NIM scale is better at detecting efforts to simulate severe psychopathology than it is at identifying malingering when milder forms of disorder are being simulated. The Rogers discriminant function appears to be more effective with efforts to simulate symptoms such as anxiety or depression.

cal populations. The item content is varied, but they share the feature that they sound dramatic and tap stereotypes of mental disorder. In fact, a few of the items are dissociative in nature, and it is has been observed that individuals with severe dissociative disorders sometimes obtain marked elevations on NIM. Idiosyncratic responses to item content can also result in NIM elevations, although in these instances INF tends also to be elevated. Regardless of the context, some inquiry about the nature of positive responses to these NIM items is merited.

Generally, low scores (below 73*t*) on NIM suggest that there is little distortion in a negative direction on the clinical scales; the respondent probably did not attempt to present a more negative impression than the clinical picture would warrant. Moderate elevations (between 73*t* and 84*t*) suggest an element of exaggeration of complaints and problems. Any interpretive hypotheses based on clinical scale elevations should be considered with caution because there is some possibility that the hypotheses will overrepresent the extent and degree of significant test findings. The likelihood of distortion increases in the range from 84*t* to 92*t*. Elevations in this range may be indicative of a cry for help or an extremely negative evaluation of oneself and one's life; some deliberate distortion of the clinical picture may also be present. The cutoff of 84*t* has been found to optimally discriminate malingerers from actual patients when the a priori probability of malingering is 50%.

High scores on NIM (at or above 92*t*) suggest that the respondent attempted to portray him- or herself in an especially negative manner. The item content suggests the strong possibility of careless responding, extremely negative self-presentation, or malingering. Research participants instructed to malinger severe mental disorders typically obtain an average NIM score in excess of 110*t*, whereas a completely random completion of the PAI would result in an average NIM score of approximately 96*t*. Regardless of the cause, however, the test results are best assumed to be invalid, and clinical interpretation of other PAI scales should focus on the desire of the respondent to report certain symptoms rather than infer that he or she actually experiences these symptoms.

The utility of NIM as an indicator of malingering has been explored in a number of research studies. The test manual (Morey, 1991) details the results of studies in which college students were instructed to simulate the responses of an individual with a severe mental disorder. The distributions of actual clinical subjects and these malingerers crossed at a score of 84*t*; this cutoff yielded a sensitivity of 88.6% in the identification of malingering, with a specificity of 89.8% among true clinical subjects. The 2 clinical standard deviations cutoff of 92*t* resulted in a sensitivity of 86.5% and a specificity of 94.1%. Subsequent studies have also been supportive of the use of NIM in detection of malingering. For example, Morey and Lanier (1998) found a 1.63 standard deviation difference on NIM between simulated and bona fide clinical groups; a cutting score of 81*t* resulted in 88.6% sensitivity and 88.9% specificity for identifying malingered responding. Along similar lines, Scragg, Bor, and Mendham (2000) reported a sensitivity of 54% and a specificity of 100% for distinguishing malingered from true posttraumatic stress disorder for the NIM scale.

However, subsequent studies have also helped to clarify situational variables that seem to limit the efficiency of NIM for identification of malingering. For example, Rogers, Ornduff, and Sewell (1993) examined the effectiveness of the NIM scale in identifying both naive and sophisticated simulators (advanced graduate students in clinical and counseling psychology) who were given a financial incentive to avoid detection as malingerers while attempting to feign specific disorders. Rogers et al. found that the recommended NIM scale cutoff successfully identified 90.9% of participants attempting to feign schizophrenia, 55.9% of participants simulating depression, and 38.7% of participants simulating an anxiety disorder. In contrast, only 2.5% of control participants were identified as simulators. Rogers et al. concluded that the NIM scale is most effective in identifying the malingering of more severe mental disorders. It is interesting to note that there was no effect of subject sophistication; the scale was equally effective in identifying naive and sophisticated malingerers. Gaies (1993) conducted a similar study of malingering, focusing on the feigning of clinical depression, and reported average scores on NIM of 92*t* for sophisticated malingerers and 81*t* for naive malingerers. Although both simulation groups were elevated relative to honestly responding groups, the results were similar to those of Rogers et al. in suggesting that individuals attempting to simulate milder forms of mental disorder (in this case, depression) will obtain more moderate elevations on NIM. A similar conclusion was reached in a study by Bagby, Nicholson, Bacchiochi, Ryder, and Bury (2002) that also examined the effects of coaching on different malingering indexes. In their sample of malingerers, who appeared to be primarily attempting to simulate depression, the effect size of the NIM difference between bona fide and malingered patients was roughly one half standard deviation—considerably less than the 1.63 standard deviations obtained in the Morey and Lanier (1998) sample that attempted to malinger more severe psychopathology. As with previous studies, the Bagby et al. results suggested that coaching had little effect on NIM efficiency.

In summary, the NIM scale has a place in the assessment of malingering on the PAI, but it also has limitations. It appears to work best with efforts to simulate severe forms of mental disorder; when milder forms of disorder are falsified, it is less sensitive. In addition to limitations associated with the type of mental disorder malingered, the NIM scale has limited utility as a specific indicator of malingering. This is because NIM was designed as a general measure of a response style leading the clinician to form a more negative impression than what might be objectively warranted; it is not a malingering scale per se.

The Malingering Index

The need for a more specific indicator of malingering led to the development of the Malingering index (Morey, 1996). The Malingering index is comprised of eight configural features of the PAI profile that tend to be observed much more frequently in the profiles of persons simulating mental disorder (particularly severe mental disorders) than in actual clinical patients; these features are presented in Rapid Reference 5.1. The Malingering index is scored by determining the number of positive features, and thus scores can range from zero to eight.

The features of the Malingering index range from basic elevations of the validity scales to particular (and peculiar) configural aspects of the clinical scales and subscales. With respect to the former, one feature is scored positive if the NIM t score is greater than or equal to

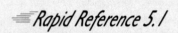

Rapid Reference 5.1

Configural Indicators of the Malingering Index

1. NIM $\geq$ 110t
2. NIM – INF $\geq$ 20t
3. INF – ICN $\geq$ 15t
4. PAR-P – PAR-H $\geq$ 15t
5. PAR-P – PAR-R $\geq$ 15t
6. MAN-I – MAN-G $\geq$ 15t
7. DEP $\geq$ 85 and RXR $\geq$ 45t
8. ANT-E – ANT-A $\geq$ 10

110t. The limitations of NIM for assessment of malingering for this use have been discussed previously. Nonetheless, although elevations on NIM are not uncommon in clinical samples, extreme elevations (such as those of 110t or above) are very uncommon in any sample of respondents completing the test under standard instructions. Elevations in this range tend to be specific to subjects instructed to simulate disorders, particularly severe mental disorders such as schizophrenia.

An example of a peculiar clinical scale configuration may be found in the item that is scored positive if DEP is greater than or equal to 85t while RXR is greater than or equal to 45t. This item reflects mistaken assumptions about individuals with mental disorders—in particular, the belief that individuals suffering from such disorders lack insight into the nature and severity of their condition. Such stereotypes often lead lay observers to underestimate the marked distress and motivation for change that characterize most forms of mental disorder. On the PAI, it is very uncommon to find respondents who report both a significant degree of distress (as indicated by elevations on DEP) and little motivation to change (as indicated by scores on RXR approximating those obtained from nonpatients). In actual clinical samples, these two scales display a strong inverse relationship, and elevations on DEP are typically associated with very low (e.g., 35t or below) scores on RXR. Scores at or above 45t on RXR are almost never associated with DEP scores of 85t or above in true patients. However, in simulation samples, RXR is often found to be close to 50t, even in the presence of indicators of marked distress.

Morey (1996) presented data demonstrating that each feature of the Malingering index was observed with far greater frequency in a simulated mental disorder group than in actual clinical or community samples, with an average score for a malingering sample of 4.41 positive items compared to a mean of 0.80 for the clinical standardization sample. A Malingering index score of 3 or above lies more than 2 standard deviations above the mean of the clinical standardization sample, and scores in this range should raise questions of malingering. Scores of 5 or more are highly unusual in clinical samples and tend to occur only when severe mental disorder is being feigned. (See Rapid Reference 5.2.)

Follow-up studies of the validity of the Malingering index have generally been supportive. Morey and Lanier (1998) found that a cutting score of 3

≡Rapid Reference 5.2

Malingering Index

Source: Morey, 1996.

Content: Sum of eight configural features of profile involving comparisons among 12 PAI scales and subscales.

Descriptive statistics: Community sample mean of 0.46 features (SD = 0.74); clinical sample mean of 0.80 (SD = 0.98).

Correlates: Correlates moderately with NIM and MMPI F and inversely with PIM; correlates modestly with Rogers discriminant function.

Interpretation: Scores of 3 or above raise questions of overt efforts to malinger more severe mental disorder; scores of 5 or above are highly specific to malingering. Score appears to show moderate relationship to respondent's true mental health status; false positive elevations are more common among hostile, suspicious, and unempathic patients.

demonstrated a sensitivity of 81.8% and a specificity of 93.3% in naive simulators who appeared to be feigning severe mental disorders; the effect size distinguishing these two groups was a sizable 1.75 standard deviations. Scragg et al. (2000) reported sensitivity of 45% and specificity of 94% of the index in distinguishing malingering individuals from those with true posttraumatic stress disorder. Feigning status in male inmates, as identified by the Structured Interview of Reported Symptoms (SIRS; Rogers, Bagby, & Dickens, 1992), has also been found to be associated with Malingering index scores in the anticipated direction (Wang et al., 1997).

The Gaies (1993) study of the malingering of depression, using a cutoff of 3 or greater as an indicator of malingering, found a sensitivity of 56.6% for identifying the informed malingerers and 34.2% for identifying the naive malingerers. Specificity of the index in a sample of patients who were actually depressed was 89.3%, while normal controls demonstrated a specificity of 100%. Bagby et al. (2000), whose simulation subjects also appeared to be feigning depression, found an effect size of roughly .5 standard deviations distinguishing bona fide patients from uncoached feigners, but the index did not distinguish between coached feigners and true patients. Similar to the results obtained using NIM, it appears that the sensitivity of the Malingering index will decline when milder forms of psychopathology (such as depression or anxiety) are being simulated, although the effects of coaching appear to be mixed. Thus, in situations in which the malingering of milder disorders is a concern, adjustments to the index cutoff may be needed to optimize the utility of decisions.

Rogers Discriminant Function

The Rogers index (Rogers et al., 1996) is a discriminant function that was developed to distinguish the PAI profiles of bona fide patients from those of individuals simulating such patients (including both naive and coached simulators). The specific function is not included here because it includes weighted combinations of 20 different PAI scores (the actual formula is included in both Rogers et al., 1996, and Morey, 1996). The formula yields a discriminant function score that has a cutting score of roughly 0. Thus, in interpreting the results of the function, scores greater than 0 suggest malingering, whereas scores less than 0 suggest that no effort at negative distortion was made. The function has the very interesting characteristic of yielding similar results when it is applied to both community and patient samples; each obtains average scores of roughly –1.00 (with a standard deviation of approximately 1.0). The similarity of community and clinical groups means that scores on this function are independent of clinical status—thus, the function (unlike NIM, for example) does not appear to confound true psychopathology and effortful negative impression management.

In deriving the function, Rogers et al. (1996) found estimates of sensitivity and specificity in excess of 80% in both derivation and cross-validation; these results were superior to those obtained with the use of the NIM scale in isolation. Morey (1996) found a close replication of the results of Rogers et al. (1996) with this function using naive college student simulators. A subsequent comparison of NIM, the Malingering index, and this index found the Rogers function to be most accurate (1.96 standard deviation effect size) in identifying simulators (Morey & Lanier, 1998); using a cutting score of +0.53 resulted in 95.5% sensitivity and 95.6% specificity. Scragg et al. (2000) reported a sensitivity of .63 and a specificity of .94 for the Rogers function in their study of malingered posttraumatic stress disorder. Bagby et al. (2002) found very large effect sizes distinguishing bona fide patients from coached feigners (1.87 standard deviations) as well as uncoached feigners (1.55 stan-

≣ Rapid Reference 5.3

Rogers Discriminant Function

Source: Rogers et al., 1996.

Content: Weighted sum of features from 20 PAI scales and subscales.

Descriptive statistics: Community sample mean of −1.00 (SD = 1.08); clinical sample mean of −1.15 (SD = 1.17).

Correlates: Correlates modestly with the Malingering index and INF; minimal correlations with NIM or MMPI's F scale.

Interpretation: Scores above 0 suggest overt efforts to malinger mental disorder. Score appears to show little relationship to respondent's true mental health status; thus, elevations are unlikely to be produced by true psychopathology.

---

dard deviations). However, Wang et al. (1997) failed to find any relationship between the Rogers index and malingering classification based on the SIRS. (See Rapid Reference 5.3.)

Negatively Distorted Responding: Interpreting Indicator Configuration

Each of the three PAI negative distortion indicators—NIM, the Malingering index, and the Rogers discriminant function—have received validity support for their ability to identify malingering. However, each indicator seems to have somewhat different properties in this regard. These differences are clearly evident in the pattern of correlations observed among the three indicators (Morey, 1996). NIM correlated .61 with the Malingering index but only .09 with the Rogers discriminant function, whereas the Malingering index correlated .26 with the Rogers function. This pattern of association appears to represent the degree to which the different indicators are free of influence from true psychopathology; the NIM scale is relatively highly saturated with influ-

DON'T FORGET

The configuration of the different PAI validity indicators may provide information to assist in distinguishing effortful distortion of test results from automatic or unconscious sources of distortion.

ences of psychopathology, the Rogers function is virtually free of such influences, and the Malingering index appears to be somewhere in between in this regard.

This pattern of properties provides interesting configural information about negative distortion that can potentially shed light on the relative contributions of covert and overt influences on the profile. There are four basic prototype configurations that may be seen. When all three negative indicators are markedly elevated (e.g., 90t or greater) to approximately the same degree, the research suggests the respondent is effortfully attempting to simulate severe psychopathology. When NIM is elevated but the Rogers function is average and the Malingering index falls somewhere in between, the pattern suggests that covert factors—probably associated with true psychopathology— may be distorting the profile in a negative direction. For example, these factors may involve cognitive distortions of the type found in severe depression, as described earlier. If the configuration is somewhere between these two patterns (NIM > Malingering index > Rogers, with Rogers still at least moderately elevated), it suggests a mixture of covert and overt influences. For example, a person with true clinical problems may be attempting to ensure, perhaps through some conscious exaggeration, that these problems are duly noted by the evaluating clinician. The fourth prototype configuration involves the Rogers function as the largest elevation (Rogers > Malingering index > NIM). This pattern suggests overt efforts at malingering; if NIM is only modestly elevated, this may suggest that the person is attempting to simulate a milder form of mental disorder, such as depression or anxiety.

Identifying Positive Distortion

As with negative distortion, the factors leading to positive distortion (i.e., distortion in the direction of psychological health) are diverse. For example, the stigma of mental illness and the limitations of psychological insight can give rise to an underreporting of clinical problems. Distortion may arise from personality traits or from situational influences on a respondent, it may involve intentional distortion or true lack of awareness, or it could involve selective defensiveness about some problem areas (e.g., substance abuse) but not others (e.g., anxiety). Identifying positive distortions has arguably been the most difficult assessment task for researchers and clinicians because most procedures that have been developed to identify defensiveness tend to show large overlap with normal functioning.

Detecting defensive response patterns with the PAI may be accomplished through the use of a number of strategies. Each strategy provides information useful in assessing profile validity, but none are infallible. The supplementation of PAI profile information with concurrent reports from family members, peers, documents or records, and other psychological and laboratory testing is recommended when situational factors press for the underreporting of clinical problems. Such situations can include but are not limited to pre-employment screenings, fitness for duty evaluations, child custody decisions, criminal dispositions, and involuntary hospitalization or treatment decisions.

PIM: Positive Impression

The content of PIM scale items involves the presentation of a very favorable impression or the denial of relatively minor faults. The items were selected by examining the distributions of scores for normally functioning individuals, patients, and research participants responding to the PAI under positive impression enhancement instructional sets. The items were selected on the basis of low endorsement frequencies in both normal and clinical participants; however, PIM items are endorsed with greater frequency in normal adults than in clinical patients. Hence, marked elevations in clinical patients are particularly rare and hence are interpretively significant if they are obtained. Both patients and community adults score considerably lower on this scale than do research participants completing the PAI under a positive impression enhancement instructional set.

For the most part, PIM items offer the opportunity for an individual to acknowledge a relatively minor personal fault. Hence, elevated scores indicate that the respondent does not take many opportunities to say negative things about him- or herself. There are a number of reasons that people completing a self-report instrument might not report negative characteristics. One possibility is that the respondent indeed does not have negative characteristics or at least has fewer such characteristics than do most respondents. A second possibility is that they are not telling the truth—that they are trying to deceive the recipient of the test results into believing that they have more positive features than they really do. A third possibility is that they are simply not aware of certain faults that they may have—that they lack insight into some of their personal shortcomings. In either of the latter two instances, the results of a self-report test will lead the interpreter to form a more positive impression of the respondent's life circumstances and psychological adjustment than would probably be merited according to an independent observer. It is these latter two characteristics that PIM was designed to measure.

It should be recognized that the tendency for favorable self-presentation appears to be fairly common in the normal population. Typically, most cutting scores on indexes of social desirability that were derived from clinical studies will identify 30–40% of the general population as faking good. Such results underscore the difficulty of distinguishing defensive responding from normality with respect to clinical instruments. A number of instruments have used scales similar to PIM to correct other scales on the test for defensive responding as if such scales tapped pure suppressor variables, but the PAI makes no such correction because attempts to eliminate social desirability from clinical scale scores tends to remove criterion-related variance and hence lowers validity.

The interpretation of PIM scores is facilitated by the results of a number of studies of the performance of participants attempting to manage their impression in a positive direction. These studies have tended to yield results that are remarkably consistent with respect to the application of cutting scores for distortion decisions. In an initial examination of PIM, Morey (1991) compared the PIM scores of college students instructed to fake good to the scores of a community sample. The point of rarity between the distributions of the impression management sample (i.e., fake good) and the community normative sample corresponded to a score of $57t$; application of this cut score resulted in a sensitivity in the identification of defensiveness of 82% and a specificity with respect to normal individuals of 70%. These findings have been replicated; for example, a study by Cashel et al. (1995) also identified $57t$ as their optimal cutting score. Their study, in which respondents were coached regarding believability of results, yielded sensitivity and specificity rates of 48% and 81%, respectively. Peebles and Moore (1998) also found a cutting score of $57t$ to be optimal for their sample, resulting in a hit rate of 85.1% in distinguishing forthright from fake-good responders. Morey and Lanier (1998) found that the $57t$ cutting score yielded a 93.3% sensitivity and a 77.8% specificity for identifying positive dissimulators. Baer and Wetter (1997) found a large 2.56 standard deviation effect size for PIM in identifying un-coached dissimulators, but this dropped to a more moderate 0.49 effect in coached underreporters. The optimum cutting score in their study was 56t, which led to an 88% hit rate for identifying uncoached and a hit rate of 64% for coached participants. Finally, a study by Fals-Stewart (1996) found that the 57t cutoff score on PIM had a sensitivity of 88% in identifying questionable responding in substance abusers (e.g., forensic patients who denied substance use but had positive urine screens), with a specificity of 80% in honestly responding groups. These studies have also converged in identifying low PIM scores as a useful exclusion criterion for defensive responding. For example, Cashel et al. (1995) found that scores below 43t could be used with very high specificity; in other words, virtually no participant attempting to manage his or her impression obtained scores below that value on PIM.

Another approach for identifying problematic protocols uses cutting scores derived from the distributions of clinical subjects. Use of the reference data from clinical patients is particularly relevant for the impression manage-ment scales because community and clinical subjects tend to differ in this re-gard. For PIM, a score of 68t or above corresponds to a score that is 2 stan-dard deviations above the mean for clinical subjects. Applying this more conservative decision rule results in decisions that are more specific to at-tempts at impression management than are those provided by the empirical cutoffs. In other words, relatively few actual protocols are identified as invalid using the cutoffs of 2 standard deviations or clinical norms; the specificity rates for this cutoff are 95% or greater. However, the sensitivity in identifying dissimulated protocols with this higher cutoff falls to 52–57% (Morey, 1991; Morey & Lanier, 1998), and this rate drops to 17% when respondents are coached regarding believability of results (Cashel et al., 1995).

Thus, low scores on PIM (< 44t) are strongly indicative of honest re-sponding. Generally, scores between 44t and 57t suggest that the respondent did not attempt to present an unrealistically favorable impression in complet-ing the test, although scores in the upper end of this range tend to be unusual in clinical settings. Moderate elevations (between 57t and 68t) suggest that the examinee responded in a manner to portray him- or herself as relatively free of the common shortcomings to which most individuals will admit. This re-sponse style could be overt, but it could also involve a covert, automatic de-fensive process. With PIM in this range, the accuracy of interpretations based on the PAI clinical scales profile may be distorted and interpretive hypotheses should be reviewed with caution. It is likely that the PAI profile will underrepresent the extent and degree of significant test findings. High scores on PIM (at or above 68t) suggest that the respondent attempted to portray him- or herself as exceptionally free of the common shortcomings to which most individuals will admit. When scores in this range are obtained, the validity of the PAI clinical scale profile is questionable, and extreme caution in the clinical interpretation of other PAI scales is recommended. As noted previously, however, such scores are usually rare, and concerns about defensiveness should be raised at even lower scores.

The Defensiveness Index

The Defensiveness index (Morey, 1996) involves a set of indicators developed to further supplement the tools for identifying defensive responding. This index is comprised of eight configural features of the PAI profile that tend to be observed with greater frequency in subjects instructed to present a positive impression as compared to either community or clinical subjects. One of the eight items is double-weighted (if the PIM scale is above average); all other items are worth 1 point if present, meaning that this index can range from 0 to 9. Rapid Reference 5.4 presents the eight features of the index.

The features shown in Rapid Reference 5.4 range from basic elevations of the PIM scale to relatively unusual configural aspects of the clinical scales and subscales. With respect to the former, the first feature listed is scored positive (either 1 or 2 points) depending upon the elevation of PIM. This item is weighted 2 points for PIM scores at or above 50t and 1 point for a score from 45t to 49t. It is unusual for individuals in clinical settings to ob-

Rapid Reference 5.4

Configural Features of the Defensiveness Index

Index Item	Item Weight
1. PIM $\geq$ 50t	2
or $\geq$ 45t	1
2. RXR $\geq$ 45t	1
3. ANT-E – ANT-A $\geq$ 10t	1
4. ANT-S – ANT-A $\geq$ 10t	1
5. MAN-G – MAN-I $\geq$ 10t	1
6. ARD-O – ANX-A $\geq$ 10t	1
7. DOM – AGG-V $\geq$ 15t	1
8. MAN-A – STR $\geq$ 10t	1

tain scores above 50*t*, and even scores of 45*t* are uncommon among this group. Elevations in this range are common in the general population because about one half of such individuals would be expected to score above the mean of 50*t*. However, nearly all individuals responding in a positive dissimulation response set will score above 50*t*. This item on the Defensiveness index recognizes the utility of PIM as an exclusion criterion for defensive responding, while underscoring the finding that in isolation PIM is not sufficient evidence of effortful defensiveness because many normally functioning individuals will also be positive for this item.

An example of an unusual clinical scale configuration may be found in the item that is scored positive if there is a 15-point discrepancy between reported levels of dominance and tendency to express anger verbally (DOM > AGG-V). The DOM scale is often elevated in dissimulation samples because it represents the reported ability to assume leadership roles effectively. A person demonstrating this difference between DOM and AGG-V is describing him- or herself as very effective in controlling other people without ever having to verbally admonish others. Such people portray themselves as naturally dominant, such that others will follow their wishes without any need for assertiveness on their part. This desirable but unlikely combination of features appears six to seven times more frequently in dissimulation samples than it does in the general population (Morey, 1996).

Morey (1996) found that the average score for a naive fake-good sample on the Defensiveness index was 6.23, as compared to 2.81 of these features in the normative community sample (Morey, 1996). A follow up study (Morey & Lanier, 1998) found that a cutting score of 5 resulted in 93.3% sensitivity and 86.7% specificity in distinguishing normal and dissimulation groups in college students. Similarly, Peebles and Moore (1998) reported a hit rate of 83.3% for the Defensiveness index in distinguishing forthright from fake-good responding. However, a study performed by Cashel et al. (1995) reported a lower mean score of 4.27 on the Defensiveness index in a group of positive dissimulators who had been coached about validity scales; this score still lies roughly 1 standard deviation above the norm for community samples. Baer and Wetter (1997) found that the effect size of the index dropped markedly from a 1.62 standard deviation difference between normal administration and uncoached dissimulators to a 0.20 difference comparing coached simulators. These results suggest that the sensitivity of the Defensiveness index is low-

≡Rapid Reference 5.5

Defensiveness Index

Source: Morey, 1996.

Content: Sum of eight configural features of profile involving comparisons among 13 PAI scales and subscales.

Descriptive statistics: Community sample mean of 2.81 features (SD = 1.52); clinical sample mean of 1.66 (SD = 1.54).

Correlates: Correlates moderately with PIM and MMPI's L; correlates modestly with the Cashel discriminant function, MMPI's K, and the Marlowe-Crowne Social Desirability Scale.

Interpretation: Scores of 6 or above raise questions of overt efforts to fake good; sensitivity appears lower in individuals coached to produce believable positive impression profiles. Score appears to show moderate relationship to respondent's true mental health status.

ered in samples coached for believability in being defensive, as noted in Rapid Reference 5.5.

The results of these studies suggest that a person scoring 6 or greater on the Defensiveness index is likely to be overtly defensive, although the sensitivity of this cutting score would appear to be limited in coached dissimulators. Thus, scores lower than 6 should not be considered to be efficient exclusion signs for defensiveness. In other words, defensive people may not score high on the index and scores within normal limits should not be considered to rule out the possibility of a dissimulated protocol. Nonetheless, the Defensiveness index displays promise and merits further study as a tool for use in addressing effortful positive impression management.

Cashel Discriminant Function

The Cashel discriminant function was derived in a detailed study of defensive responding on the PAI conducted by Cashel et al. (1995). They instructed two types of participants (college students and jail inmates) to answer the PAI in a fashion that would portray them in the best possible manner, but the instructions also stressed the believability of the resulting profile. The authors constructed a discriminant function that was designed to optimally distinguish between defensive and honest responding, reporting that this function was more accurate in identifying dissimulated responding than either the PIM score in isolation or the score on the Defensiveness index. The scales and the relevant weights are presented in Rapid Reference 5.6.

This function involves multiplying the t scores for six PAI scales by the weights presented in Rapid Reference 5.6 and then summing these products to create a function score (note that the weights for two scales—ALC and STR—are negative, meaning that these scores are subtracted from the function total rather than added). Morey (1996) applied this function to the normative community sample of the PAI, which resulted in a mean value of 138.14 and a standard deviation of 14.91 for this composite. Morey also found that the function had the interesting characteristic of yielding similar results when applied to both community and patient samples (which had a mean value of 135.28). The similarity of community and clinical groups suggests that scores on this function are independent of actual mental health status; thus, the function (unlike PIM, for example) holds the promise of disentangling true mental health from effortful positive impression management.

Cashel et al. (1995) found that this discriminant function demonstrated sensitivities ranging from 79% to 87% in identifying falsified profiles, with specificity of 88%. Close replication of the results of Cashel et al. (1995) with this function have been found using naive dissimulators (Morey, 1996). Morey and Lanier (1998) found that a score of 148.44 demonstrated a 97.8% sensitivity and a 71.1% specificity in distinguishing normal and dissimulation groups in college students. Surprisingly, the Morey and Lanier study also found that the Cashel function was effective in distinguishing malingering simulators from both bona fide clinical patients and community respondents.

≡Rapid Reference 5.6

....

Calculating the Cashel Discriminant Function

Cashel score =   1.67 multiplied by BOR t score
plus .97 multiplied by PIM t score
plus .72 multiplied by MAN t score
plus .60 multiplied by RXR t score
minus .52 multiplied by ALC t score
minus .68 multiplied by STR t score

However, the malingering study by Bagby et al. (2002) did not replicate this finding. Thus, it is unclear whether the Cashel function can be used effectively in identifying negative as well as positive distortion, but the possibility that it may be a nonspecific indication of effortful distortion in either direction should be considered when interpreting the function results. Rapid Reference 5.7 provides important summary information about this function.

Thus, low scores on the Cashel function (< 135) indicate honest responding. Generally, scores between 145 and 160 suggest some efforts at impression management in completing the test. With scores in this range, the accuracy of interpretations based on the PAI clinical scales profile may be distorted and interpretive hypotheses should be reviewed with caution; certain aspects of the PAI profile may underrepresent the degree of problems in selected areas. It should be noted that scores in the lower end of this range tend to be more common in younger participants (i.e., 18–25 years old), in part due to the higher BOR scores that tend to be obtained in these groups. High scores on the Cashel function (> 160) suggest that the respondent overtly attempted to portray him- or herself in a distorted way and that the profile probably reflects the way the respondent desired to appear rather than the true experiences of the respondent.

≡Rapid Reference 5.7

Cashel Discriminant Function

Source: Cashel et al., 1995.

Content: Weighted sum of features from six PAI full scales.

Descriptive statistics: Community sample mean of 138.14 (SD = 14.91); clinical sample mean of 135.28 (SD = 18.79).

Correlates: Correlates modestly with the Defensiveness index and Marlowe-Crowne Social Desirability Scale; minimal correlations with PIM or MMPI's K scale.

Interpretation: Scores above 160 suggest overt efforts to distort profile, typically in a healthy direction, although examinees instructed to malinger severe mental disorder may also score high. Score appears to show little relationship to respondent's true mental health status. Scores in the 140–150 range are more common among 18- to 21-year-olds.

Defensive Responding: Interpreting Indicator Configuration

The three PAI positive distortion indicators—PIM, the Defensiveness index, and the Cashel discriminant function—have received validity support for their ability to identify defensive individuals in simulation studies. However, as with the negative distortion indicators, these positive distortion indicators seem to have somewhat different properties. The differences are evident from the intercorrelations among the three indicators (Morey, 1996): PIM correlated .56 with the Defensiveness index but only .06 with the Cashel discriminant function, whereas the Defensiveness index correlated .32 with the Cashel function. This pattern of association appears to represent the degree to which the different indicators are independent of true mental health status; the PIM scale is relatively influenced by true adjustment status, the Cashel function is largely independent of mental health status, and the Defensiveness index appears to fall somewhere between the other two indexes in this regard.

The configuration of these three indexes can thus potentially clarify the relative contributions of covert and overt defensiveness to the PAI profile. As with the negative indicators, there are four basic prototype configurations that may be seen with the positive distortion indicators. When all three indicators are markedly elevated, the research suggests the respondent is effortfully attempting to present a favorable impression (i.e., fake good). When PIM is elevated but the Cashel function is average and the Defensiveness index falls somewhere in between, the pattern suggests that covert factors, such as a lack of insight or awareness of difficulties, may be distorting the profile in the direction of mental health. When the configuration is somewhere between these two patterns (PIM > Defensiveness index > Cashel, with the Cashel function still displaying some elevation), a mixture of covert and overt influences is likely. For example, a person may be consciously trying to present a favorable image but may also be unaware that problems are more serious than such a person will acknowledge even to him- or herself. The fourth prototypical configuration involves the Cashel function as the largest elevation (Cashel > Defensiveness index > PIM). This pattern suggests overt positive dissimulation. If neither the Defensiveness index nor PIM displays any elevation, it is also possible that there is overt negative profile distortion, as suggested by the results of the Morey and Lanier (1998) study described previously.

Examining Substance Abuse Denial

One content area that represents a particularly salient issue for positive profile distortion involves the assessment of substance abuse. Both the ALC and DRG scales include items that address substance use and problems related to substance use directly. In other words, the item content is not subtle; hence, the scales are susceptible to denial, a problem of concern to many in the substance abuse field. This denial can be either overt (e.g., a person denying use of illicit drugs in a forensic context) or covert (e.g., an alcoholic defensively minimizing the negative consequences of drinking).

There are three general strategies for detecting substance use underreporting on the PAI. The first strategy is simply to consider that elevations on the positive distortion indicators might signify substance abuse underreporting. For example, as noted earlier, a study by Fals-Stewart (1996) found that the 57t cutoff score on PIM had a sensitivity of 88% and a specificity of 80% in distinguishing questionable responding in substance abusers (e.g., forensic patients who denied substance use but had positive urine screens) from honestly responding groups. With a PIM score elevated in this range, the combination of low ALC and DRG scales in the presence of elevations on other clinical scales may be suggestive of substance abuse denial.

The remaining two strategies involve actuarial functions for identifying substance abuse underreporting. In his study, Fals-Stewart (1996) combined ALC, DRG, and PIM into multivariate composite scores to distinguish substance abuse patients, defensive substance abuse patients, and nonclinical controls. This procedure involved the use of the following three equations:

$$\text{Standard substance abuse patient} = .0269(\text{DRG}) + .0029(\text{ALC}) - .0022(\text{PIM}) - 1.3429$$

$$\text{Defensive substance abuse patient} = .0067(\text{DRG}) + .0015(\text{ALC}) + .0437(\text{PIM}) - 2.537$$

$$\text{Nonclinical control} = -0.0337(\text{DRG}) - .0044(\text{ALC}) - .0416(\text{PIM}) + 4.88$$

The result of each of these equations reflects the probability of being assigned to each of the three groups. Fals-Stewart (1996) assigned the cases in his study to the group for which the highest of the three scores was obtained.

This procedure correctly classified 82.2% of his derivation cases. However, this hit rate demonstrated shrinkage to 68% accuracy in a cross-validation study (Fals-Stewart & Lucente, 1997); thus, the generalizability of the procedure may be limited.

The final strategy for detecting substance abuse underreporting involves a comparison of observed scores on ALC and DRG with scores anticipated based on other personality features present in the PAI profile. In this approach, low scores on ALC or DRG are regarded with suspicion if the person has other characteristics that would lead one to expect the person to have at least experimented with alcohol or controlled substances. Morey (1996) developed a linear regression strategy to identify potential underreporting of alcohol and substance use problems, based on the finding that BOR-S (indicating impulsivity), ANT-S (sensation-seeking), ANT-A (history of antisocial behavior), ANT-E (interpersonal callousness), and AGG-P (history of physical aggression) all tend to display moderate correlations with both ALC and DRG. Thus, if these five scales are elevated, one would also expect ALC, DRG, or both to be elevated to some extent. The degree of this elevation could be predicted by summing the t scores from these five PAI subscales (BOR-A, ANT-A, ANT-E, ANT-S, AGG-P) and applying the following formulas:

$$\text{Estimated ALC } t \text{ score} = 0.162184 \text{ (sum of 5 scales)} + 14.39$$

$$\text{Estimated DRG } t \text{ score} = 0.199293 \text{ (sum of 5 scales)} + 3.07$$

When Morey (1996) applied the results of these equations to the mean profiles of the samples obtained by Fals-Stewart (1996), the defensive responding groups obtained estimated DRG and ALC scores that were 10 to 15t points (1–1.5 standard deviations) higher than their actual scores. In contrast, the standard administration substance abuse patients obtained estimated scores that were markedly lower than their actual ALC and DRG scores. Thus,

DON'T FORGET

When the observed scores on ALC or DRG are 10t or more below what is estimated from predictor scales, the possibility of underreporting of substance use and its consequences should be considered.

Morey (1996) recommended that a discrepancy of 10*t* or more (when estimated exceeds observed) should raise questions of substance abuse denial. When such discrepancies are obtained, discussing substance use with some type of collateral informant (such as a spouse or family member) might be worthwhile.

 TEST YOURSELF

1. **A client completes the PAI carelessly. You should expect elevations on scales**
   (a) ICN.
   (b) INF.
   (c) PIM.
   (d) both a and b.

2. **NIM is most likely to identify individuals**
   (a) malingering milder mental disorders such as anxiety or depression.
   (b) malingering severe mental disorders such as schizophrenia.
   (c) who malinger, but only if they have not been coached.
   (d) only with cognitive distortions; it is ineffective for malingering.

3. **Concerns about positive impression management should begin to be considered when PIM is**
   (a) greater than or equal to 50t.
   (b) greater than or equal to 57t.
   (c) greater than or equal to 68t.
   (d) greater than or equal to 70t.

4. **Which of the following may elevate in the presence of both malingering and positive response distortion?**
   (a) Cashel function
   (b) Rogers function
   (c) NIM
   (d) PIM

(continued)

5. Which of the following accurately describes normative data for the Cashel and the Rogers discriminant functions?

   (a) Clinical and community groups differ little.

   (b) Clinical groups score higher on both than do community groups.

   (c) Community groups score higher on both than do clinical groups.

   (d) Clinical groups score higher on the Rogers index but not on the Cashel index.

6. If NIM is elevated and the Rogers function yields an average score, what is the recommended interpretation?

7. Concern about substance abuse denial should result when

   (a) $PIM > 57t$.

   (b) observed ALC > estimated ALC.

   (c) estimated DRG – observed DRG > $10t$.

   (d) a and c.

8. The Fals-Stewart discriminant function for identifying substance abuse denial performed as well upon cross-validation as it did when it was derived. True or False?

9. The Cashel discriminant function for identifying defensiveness performed as well upon cross-validation as it did when it was derived. True or False?

Answers: 1. d; 2. b; 3. b; 4. a; 5. a; 6. The respondent has true psychopathology that may be negatively distorting the profile; 7. d; 8. False; 9. True

Six

THE INDIVIDUAL PAI SCALES

The basic step in interpreting the PAI involves a consideration of the individual scales. Each scale on the test was designed to measure the major facets of a particular clinical construct, as determined by current theoretical and empirical work on that construct. Because most of the clinical scales offer subscales, configural interpretation of the test is possible even at the level of the individual scales because two identical elevations on a particular scale may be interpreted differently depending on the configuration of the subscales. The following sections describe the logic behind the substantive scales of the PAI and the interpretations of different ranges and configurations of scores on the scale.

SOM: SOMATIC COMPLAINTS

The target features assessed by SOM reflect complaints and concerns about physical functioning and health matters in general. As discussed later in this section, the nature of the physical problems varies somewhat as a function of the configuration of the SOM subscales, but a full-scale elevation suggests that the physical conditions are a central concern in an individual's life. Patients with very similar physical conditions can differ in their adaptation to the condition; one person might react stoically, whereas another person might ruminate bitterly about his or her limitations, perhaps even using the problems as a means of controlling those around him or her. In both situations there may well be valid physical problems, but the psychological reaction to the problems is markedly different. The SOM scale provides information about the latter, but it should not be used in isolation to determine the veracity of any somatic complaints. Self-report questionnaires such as the PAI simply have little demonstrated ability to distinguish between functional and organic somatic features. Like all such tests, the PAI is not sufficient for establishing a diagnosis of a physical condition.

The full-scale score of SOM reflects the degree of concern about physical functioning and health matters and the extent of perceived impairment arising from somatic symptoms. Average scores on SOM (below 60*t*) reflect a person with few bodily complaints. Such individuals are typically seen as optimistic, alert, and effective. Scores between 60*t* and 70*t* indicate some concern about health functioning; such scores are relatively common in older adults and in medical patients with relatively specific organic symptoms. Scores above 70*t* suggest significant concerns about somatic functioning and probably impairment arising from somatic symptoms. Such a person will feel that he or she is in poor health, with the health problems perceived as complex and difficult to treat. For such people, social interactions and conversations are likely to focus on their health problems, and their self-image may be largely influenced by the belief that they are handicapped by poor health. Individuals scoring in this range may be seen as unhappy, complaining, and pessimistic, and they may be using somatic complaints to control others in a passive-aggressive manner. SOM scores that are markedly elevated (above 87*t*) are unusual even in clinical samples; such scores suggest a ruminative preoccupation with physical functioning and health matters and severe impairment arising from somatic symptoms. In that range, the somatic complaints are likely to be chronic and accompanied by fatigue and weakness that render the individual incapable of performing even minimal role expectations. Such scores reflect a large number of somatic complaints affecting most organ systems. The self-image of individuals scoring in this range may focus on the belief that they are handicapped; such individuals are likely to be accustomed to the patient role.

Subscale Structure

As shown in Rapid Reference 6.1, the SOM scale has three subscales: Conversion, Somatization, and Health Concerns.

SOM-C: Conversion

The Conversion subscale includes items corresponding to the dramatic physiological symptoms that have been found to be prevalent in conversion disorders. Most of these symptoms involve unusual sensory and motor prob-

≡ Rapid Reference 6.1

....

Subscales for Somatic Complaints (SOM)

Conversion (SOM-C): Focuses on rare symptoms of sensory or motor dysfunctions associated with conversion disorder; can elevate in certain medical conditions.

Somatization (SOM-S): Focuses on the frequent occurrence of various common physical symptoms and vague complaints of ill health and fatigue.

Health Concerns (SOM-H): Focuses on a preoccupation with health status and physical problems.

lems: impairments in perception (vision problems, hearing problems, or numbness) or motor problems such as paralysis. The mean raw score in the normative sample on the Conversion subscale is very low, confirming that these symptoms are unusual in the general population. Although such symptoms may be rare, there are some populations in which these symptoms are more common because there are a variety of physical conditions that result in sensory and motor problems. For example, people with multiple sclerosis, stroke survivors, and those with other neurological disorders all may have sensory and motor problems. It has been observed that the SOM-C subscale is probably the most sensitive scale on the PAI to various forms of central nervous system impairment. One diagnostic group that frequently obtains elevations on SOM-C involves chronic alcoholics who are beginning to experience some neuropsychological compromise associated with their drinking. Many times clinicians will use indicators on self-report personality inventories to distinguish a conversion reaction from a genuine organic problem or to distinguish functional from organic pain, but in actuality this diagnostic distinction should never be based solely on the results of such tests. In such instances, a thorough medical evaluation is recommended.

SOM-S: Somatization

The Somatization subscale inquires about routine physical complaints, such as headaches, back problems, pain, or gastrointestinal ailments; these complaints are diagnostic by virtue of their frequency rather than their presence. In comparison to SOM-C, the Somatization subscale consists of complaints that are more vague and diffuse, not localized in any one organ system. There are two components to elevations on the subscale—one involving the physical symptoms (which can include a general lethargy and malaise), and a second element that is related to a more general complaintiveness and dissatisfaction. The SOM-S subscale yields substantial correlations with measures of both psychological as well as physical distress, and individuals with elevations are likely to have a litany of complaints. They will report particular problems with the frequent occurrence of various minor physical symptoms and vague complaints of ill health and fatigue that impede daily functioning, often accompanied by unhappiness and bitterness about their health. This pattern of symptoms is often consistent with a somatization disorder.

SOM-H: Health Concerns

The Health Concerns subscale indicates a preoccupation with health and physical functioning. Items on this subscale are related to the self-perceived complexity of the individual's health problems and the intensity of his or her efforts to ameliorate these problems. The scale is a measure of focus rather than of severity; a general medical population has a very wide range of scores on this subscale and individuals with very serious health problems can still obtain low scores. Such people will tend to strike others as stoic about their problems, whereas a person who is elevated on SOM-H will tend to focus a great deal upon his or her health issues. Individuals with elevations on SOM-H are likely to report that their daily functioning has been compromised by numerous and varied physical problems. If the other subscales are not elevated, such individuals may appear to be relatively healthy to other observers but see themselves as having a history of complex medical problems. They will tend to feel that their health is not as good as that of their age peers, who may view the person as rather hypochondriacal. There are likely to be continuous concerns with health status and physical problems, and the poor health may be a major component of the self-image, with the person accustomed to being in the patient role.

Noteworthy Subscale Configurations

One revealing comparison among the SOM subscales involves the relative elevations of SOM-C and SOM-H; a markedly elevated SOM-C with no accompanying SOM-H elevation reflects the classic configuration of indifference thought to typify conversion hysteria. When SOM-S and SOM-H are high relative to SOM-C, complaintiveness and bitterness are a much more prominent part of the clinical picture; look for particular dissatisfaction with previous treatment efforts.

Diagnostic Considerations

Prominent elevations on this scale are most typically associated with somatoform disorders, such as somatization disorder, hypochondriasis, or conversion disorder. Elevations may also be seen with serious medical conditions, with the average SOM score in such conditions tending to be around 65t (Osborne, 1994). However, physical disorders with a more chronic course or those with some central nervous system involvement (such as multiple sclerosis or traumatic brain injuries) would be expected to yield higher elevations. Chronic alcoholism can lead to physical symptoms (such as peripheral neuropathy) that can manifest as elevated SOM scores. In contrast, elevations among drug abusers are much more infrequent; such individuals may have a blatant disregard for their health status (look for a relatively low SOM-H). Some Cluster B personality disorders, such as histrionic and borderline personality disorders, can demonstrate elevations on this scale, particularly during stressful events that might lead to a concomitant adjustment disorder diagnosis. Symptoms of obsessive-compulsive disorder can focus upon the health-related implications of certain compulsive behaviors and may be noted here, particularly on SOM-H. Finally, elevations on SOM may also be observed in schizophrenia and related disorders; here, the somatic complaints may be related to somatic delusions but may also involve the side effects of antipsychotic medications.

Treatment Considerations

The central treatment challenge for the individual with a SOM elevation involves the preoccupation with somatic functioning and physical explanations of problems, typically coupled with a resistance to examining the role of psychological factors. Such individuals have often been treated by a wide array of health professionals before arriving for the current evaluation and probably view the mental health specialist with skepticism and distrust—fully expecting the results of the evaluation to suggest that "it's all in your head." Thus, the establishment of rapport and a therapeutic alliance is a critical goal for the initial stages of any intervention, which can be aided by a supportive and sympathetic listening to the health concerns of the patient as well as an acknowledgment of his or her dissatisfaction with previous treatment efforts.

When the somatization tendency reflects a tendency on the patient's part to avoid the emotional and psychological realm, verbally oriented therapies will probably prove difficult. Such patients are much more likely to be receptive to the idea of pharmacological interventions, but their sensitivity to physical functioning means that side effects may be poorly tolerated. Such patients may also be taking many medications prescribed from numerous sources, and these medications should be evaluated carefully for any undesirable interactive effects. Interventions that focus on the integration of psychological and physical functions, such as biofeedback or relaxation training, may be a particularly useful step toward an exploration of the cognitive, emotional, and interpersonal aspects of their problems.

ANX: ANXIETY

ANX is a nonspecific indicator of the degree of tension and negative affect experienced by the respondent. The scale includes an examination of different ways in which anxiety is expressed. The differentiation of anxiety modalities was pioneered by Peter Lang (e.g., 1971), who viewed cognitive, somatic, and behavioral as related but independent modes of anxiety expression. Although Lang included the subjective feeling of anxiety as part of the cognitive component of anxiety, others (e.g., Koksal & Power, 1990; Zajonc, 1980) have distinguished between the affective and cognitive experiences of emotion, suggesting that a comprehensive assessment of anxiety includes an assessment of all four systems. The ANX scale of the PAI was designed to assess three of these components of anxiety; several behavioral aspects of anxiety, which often serve as the basis of making different diagnostic decisions, may be found on the ARD scale. Not including such behaviors on the ANX scale makes the scale a more general, nonspecific index of anxiety that does not have specific ties to a particular diagnostic construct. Rather, it relates broadly to the experience of anxiety and to how it is typically expressed.

The full-scale score of ANX gives a broad indication of the involvement of anxiety in the overall clinical picture. Average scores on ANX (below 60t) reflect a person with few complaints of anxiety or tension. Such individuals describe themselves as calm, optimistic, and effective in dealing with stress. Very low scores (below 40t) are indicative of a person reporting remarkable freedom from fear, and it is possible that such a score could represent a reckless lack of prudence in certain situations. Scores between 60t and 70t are indicative of a person who may be experiencing some stress and is worried, sensitive, and emotional. Scores above 70t suggest significant anxiety and tension. With scores in this range, the examinee is probably tense much of the time and ruminative about anticipated misfortune. These individuals may be seen as high-strung, nervous, timid, and dependent. With scores above 70t, at least one subscale is likely to be elevated, and these subscales should be examined to determine the typical modality in which anxiety is expressed. ANX scores that are markedly elevated (above 90t) will probably have elevations on all three subscales, reflecting a generalized impairment associated with anxiety. Such a person's life will be seriously constricted, and he or she may not be able to meet even minimal role expectations without feeling overwhelmed. Mild stressors are likely to precipitate a crisis, and this repeating pattern of crises may present difficulties for psychotherapy despite the motivating nature of the distress. Scores in this range will reflect a diagnosable anxiety disorder in most instances; their scores on ARD may suggest a specific focus for the fears, or a lack of elevation on ARD may suggest that the anxiety is free-floating and generalized.

Subscale Structure

The ANX scale has three subscales as shown in Rapid Reference 6.2, relating to different modes of anxiety expression: Cognitive, Affective, and Physiological.

≡ Rapid Reference 6.2

Subscales for Anxiety (ANX)

Cognitive (ANX-C): Focuses on ruminative worry and concern about current issues that results in impaired concentration and attention.

Affective (ANX-A): Focuses on the experience of tension, difficulty in relaxing, and the presence of fatigue as a result of high perceived stress.

Physiological (ANX-P): Focuses on overt physical signs of tension and stress, such as sweaty palms, trembling hands, complaints of irregular heartbeats, and shortness of breath.

ANX-C: *Cognitive*

The Cognitive subscale of ANX includes items that tap an expectation of harm, ruminative worry, and cognitive beliefs of the type described by Beck and Emery (1979) within the context of cognitive therapy of anxiety disorders. This cognitive component involves a ruminative form of anxiety expression; people operating in this mode of expression tend to dwell on events, running them over and over in their minds. This mode is an internalizing approach to anxiety; such people tend to be vigilant to the experience of anxiety rather than repressing it, and these feelings of being ill at ease will tend to have an ideational target or source. This mode of anxiety expression also tends to have strong trait aspects, meaning that it is a characteristic style of dealing with anxiety as well as an indication of current distress.

Elevated scores on ANX-C indicate worry and concern about current issues to the degree that may compromise the person's ability to concentrate and attend. Such people are likely to be overconcerned about issues and events over which they have no control. As scores get above 85*t*, the worry and negative expectations are likely to be debilitating, and the possibility of intrusive obsessions should be investigated.

ANX-A: *Affective*

The Affective subscale includes items that measure the feelings of tension, apprehension, and nervousness that are characteristic of anxiety. This anxiety tends to be free-floating rather than attached to specific objects or events. Also, the anxiety reflected in this subscale tends to be rather persistent and trait-like; it reflects a dispositionally low threshold for the experience of events as dangerous or threatening. High scorers on this scale experience a great deal of tension, have difficulty in relaxing, and tend to be easily fatigued as a result of high perceived stress.

ANX-P: *Physiological*

The Physiological subscale of ANX includes items that assess the somatic expression of anxiety, such as racing heart, sweaty palms, rapid breathing, and dizziness. This subscale has a pattern of relationships to other constructs that is fairly different from the patterns of ANX-C and ANX-A. For example, the ANX-P subscale is associated much less with indicators of depression and higher with physical symptom expression as compared to ANX-C or ANX-A. This distinction captures the difference between somatization and ideation. ANX-P correlates most highly with the expression of physical symptomatology; people with this pattern may not psychologically experience themselves as anxious, but they show physiological signs that most people associate with anxiety. This pattern suggests a repressive style of dealing with stress; the person may notice overt physical signs such as sweaty palms and shortness of breath but not recognize them as signs of anxiety and stress.

Noteworthy Subscale Configurations

Perhaps the most interesting comparison within these subscales is the relative elevation of ANX-C and ANX-P. This comparison parallels the distinction of "repression versus sensitization" to threat (e.g., Byrne, 1961), with sensitizers displaying ANX-C > ANX-P and repressors demonstrating the reverse pattern. This distinction represents different cognitive strategies for reducing discomfort. Repressors seek to avoid thinking about threatening situations and thus avoid the experience of anxiety. In contrast, sensitizers seek to be vigilant to threat, thereby putting themselves in a position to take effective action when the threat is encountered. In either instance, the relative elevation of ANX-A provides an index of the effectiveness of the strategy; when ANX-A is elevated, the preferred strategy appears to be failing to manage the anxiety. Elevations on ANX-A in the absence of elevations on the remaining ANX subscales are suggestive of generalized anxiety rather than more specific fears such as phobias, obsessive thoughts, or somatic preoccupations.

Diagnostic Considerations

Because anxiety is a prominent part of many clinical conditions, a number of different diagnoses may be associated with elevations on this scale. The most obvious diagnostic correlates involve anxiety disorders of various types. Although these disorders all tend to yield elevated ANX scores, the subscale configurations tend to be different for the differing types of disorders. Anxiety disorders that have a prominent ideational component, such as obsessive-compulsive disorder (in which the ideational activity involves intrusive thoughts) or phobias (in which the ideation centers around avoidance of dreaded situations) will tend to demonstrate prominent ANX-C elevations. Those anxiety disorders in which physiological reactivity is prominent, such as panic disorder, agoraphobia, or posttraumatic stress disorder, often will have ANX-P significantly elevated.

However, ANX elevations can be seen in numerous other diagnostic groups as well. Anxiety is often the prominent symptomatic aspect of an adjustment disorder (look for accompanying elevations on STR). Sensitivity to physiological symptoms of anxiety is typical of many somatoform disorders. In individuals with a diagnosis of schizophrenia, ANX elevations may reflect distress signifying deterioration into a psychotic episode or a recovery from one. Finally, very low scores on ANX may reflect an imperturbability often noted in persons with antisocial personality disorder.

Treatment Considerations

A prominent ANX elevation represents considerable subjective distress and a recognition that the experienced symptoms are disabling. As a result, to an extent these features provide important motivation for treatment and can be favorable prognostic signs. However, at extreme elevations, interventions will need to be supportive and probably oriented toward dealing with immediate crises. The subscale configuration may provide some information about therapeutic targets as well as about the potential usefulness of different treatment modalities. For example, ANX-C elevations may reflect problematic cognitions that can be profitably addressed in cognitive-behavioral therapy. Also, ANX-P elevations reflect poorly controlled autonomic arousal that may be addressed through desensitization procedures or through anxiolytic medications.

ARD: ANXIETY-RELATED DISORDERS

Anxiety is typically a feature in most clinical disorders, and as such it is of limited use in distinguishing between the many specific disorders in which anxiety may be prominent. The behavioral expression of anxiety, however, varies across different disorders; thus, these different diagnostic syndromes are typically defined by characteristic behaviors. The ARD scale assesses phenomena central to three important anxiety-related disorders that—in conjunction with marked anxiety as measured by ANX—can serve as a more specific indicator of these disorders.

The full-scale score of ARD is perhaps the most difficult to interpret of any score on the PAI because of its composition of three fairly diverse conditions. In general, it is a measure of the extent of behavioral expression of anxiety. Average scores on ARD (below 60*t*) reflect a person who reports little distress across many situations. Such individuals are typically seen as secure, adaptable, and calm under fire. Scores between 60*t* and 70*t* reflect a person who occasionally experiences (or experiences only to a mild degree) maladaptive behavior patterns aimed at controlling anxiety. Such people will have some specific fears or worries and also may have little self-confidence. Scores above 70*t* suggest impairment associated with distress and fear surrounding some situation; specific subscale elevations should reveal more precisely the nature of these fears. These individuals may be seen as insecure and self-doubting, ruminative, and particularly uncomfortable in social situations. ARD scores that are markedly elevated (above 90*t*) are likely to reflect multiple anxiety disorder diagnoses and broad impairment associated with anxiety. These clients are in severe psychological turmoil; they are faced with constant rumination and often are guilt ridden over past transgressions, real or imagined. A number of maladaptive behavior patterns aimed at controlling anxiety are probably present, but these patterns are having little effect in preventing anxiety from intruding into experience and functioning.

Subscale Structure

The ARD scale has three subscales as shown in Rapid Reference 6.3: Obsessive-Compulsive, Phobias, and Traumatic Stress.

≡Rapid Reference 6.3

Subscales for Anxiety-Related Disorders (ARD)

Obsessive-Compulsive (ARD-O): Focuses on intrusive thoughts or behaviors, rigidity, indecision, perfectionism, and affective constriction.

Phobias (ARD-P): Focuses on common phobic fears, such as social situations, public transportation, heights, enclosed spaces, or other specific objects.

Traumatic Stress (ARD-T): Focuses on the experience of traumatic events that cause continuing distress and that are experienced as having left the client changed or damaged in some fundamental way.

ARD-O: Obsessive-Compulsive

The Obsessive-Compulsive subscale includes items related to both the symptomatic features of the disorder (such as fears of contamination and performance of rituals) and the personality elements of the disorder (such as perfectionism and hyperattentiveness to detail). These two components represent both Axis I and Axis II aspects of the disorder. The Axis I component involves intrusive, recurrent thoughts, images, or behaviors; the literature suggests a number of common themes to these thoughts—for example, fears of contamination, leading to characteristic avoidance behaviors such as hand washing. The Axis II component involves a personality style that is rigid, dogmatic, and affectively constricted. Both types of behavioral patterns are represented on ARD-O.

The ARD-O scale is less correlated with traditional markers of anxiety and neuroticism than are the other ARD subscales. This suggests that high scorers are using obsessional tactics to try to control anxiety through order and predictability. If the full-scale of ANX is within normal limits, the obsessional tactics may be working with reasonable effectiveness. However, this control of anxiety may arrive at a cost; other aspects of the test may reveal pronounced interpersonal problems associated with rigidity and strong needs for control. However, if both ANX and ARD-O are elevated, this is a sign that the obsessions are failing to control the anxiety.

By comparison to most other clinical subscales, elevations on ARD-O are less frequent in clinical samples. This pattern suggests that these behaviors and defenses are more unusual in clinical samples as compared to the straightforward experience of anxiety. Thus, relatively moderate elevations (e.g., 55–65*t*) may be interpretively significant in clinical settings. Others may see such people as being ruminating, detail-oriented, conforming, and somewhat rigid in attitudes and behavior. Scores ranging from 65*t* to 75*t* suggest a fairly rigid individual who follows his or her personal guidelines for conduct in an inflexible and unyielding manner. Such people ruminate about matters to the degree that they often have difficulty in making decisions and in perceiving the larger significance of decisions that are made. Changes in routine, unexpected events, and contradictory information are likely to generate untoward stress, and such individuals will be particularly wary of situations with strong affective demands. Scores at about 75*t* indicate marked rigidity and significant ruminative concerns; intrusive thoughts are likely to be present. Such people may fear their own impulses and doubt their ability to control these impulses. Such people are likely to be extremely indecisive, and obsessional defenses are probably failing to control marked anxiety.

ARD-P: Phobias

The Phobias subscale assesses several of the more common phobic fears, including fears of heights, enclosed places, public transportation, and social exhibition. These fears were selected based on prevalence of reported phobic fears within treatment settings. For example, given the prevalence of social phobias, relevant items are heavily represented on the scale; thus, elevations may indicate marked social anxiety. The ARD-P subscale correlates well with most other indicators of phobic fears as well as with indicators of more general anxiety.

The ARD-P scale is interesting in that it has interpretive significance at very low scores as well because the scale has a rather soft floor. Raw scores of 0 or 1 place a person at roughly 35t; such scores are typically obtained in people who regard themselves as fearless and unafraid of anything, even sometimes when it is merited. In such people there is a possibility of recklessness because they are not likely to be inhibited by appropriate caution; such scores are sometimes obtained in psychopathic individuals. Scores in the range from 60t to 70t suggest the possibility of specific fears, but avoidance behaviors are not likely to be severe and will probably not preclude a relatively successful level of daily functioning. As scores elevate beyond 70t, phobic behaviors are likely to interfere in some significant way, and such people will tend to monitor their environment in an effort to avoid contact with the feared object or situation. Marked elevations indicate the likelihood of multiple phobias or a more pervasive phobia, such as agoraphobia, as opposed to a simple, more circumscribed phobia.

ARD-T: Traumatic Stress

The Traumatic Stress subscale concerns phenomena related to reactions to traumatic stressors, including nightmares, sudden anxiety reactions, and feelings of being irreversibly changed by a traumatic event. Items were not written to detail the nature of the traumatic event; these events might include combat experiences, rape or abuse, or some other highly stressful experience. With significant elevations on this subscale, the precise nature of the event should be determined through a follow-up inquiry. In this fashion, the test score can serve as a useful means of broaching a topic that an individual may not be willing to disclose during an intake interview. On occasion, ARD-T may be elevated even in cases in which the patient cannot currently report specific traumatic memories. In cases in which no obvious stressors are known, this pattern has sometimes been observed to indicate the imminent emergence of suppressed memories of childhood abuse.

ARD-T is frequently elevated in clinical settings; the average score for clinical subjects is 64t. It should be recognized that individuals in treatment settings tend to have very high rates of traumatic events. However, the frequency of this elevation also should serve as a caution against an indiscriminate use of this scale as an indication of posttraumatic stress disorder, which tends to have a characteristic profile that includes other features as well as ARD-T elevations.

Scores in the moderately elevated range on ARD-T (65–75t) suggest that the respondent has probably experienced a disturbing traumatic event in the past—an event that continues to be a source of distress and continues to produce recurrent episodes of anxiety. As scores become increasingly elevated, preoccupation with the trauma increases, and scores above 90t indicate that the trauma (single or multiple) is the overriding focus of the person's life and that the person views him- or herself as having been severely damaged—perhaps irreparably—by having experienced it.

Noteworthy Subscale Configurations

Because of the disparate nature of the three ARD subscales, they tend to be interpreted additively rather than configurally. Perhaps the most interesting combination involves an elevated ARD-O accompanied by a below-average ARD-P, a combination that suggests a rigid, perhaps counterphobic response to potential threat. Such a pattern is also obtained in positive impression management conditions, particularly when an individual wishes to convey positive (but in actuality, inversely related) personality characteristics such as orderliness and calmness to the recipient of the evaluation.

Diagnostic Considerations

To a great extent, the diagnostic implications of ARD elevations are subscale dependent. As mentioned earlier, an ARD-O elevation may alternatively signify obsessive-compulsive disorder or obsessive-compulsive personality disorder; differential diagnosis in this regard can be aided through the inspection of individual items. Also, an accompanying ANX elevation is more typical of the Axis I (obsessive-compulsive disorder) types of problems because many of the characteristics of the personality disorder are aimed at suppressing the experience of affects such as anxiety. The fears described by ARD-P are consistent with diagnoses such as specific phobia and social phobia, but they can also reflect shyness and inhibition characteristic of any disorder with marked interpersonal disruption, such as avoidant personality disorder or schizophrenia. Finally, ARD-T elevations are often found in patients with posttraumatic stress disorder, particularly when accompanied by PAI indications of other elements of the syndrome (e.g., ANX-P, DEP-P, SCZ-S, PAR-H, MAN-I and AGG-P). ARD-T elevations are also common in diagnostic groups with high reported rates of childhood abuse, such as borderline personality disorder or dissociative disorder.

Treatment Considerations

As with the diagnostic hypotheses, the treatment implications of the ARD scale tend to be subscale specific. The ARD-O scale could signify a cognitive rigidity that might lead the person to feel uncomfortable in unstructured forms of therapy; such clients might be receptive to more structured types of interventions (such as cognitive-behavioral methods), particularly in the early stages of treatment. When an elevation on ARD-T reflects trauma occurring within the context of a close attachment relationship (e.g., abuse) as opposed to a more impersonal event (e.g., car accident or natural disaster), the client may approach the therapy relationship itself with considerable wariness. In such instances, an open and supportive approach may be particularly important in the early stages of treatment.

DEP: DEPRESSION

The DEP scale of the PAI was assembled with the goal of providing content coverage of the major elements of the depressive syndrome while also providing items that would prove useful across the full range of severity of symptomatology. The clinical syndrome of depression is typically found to have three components: an affective component, characterized by unhappy and apathetic mood; a cognitive component, marked by negative expectancies; and a physiological component, characterized by sleep and appetite disturbances and low energy (e.g., Moran & Lambert, 1983). Historically, the widely used measures of depression—although they are positively correlated—have tended to emphasize one of these components, often at the expense of other aspects of the disorder. The PAI DEP scale attempted to address this issue by using the subscale composition of the scale to provide a balanced weighting of these different syndromal elements in arriving at an overall estimate of symptom severity.

Thus, the DEP full-scale score indicates the broad spectrum of diagnostic depressive symptomatology. Average scores on DEP (below 60*t*) reflect a person with few complaints about unhappiness or distress. Such individuals are typically seen as stable, self-confident, active, and relaxed. Scores between 60*t* and 70*t* are indicative of a person who is unhappy at least part of the time, and is sensitive, pessimistic, and prone to self-doubt. Scores above 70*t* suggest prominent unhappiness and dysphoria. With scores in this range, the examinee is probably despondent much of the time and withdrawing from activities that had been enjoyed previously. Such individuals tend to be viewed by others as guilt ridden, moody, and dissatisfied. As scores become elevated above 80*t*, there is increasing likelihood of a diagnosis of a major depressive episode, with marked elevations (above 95*t*) strongly indicative of this diagnosis. These individuals feel hopeless, discouraged, and useless. Interpersonally, they are socially withdrawn and feel misunderstood by and unimportant to others. Typically, there is little energy to pursue social role responsibilities, let alone outside interests, and there is also little motivation with which to do either. Suicidal ideation is common with scores in this range, and particular attention should be given to SUI elevations when DEP is markedly elevated.

Subscale Structure

The DEP scale has three subscales, shown in Rapid Reference 6.4, relating to the three different elements of depressive symptomatology.

DEP-C: Cognitive

The cognitive component of depression involves expectancies or beliefs of one's inadequacy, powerlessness, or helplessness in dealing with the demands

≡ Rapid Reference 6.4

Subscales for Depression (DEP)

Cognitive (DEP-C): Focuses on thoughts of worthlessness, hopelessness, and personal failure as well as indecisiveness and difficulties in concentration.

Affective (DEP-A): Focuses on feeling of sadness, loss of interest in normal activities, and anhedonia.

Physiological (DEP-P): Focuses on level of physical functioning, activity, and energy, including disturbance in sleep pattern, changes in appetite, and weight loss.

of the environment. According to cognitively oriented theorists, the root of depressive symptomatology lies in these beliefs. Individuals with this cognitive style tend to globally attribute negative events in their life to their own incompetence or inadequacy, whereas any positive events are minimized or attributed to some external source (e.g., good luck or assistance from others). Other characteristics of the depressive cognitive style include a tendency to think in dichotomies, with events viewed as extremes (good or bad, black or white); self-referential assumptions, such as believing everyone notices if one makes a small mistake; and selective abstraction of negative events.

The beliefs and attitudes tapped by the DEP-C scale reflect a personally evaluative component of self-esteem, one involving a sense of personal competence or self-efficacy. Individuals with DEP-C elevations are likely to report feeling worthless, hopeless, and as though they have failed at most important life tasks. They are likely to be pessimistic and have very little self-confidence. Thus, they feel helpless and powerless to bring about positive changes in their life. Concentration problems and indecisiveness are also likely to be present as scores become increasingly elevated. Conversely, people with very low scores on DEP-C (e.g., below 40*t*) report that their abilities have few limits; such a pattern could reflect either grandiosity or narcissism.

DEP-A: Affective

The affective component of depression refers to the experience of feeling distressed, unhappy, sad, blue, and down in the dumps. Elevations on DEP-A suggest sadness, a loss of interest in normal activities, and a loss of sense of pleasure in things that were previously enjoyed. This scale is probably one of the most direct measures of overall life satisfaction on the PAI. Thus, as a relatively pure measure of distress, DEP-A can be considered a positive prognostic indicator because it reflects significant dissatisfaction with current circumstances and such distress can serve as a motivator for change.

DEP-P: Physiological

The DEP-P subscale involves what are called the vegetative signs of depression: sleep problems, appetite problems, and lack of energy or drive. Elevations on DEP-P suggest that the respondent has experienced a change in level of physical functioning. Such people are likely to show a disturbance in sleep pattern; a decrease in energy and level of sexual interest; and a loss of appetite, weight loss, or both. Motor slowing may also be present, and the lack of energy often fuels the apathy represented by a DEP-A elevation because the respondent may feel unable to overcome the inertia obstructing his or her participation in most activities.

Noteworthy Subscale Configurations

The DEP-C and DEP-A subscales tend to be fairly highly correlated, and the most typical variant in DEP subscale configurations involves the contrast of these two subscales with the DEP-P score. When the former two subscales are elevated but DEP-P is within normal limits, the client may be experiencing considerable distress and unhappiness, but the depressive symptoms may be secondary to problems noted on other scales. If no such other elevations are noted, this pattern may suggest a milder but more persistent form of dysphoria, particularly if BOR is among the higher clinical scales.

If DEP-P is elevated but the other subscales are not, two possibilities should be considered. First, this configuration may suggest that the client tends to repress negative affective experiences but that the distress is being expressed in somatic form. As a general tendency, this pattern is typically accompanied by elevations on at least one of the SOM subscales. The second possibility is that other problems are leading to disruptions in vital functions such as appetite or sleep; for example, sleep patterns could be impaired by posttraumatic nightmares, mania, or obsessive ruminations.

One other configuration worthy of note is one in which DEP-A is considerably elevated while DEP-C falls within normal limits. This pattern suggests prominent unhappiness accompanied by intact self-esteem and suggests that the cause for the distress is viewed as external in origin. This configuration can occur in situations such as uncomplicated bereavements, but it can also occur when there is projection of responsibility for problems and an unwillingness to accept a personality involvement in the factors that are leading to the person's current dissatisfaction.

Diagnostic Considerations

Obviously, the first diagnosis to come to mind with DEP elevated is some form of depressive mood disorder. When all three subscales exceed 70t, the client is likely to meet criteria for a major depressive episode, whereas a DEP elevation without a contribution from DEP-P may be more likely to indicate a milder form of problem, such as dysthymic disorder. The relationship of DEP to other scales can be useful in distinguishing among different depressive subtypes. When STR and DEP are both elevated at comparable levels (particularly in the absence of other elevations), this pattern suggests a depression that is reactive or situational in nature. In contrast, when BOR and DEP are both elevated and at comparable levels, the depression is likely to be long-standing and more characterological in nature. Endogenous or melancholic depressions are characterized by prominent DEP-P elevations accompanied by very low MAN elevations, signifying the motor retardation and apathy of this subtype.

However, as a broad measure of subjective distress, the DEP scale also tends to be elevated in many psychiatric conditions, and as such a DEP elevation should not be considered to be specific to a depressive disorder (although this specificity should increase in the absence of other PAI scale elevations). A DEP elevation could reflect distress secondary to other conditions such as anxiety disorders, posttraumatic stress disorder, a somatoform disorder, or a substance abuse disorder. Severe depression can also be observed in patients with schizophrenia, particularly following the resolution of a psychotic episode. The described symptoms could reflect historical symptoms described during a current manic episode.

Treatment Considerations

DEP elevations are associated with a degree of subjective distress that often serves as a powerful motivation for treatment, and as such some degree of DEP elevation is often a favorable prognostic sign. However, with markedly elevated scores the respondent may be apathetic and lack the energy to actively participate in the treatment process; in such instances antidepressant medication may be needed in the early stages of treatment to facilitate participation in psychosocial interventions. Another consideration in the treatment of individuals with DEP elevations is that suicidal ideation typically accompanies this presentation; the SUI scale and other indications of suicide potential should be carefully evaluated in such individuals. In these patients, support and crisis intervention may be the focus of the initial phase of treatment, moving on to more focused techniques as the initial presenting crisis begins to abate.

There are a variety of different forms of tested treatments for depression, and the DEP subscales can be useful in identifying treatment targets associated with these different interventions. For example, DEP-C elevations suggest that the person is likely to be experiencing distorted thoughts surrounding his or her self-efficacy, which provide targets for intervention with cognitive therapy. Similarly, the DEP-P subscale identifies vegetative depressive signs that have been demonstrated to be particularly responsive to many forms of antidepressant medication. Finally, the DEP-A subscale can be particularly helpful in tracking a patient's subjective response to treatment because it provides a relatively direct summary statement of the respondent's current life satisfaction.

MAN: MANIA

The MAN scale of the PAI was designed to assess prototypical signs of a manic episode. However, because mania is a disorder with a fluctuating presentation of symptomatology, it represents a particular measurement challenge for cross-sectional assessment methods that are capturing the respondent's mental state at a particular point in time. Even within a particular manic episode, symptoms can vary widely; for example, mood can be alternatively elevated, irritable, or depressed within a brief time span. Goodwin and Jamison (1990), in a comprehensive description of the manic-depressive syndrome, divided symptoms into four broad areas: (a) mood, (b) cognitive symptoms, (c) activity and behavior, and (d) psychotic symptoms. These authors examined the diagnostic sensitivity of different signs and symptoms within each of the four areas. With respect to mood symptoms, the most commonly observed symptoms were irritability, depression, and euphoria. For cognitive symptoms, grandiosity, racing thoughts, and poor concentration were most common; and behaviorally, hyperactivity typically involving pressured speech and decreased sleep was often observed. However, psychotic symptoms such as delusions or hallucinations were much less frequently observed. As such, the PAI MAN scale focused on disruptions in mood, cognition, and behavior, and the assessment of psychotic features received relatively little weight in the final scale.

Elevations on the full scale of MAN tend to be rarer in clinical settings than are any of the other clinical scales of the PAI. Indeed, the average scores for clinical and community examinees are nearly identical, which is certainly not the case with any other PAI clinical scale. Therefore, the critical thresholds for identifying MAN scores as a prominent issue are lower than the thresholds for any other clinical scale when the instrument is being used in a typical clinical setting.

Average scores on MAN (below 55t) reflect a person with few features of mania or hypomania. Although depressed individuals are rarely grandiose and do not have heightened activity levels, they can be irritable; hence, depression will not invariably be associated with very low MAN scores. Scores between 55t and 65t suggest a person who may be seen as active, outgoing, ambitious, and self-confident; however, toward the upper end of this range the person may also be rather impatient and hostile, with a quick temper. Scores in the 65–75t range are associated with increasing restlessness, impulsivity, and high energy levels. Others are likely to perceive such individuals as unsympathetic, moody, and hot-headed. MAN scores that are markedly elevated (above 75t) are typically associated with disorders such as mania, hypomania, or cyclothymia. Such individuals take on more than they can handle and react with frustration and anger to suggestions that they reduce their activities. They are typically impulsive and have little capacity to delay gratification; their lack of judgment in such situations is likely to lead to significant impairment in role functioning. They may experience flight of ideas, and their grandiosity may be delusional in proportion. Interactions with others are likely to be problematic for such individuals because their self-importance, hostility, and narcissism impede their ability to be empathic in relationships.

Subscale Structure

As shown in Rapid Reference 6.5, the MAN scale has three subscales: Activity Level, Grandiosity, and Irritability.

MAN-A: Activity Level

The activity level of individuals in a manic episode is heightened, both in the ideational as well as the behavioral realm. Thus, both ideas (e.g., flight of ideas) and behaviors (e.g., motor activity) show increases in intensity and rapidity. However, this increase in *quantity* of behavior is accompanied by a decrease in quality; both the ideation and the overt actions become increasingly pressured and disorganized as the activity level increases. Thus, high scorers on the MAN-A scale are not merely involved in many activities; rather, they are overinvolved and ineffective at managing all their commitments and self-imposed obligations.

The MAN-A subscale has one of the softest floors of the PAI clinical scales, meaning that it is possible to obtain very low scores. Scores in this range (below 30*t*) represent very low activity levels and marked apathy and indifference that suggest a severely depressed individual. Scores in the moder-

⩵Rapid Reference 6.5

Subscales for Mania (MAN)

Activity Level (MAN-A): Focuses on overinvolvement in a wide variety of activities in a somewhat disorganized manner and the experience of accelerated thought processes and behavior.

Grandiosity (MAN-G): Focuses on inflated self-esteem, expansiveness, and the belief that one has special and unique skills or talents.

Irritability (MAN-I): Focuses on the presence of strained relationships due to the respondent's frustration with the inability or unwillingness of others to keep up with their plans, demands, and possibly unrealistic ideas.

ate range (55*t*–65*t*) suggest an activity level somewhat higher than normal; in the upper end of this range, the person may be overinvolved in a wide variety of activities but not necessarily in a disorganized fashion. Scores between 65*t* and 75*t* represent an activity level that is noticeably high to even a casual observer. Such people tend to be involved in a wide variety of activities but in an increasingly disorganized manner, and performance in at least some of these activities is likely to be suffering. With these modest elevations, the respondent may be experiencing accelerated thought processes. As scores exceed 75*t*, this acceleration renders the person confused and difficult to understand; scores in this range are unusual because such people often have difficulty focusing their attention for the time required to complete lengthier self-report questionnaires such as the PAI.

MAN-G: Grandiosity

The grandiosity component of mania involves an overevaluated self-image—an overestimation of one's talents and capabilities. Hence, MAN-G items inquire about the person's self-evaluation of many talents and abilities. Grandiose individuals tend to believe that they are good at virtually anything, and thus they obtain elevated scores. In milder forms, this elevation may merely reflect optimism and an unwillingness to be hampered by one's limitations. In more extreme forms, this pattern represents the incapacity to recognize one's limitations, to such a degree that one is not able to think clearly about one's capabilities.

The MAN-G subscale, like MAN-A, is interpretively useful at the lower end. Because the scale has a major component of self-evaluation, it can be useful in identifying persons with low self-esteem who are not necessarily depressed. Very low scores on MAN-G can render individuals vulnerable to depression because they tend to feel rather inadequate and unwilling to accept or acknowledge positive aspects of themselves. Conversely, when DEP is elevated and MAN-G is not suppressed, this pattern may indicate that blame for the current circumstances is being externalized. For example, paranoid individuals may be pessimistic about their ability to deal with the forces that beset them, yet their self-esteem will remain intact because they simply project blame outward. Thus, even more than DEP-C, the MAN-G score may reflect the extent to which a low self-concept has been internalized.

Scores on MAN-G that are in the moderately elevated range (60–70*t*) represent an optimistic and perhaps driven type of individual. Content of thought is likely marked by an element of expansiveness and self-confidence, with a focus on strategies for success or achievement. Toward the upper end of this range, the possibility of inflated self-esteem increases. As scores exceed 70*t*, the likelihood of grandiosity must be considered because scores in this range are unusual in clinical settings. Such elements may range from beliefs of having exceptionally high levels of common skills to beliefs that border on delusional in terms of having special and unique talents that will lead to fame and fortune. Others may view such people as self-centered and narcissistic.

MAN-I: Irritability

Although elevated mood is one of the more striking affective features of mania, it is actually not as characteristic of mania as might be expected. More typical of manic affect is volatility; the mood can change rather abruptly, particularly in response to frustration. Thus, MAN-I items tap a frustration-responsive irritability that is typical of manic patients. There tend to be two aspects to these items—one involving a certain degree of ambition and the second involving low frustration tolerance. It is this combination of features that makes the scale reasonably specific, rather than a more general marker of trait hostility, which may be more directly addressed by some of the PAR subscales.

Low scores on MAN-I (40*t* and below) represent an individual who portrays him- or herself as very patient and rather immune to frustrations. Milder elevations (60–70*t*) suggest a person who is impatient and easily frustrated; others may see those in the upper end of this range as demanding. Such people may have difficulty with others who do not cooperate with them or who do not keep up with the respondent's plans and schedule of activities. As scores exceed 70*t*, relationships with others are probably under stress due to the demanding presentation of the respondent. Such people are easily frustrated by lack of ability or cooperation in other people, and these others will tend to be blamed for failures and accused of attempting to thwart the respondent's possibly unrealistic plans for success and achievement. With scores above 80*t*, the person is very volatile in response to frustration, and his or her judgment in such situations may be poor. The quality of mood state in such people can change very rapidly, and they are prone to lash out at people whom they view as the source of their frustrations.

Noteworthy Subscale Configurations

Of the three subscales, MAN-I appears to be most likely to elevate indepen-
dently of the other two; when this occurs, it is typically a sign of impatience
and poor frustration tolerance that can occur in depressed individuals and in
individuals with anger management problems. When MAN-I is low relative
to MAN-A and MAN-G, this pattern can be a more favorable sign in that it
suggests a perseverance that may increase the possibility that some of the person's energy and enthusiasm can be translated into effective action. Combined elevations on MAN-G and MAN-I reflect an inflated self-esteem manifested by haughtiness and arrogance; this self-esteem may be particularly
vulnerable to insult (particularly if BOR-I is elevated), and when it is threatened they may lash out in frustration at those around them. Such people probably view themselves not as hostile but rather as acting in a manner merited
by the strengths and importance of their ideas and convictions.

Diagnostic Considerations

Elevations on the MAN scale tend to be relatively rare in most clinical diagnostic groups because few clients with emotional problems experience heightened activity levels or increased self-esteem. However, the diagnostic implications of MAN vary somewhat depending upon the subscale configuration.
When all three subscales are elevated, a manic episode within a bipolar affective disorder must be a central consideration. When a MAN elevation is
driven primarily by a strong MAN-G elevation, it is more likely that the difficulties involve a disorder with prominent narcissistic pathology, such as narcissistic or antisocial personality disorders. Finally, a MAN elevation that is
primarily driven by MAN-I may reflect prominent difficulties with impulse
control and particular problems with anger management; when this pattern is
accompanied by a marked elevation on AGG, it may indicate a diagnosis such
as intermittent explosive disorder.

Treatment Considerations

Elevations on the MAN scale are generally a negative prognostic sign for psychosocial interventions. Often, there is insufficient distress to serve as a motivation for treatment; responsibility for any disruptions or difficulties tends

to be attributed to external sources, and the need for personal change is questioned. Even when a commitment to treatment can be elicited, such individuals lack the patience or frustration tolerance to deal with the perceived slow pace of treatment. The incentive to defensively avoid the experience of any negative affects can also increase treatment resistance and can lead to clients' leaving treatment prematurely just as progress appears to be made. With subscale configurations suggestive of a manic episode, the initial stages of treatment should focus on medication adherence and a supportive monitoring of the client's judgment and decision making. With configurations more indicative of narcissistic pathology, the initial challenge of treatment will probably involve alliance formation because the client may question the therapist's expertise and adopt a competitive or devaluative stance toward the therapist. In either case, an active and more direct therapeutic stance in the early stages of treatment may be more successful for engaging the client in treatment.

PAR: PARANOIA

The PAR scale focuses on symptoms and enduring characteristics of paranoia. Features of paranoia are found in a variety of diverse and more severe psychopathological conditions. Manifestations can range from characterological suspiciousness (such as that found in paranoid personality disorder) to the frank persecutory delusions that characterize paranoid psychosis. However, paranoid symptoms are not specific to these syndromes; these beliefs are often encountered in schizophrenia, mania, other personality disorders such as antisocial and borderline personality disorders, and certain organic conditions. Regardless of the primary diagnosis, paranoid characteristics present a difficult assessment challenge because the patient is by definition defensive and suspicious of diagnostic and treatment efforts. In identifying the relevant components of the paranoia construct for the PAI, a decision was made to place an emphasis on the phenomenology of the disorder rather than on more overt symptomatology in an effort to reduce the impact of defensiveness on scale performance.

The items of the scale measure the typical experiences of the paranoid individual, with respect to both transient symptoms and stable personality elements. The item content addresses a vigilance in monitoring the environment for potential harm, a tendency to be resentful and to hold grudges, and a readiness to spot inequities in the way that the respondent has been treated by others. At the full-scale level, PAR represents a direct measure of interpersonal mistrust and hostility. Average scores on PAR (below 60t) reflect a person who reports being open and generally forgiving in relationships with others. Scores between 60t and 70t indicate persons who are sensitive, tough-minded, and skeptical. Toward the upper end of this range, they may also be rather wary and cautious in their interpersonal relationships. With scores above 70t, the person is likely to be overtly suspicious and hostile. Such a person tends to be distrustful of close interpersonal relationships and probably has few close friends. As scores become markedly elevated (above 84t), the probability increases that the paranoia is potentially delusional in proportion. These individuals are bitter and resentful of the way they have been treated by others, and they anticipate that others will attempt to exploit them at every opportunity. Jealousy and accusations probably trouble any close relationships that have endured. Ideas of reference and delusions of persecution or grandiosity may be present when scores are in this range.

Subscale Structure

The PAR scale has three subscales, as shown in Rapid Reference 6.6: Hypervigilance, Persecution, and Resentment.

≡Rapid Reference 6.6

Subscales for Paranoia (PAR)

Hypervigilance (PAR-H): Focuses on suspiciousness and the tendency to monitor the environment for real or imagined slights by others.

Persecution (PAR-P): Focuses on the belief that one has been treated inequitably and that there is a concerted effort among others to undermine one's interests.

Resentment (PAR-R): Focuses on a bitterness and cynicism in interpersonal relationships and a tendency to hold grudges and externalize blame for any misfortunes.

PAR-H: *Hypervigilance*

The paranoid individual carries the predisposition to distrust people that he or she does not know well. As a result, such persons tend to be vigilant and guarded in their interactions with others, looking for warning signs that the person with whom they are dealing is not completely trustworthy. This tendency is more of an interpersonal set—a way of relating to others—than it is a specific belief, and so elevations should not be interpreted as indicative of a delusional system. Rather, it represents a wariness in interactions with others, and a reluctance to let one's guard down in relationships.

PAR-H has a reasonably soft floor, and very low scores are possible. When scores below 40*t* are obtained, this pattern suggests a person who reports being exceedingly trusting and open in relationships. If this self-report is accurate, such people are vulnerable to interpersonal exploitation, particularly if DOM is low. However, such scores may also be obtained in individuals motivated to appear as trusting. Moderate elevations (60–70*t*) suggest a person who is pragmatic and skeptical in relationships with others; these people may be difficult to know well and keep casual acquaintances at arm's length. Scores above 70*t* indicate a person who spends a great deal of time monitoring the environment for evidence that others are not trustworthy and may be trying to harm or discredit them in some way. Others will view such people as hypersensitive and easily insulted in their interactions. Such people will question and mistrust the motives of those around them as a matter of course, despite the nature or history of the relationships. As a result, working relationships with others are likely to be strained and may require an unusual degree of support and assistance in order to succeed.

PAR-P: *Persecution*

The items on the Persecution subscale directly address beliefs that others are attempting to obstruct or impede the respondent's efforts. These beliefs can range from mild feelings of jealousy to delusional beliefs of conspiracy and intrigue. Of the three PAR subscales, PAR-P is most closely tied to Axis I manifestations of delusional disorders involving paranoia.

Because item content on PAR-P is unusual, raw scores tend to be low in the general population and the standard deviation tends to be small. Hence, the scale can elevate rapidly even if relatively few items are answered in the positive direction. Elevated scores suggest individuals who are quick to feel that

they are being treated inequitably and easily believe that there is a concerted effort among others to undermine their best interests. Working and social relationships are likely to be very strained, despite any efforts of others to demonstrate support and assistance. As scores increase above 85*t*, the possibility of
delusional beliefs should be investigated, particularly if SCZ-P is also elevated.

PAR-R: Resentment

The third PAR subscale captures the hostility and bitterness of the paranoid
character—the tendency to approach life with a chip on one's shoulder. The
obstructions provided by others (reflected in the scores on the other subscales) are a source of lingering resentment for such people. These people feel
that they have not been treated fairly in their lives, and they nurse grudges
against all who have transgressed against them in the past. Blame for any failures is projected outwards, and forgiveness from the respondent is not likely.
Indeed, getting even with the objects of this resentment may be a major preoccupation for such people.

   Scores on PAR-R that are moderately elevated (60–70*t*) suggest a sensitive
person who is easily insulted or slighted and responds by holding grudges toward the offending party. As scores elevate above 70*t*, such individuals are increasingly inclined to attribute their misfortunes to the neglect of others and
to discredit the successes of others as being the result of luck or favoritism.
They are likely to be envious of others and disinclined to assist others in
achieving their goals and successes. As scores exceed 80*t*, the person may
dwell on past slights by others and be preoccupied with evening the score. Examination of scores on DOM and AGG may suggest whether this hostility is
likely to be expressed directly or in more passive-aggressive form.

Noteworthy Subscale Configurations

As noted previously, the PAR subscales can be divided into the personological
(PAR-H and PAR-R) and the symptomatic (PAR-P) elements of paranoia.
The typical subscale patterns of PAR tend to reflect this grouping. When the
personological subscales are elevated but PAR-P lies within normal limits,
it suggests a characterologically suspicious individual who is predisposed to
question and mistrusts the motives of others. Although such individuals may
not view themselves as unduly suspicious, others are likely to view them as hostile and unforgiving. If such people experience sufficient stress, their judgment
and reality testing may deteriorate, in which case the PAR-P score will rise to

match and ultimately exceed the score on the remaining two subscales. Sometimes PAR-P and PAR-R may be high in the absence of a PAR-H elevation—a configuration often seen in individuals with acting-out behaviors who project responsibility for these behaviors onto others. It is very unusual for PAR-P to be markedly elevated with the remaining two subscales falling within normal limits; this latter configuration is typically seen only in simulation samples of malingering, and items on the Malingering index reflect this configuration.

Diagnostic Considerations

Elevations on the PAR scale are suggestive of diagnoses with a prominent degree of hostility and suspiciousness, although the centrality of these clinical features can vary in different diagnoses. The most obvious initial diagnostic hypotheses with a marked PAR full-scale elevation are paranoid personality disorder or paranoid delusional disorder. These disorders are typically distinguished by the relative positioning of the PAR-P subscale relative to the remaining two PAR subscales. In the personality disorder, PAR-P is typically within normal limits even when PAR-H and PAR-R are elevated, whereas in a disorder characterized by paranoid delusions all three subscales are likely to be elevated, with PAR-P at (or more typically, above) the scores from the other two subscales. The latter configuration may suggest schizophrenia, paranoid subtype, if the SCZ scale is also elevated. A concomitant elevation of MAN may indicate that paranoid beliefs accompany grandiosity and reflect deterioration in judgment consistent with a manic episode.

Other personality disorders with prominent hostility, such as borderline or antisocial personality disorder, may also display elevations on PAR, with PAR-R a particularly likely candidate for a subscale elevation. For the antisocial personality, this pattern represents the projective externalizing of responsibility that is a typical response to problems that arise. For the borderline personality, the PAR elevation is an expression of the perception of poor treatment by important others in the past and the expectation that such poor treatment will continue in future relationships.

Treatment Considerations

Elevations on PAR are rarely a favorable prognostic sign for treatment; the suspiciousness of such clients invariably leads to difficulty in forming a trusting relationship with a mental health professional. Therapy process is likely to be impeded by repeated tests of the therapist's trustworthiness. A firm and open approach to such clients in particularly important, but it is easy to err in either respect; neither an overly energetic confrontation of the accuracy of the client's beliefs nor a sympathetic collusion with those beliefs is likely to gain the client's trust. The tendency of such clients to focus on the behaviors and intentions of others may appear to further hamper treatment progress, but because these perceptions typically involve considerable projection, they can also provide opportunities for important communications to occur between clients and therapists that might be too threatening if they occurred directly.

SCZ: SCHIZOPHRENIA

The SCZ scale of the PAI was designed to assess three aspects of schizophrenia that appear to represent different elements or forms of the disorder. Schizophrenia is perhaps one of the most heterogeneous of all clinical syndromes, and this heterogeneity poses a number of problems for assessment. Historically, there have been many schemes for subtyping schizophrenia, with number of subtypes ranging from the three originally described by Kraepelin (i.e., paranoid, catatonic, hebephrenic) to the dozens of subtypes described by Leonhard (e.g., Ban, 1982). A distinction that has received considerable research support in recent years involves that between positive and negative symptoms in schizophrenia. Positive symptoms involve features that are normally not present in individuals and include phenomena such as hallucinations, delusions, and bizarre behavior. Negative symptoms represent the absence of features that normally are present in individuals, such as social behavior and affective responsiveness (Andraesen, 1985). The clinical import of the distinction can be found in a wide variety of areas; for example, patients with predominantly negative symptoms often show little response to neuroleptic medication and have poorer prognoses (Angrist, Rotrosen, & Gershon, 1980). However, thought disorder is an important diagnostic feature of schizophrenia that does not fit neatly into the positive-negative distinction, and some have suggested that it be considered a third, relatively independent pattern of impairment in schizophrenia. The PAI thus includes a distinct assessment of thought disorder as well as positive and negative symptomatology.

Because the SCZ scale was designed to measure these different facets of schizophrenia, elevations on the full scale could occur for numerous reasons: unusual beliefs and perceptions, poor social competence and social anhedonia, or inefficiency and disturbances in attention, concentration, and associational processes. Perhaps because of this heterogeneity, the limited research thus far on SCZ suggests that it may have adequate convergent validity but limited discriminant validity. Rogers, Ustad, and Salekin (1998) found that although SCZ scores correlated reasonably well with diagnoses of schizophrenia arrived at via structured clinical interview, similar correlations were observed with diagnoses of depression. Boyle and Lennon (1994) also found discriminant validity problems for the SCZ scale, although certain characteristics of their criterion group (patients on medication maintenance) and their comparison group (alcoholics undergoing detoxification) might have in part accounted for their findings (Morey, 1995). Further research along these lines is needed; at this point, combining the PAI profile with information from other assessment sources may be particularly important for differential diagnosis of schizophrenic disorders.

In general, average scores on SCZ (below 60t) reflect a person who reports being effective in social relationships and has no trouble with attention or concentration problems. Scores between 60t and 70t are indicative of a person who may be seen as withdrawn, aloof, and unconventional. Toward the upper end of this range, such persons may be cautious and hostile in their few interpersonal relationships. With scores above 70t, the person is likely to be isolated and feel misunderstood and alienated from others. Some difficulties in thinking, concentration, and decision making are probable with scores in this range. Specific subscale elevations may reveal the presence of unusual perceptions or beliefs that may be psychotic in nature.

SCZ scores that are markedly elevated (above 90t) are typically associated with an active schizophrenic episode. These individuals are confused, withdrawn, and suspicious, and they tend to have poor judgment and reality testing. Active psychotic symptomatology is likely with scores in this range, and specific elevations on other scales may

---

CAUTION

Although elevations on SCZ typically indicate severe psychopathology, they may not be specific to schizophrenia. Information from other assessment sources may provide important supplements for differential diagnosis of schizophrenia.

be helpful in identifying the precise nature of such symptoms. For example, concomitant elevations on PAR may indicate the presence of delusions of persecution. With increasing *t*-score elevations, delusions of thought broadcasting, thought insertion, thought withdrawal, and thought control become more likely. These patients may often require referral to evaluate the need for psychotropic medications.

Subscale Structure

The SCZ scale has three subscales as shown in Rapid Reference 6.7: Psychotic Experiences, Social Detachment, and Thought Disorder.

SCZ-P: Psychotic Experiences

Positive symptoms of schizophrenia involve delusions and hallucinations as well as characteristic bizarre thought content. The positive symptoms tend to have a rather distinct course, with episodic exacerbation and often complete remissions, and persons with predominantly positive symptomatology do not tend to show intellectual impairments. These symptoms also tend to respond favorably to antipsychotic medications.

The SCZ-P items tap various positive symptoms of schizophrenia that vary in severity from unusual perceptions and magical thinking to characteristic first-rank psychotic symptoms of schizophrenia. In keeping with efforts to maintain discriminant validity, the features are designed to be relatively specific to schizophrenia rather than more broadly defined, nonspecific symp-

---

≋Rapid Reference 6.7

Subscales for Schizophrenia (SCZ)

Psychotic Experiences (SCZ-P): Focuses on the experience of unusual perceptions and sensations, magical thinking, and other unusual ideas that may involve delusional beliefs.

Social Detachment (SCZ-S): Focuses on social isolation, discomfort, and awkwardness in social interactions.

Thought Disorder (SCZ-T): Focuses on confusion, concentration problems, and disorganization of thought processes.

toms that might be found in other syndromes (such as delusions of grandeur or nihilistic delusions). Scores that are moderately elevated (60–70*t*) suggest that the respondent may entertain some ideas that others find unconventional or unusual; toward the upper end of this range, the person may strike others as peculiar and eccentric. Scores above 70*t* indicate the experience of unusual perceptual or sensory events or unusual ideas that may involve delusional beliefs. Scores exceeding 85*t* are often associated with an active psychotic episode, with poor judgment and breakdown in reality testing as hallmark features; full-blown hallucinations or delusions are probable.

SCZ-S: Social Detachment

The negative symptoms of schizophrenia involve behavioral deficits that include poor interpersonal rapport, flattening of affect, and poverty of communication. Such individuals are apathetically indifferent to others, generally speaking only when necessary and avoiding interpersonal contact if possible. In schizophrenia, the course of these negative symptoms tends to be enduring as opposed to episodic, and they are less responsive to pharmacological interventions than are positive symptoms. This pattern of behaviors is also consistent with the features of schizoid personality disorder, which may simply be an alternative name for the same phenomenon.

The SCZ-S items focus on the features of social disinterest and lack of affective responsivity. Moderate scores (60–70*t*) suggest a quiet, impassive individual who exhibits little interest in the lives of other people. Toward the upper end of this range, the score may indicate a lack of ability to interpret the normal nuances of interpersonal behavior that provide the meaning to personal relationships. Scores above 70*t* reflect a person who neither desires nor enjoys close relationships; social isolation and detachment may serve to decrease the sense of discomfort that interpersonal contact fosters. Their lack of interest in others is mirrored in a lack of self-interest; they are generally indifferent to how others view them and disinterested in introspection. They are particularly discomfited by strong emotions, which they themselves tend not to experience and do not understand in others.

SCZ-T: Thought Disorder

Schizophrenia is characterized by disruptions in thought process that do not seem to covary with either positive or negative symptoms. At its extreme, thought disorder can render the patient incoherent and unable to string together an intelligible sentence. In its milder forms, difficulties in concentration, decision making, and memory will take place. It should be recognized that these milder features tend to be nonspecific and associated with severe affective disorders in particular. Thus, SCZ-T elevations are commonly observed in severe major depression, without accompanying elevations on SCZ-P.

The SCZ-T items sample across the range of clarity and freedom from confusion in thought processes. Moderate elevations (60–70*t*) suggest problems in concentration and decision making; such scores would not be unexpected among depressed or anxious individuals. However, toward the upper end of this range there is increasing likelihood of confusion and perplexity in addition to the more benign cognitive inefficiencies. Scores above 70*t* reflect a loosening of associations and increased difficulties in self-expression and communication. However, in the absence of a clinical elevation of the full SCZ scale, this finding can reflect various causes outside of schizophrenic disorder. Severe depression or mania, the sequelae of brain injury or disease, the effects of medication, and the consequences of drug or alcohol abuse should all be explored as potential causes of elevations on this subscale.

Noteworthy Subscale Configurations

With respect to the diagnosis of schizophrenia, the SCZ-P subscale probably has the greatest specificity (and perhaps the lowest sensitivity) of the three SCZ subscales. Thus, it is fairly common to observe SCZ-S and SCZ-T to be elevated in the absence of a high SCZ-P score; this pattern suggests a socially isolated individual who is generally apathetic and disinterested in other people and their emotional states. Such a configuration may suggest a residual phase of schizophrenia, but it may also represent a manifestation of a severe depression or a personality disorder such as schizoid or schizotypal personality disorder. Individuals with a well-integrated delusional system may sometimes present with elevations on SCZ-P and SCZ-S but show no abnormalities on SCZ-T; when PAR-P is also elevated, these ideas may involve persecutory beliefs that would account for the person's presentation as being a socially isolated individual who has few (if any) close relationships.

Diagnostic Considerations

As noted earlier, until more discriminant validity data have been collected, the SCZ scale should be used cautiously as a diagnostic indicator of schizophrenia. In addition, the relatively low prevalence rate of this diagnosis in most settings also suggests that relatively high scores would be indicated before the diagnosis would emerge as a primary consideration. In particular, a sole reliance on the full-scale score of SCZ is discouraged because features such as disrupted thought processes (SCZ-T) or social anhedonia (SCZ-S) can be observed in other diagnoses, such as severe affective disorders or cognitive disorders. However, when all three SCZ subscales display simultaneous prominent elevations, a diagnosis of schizophrenia should receive careful consideration.

Treatment Considerations

Elevations on SCZ are typically a negative prognostic sign for most interventions because the confusion and withdrawal represented by the item content pose significant compliance problems, regardless of the nature of the treatment. With marked elevations accompanied by other indications of psychotic features, antipsychotic medication is an obvious consideration. In particular, a prominent SCZ-P elevation may suggest a need for medication to address target symptoms of psychosis, but SCZ-T elevations that reflect cognitive disruption may also be a target for medication.

A SCZ-S elevation poses a particular difficulty in treatment because such individuals tend to be uncomfortable with the relational aspects that are a critical part of even the most highly structured forms of treatment. In the treatment of such patients, alliance formation will probably be a slow process and will require considerable patience on the part of the therapist. Although such individuals will tend to feel most at ease with a reliable and predictable structure to the treatment, the interaction itself will need to be supportive. The therapist must guard against expecting rapid progress in the early stages of treatment. Although the therapist may view revisiting the same material or the same technique as a repetitious and perhaps frustrating lack of progress, such repetition lends predictability to treatment that can greatly enhance the patient's comfort level in the early stages. As the treatment matures, the effects of specific techniques (such as social skills training, contingency management, or cognitive interventions) are more likely to take hold as they proceed from the base of a firm alliance between patient and therapist.

BOR: BORDERLINE FEATURES

The BOR scale assesses a number of elements related to severe personality disorder; although all of these elements are a part of the borderline syndrome, individually they are also common to numerous other disorders. The scale is the only scale on the PAI that has four subscales, largely due to the complexity of the construct as it has been represented in the literature. Part of the reason for this complexity is that it is inherently a more nebulous construct than some that have been recognized far longer, such as depression or schizophrenia. The borderline concept has always been one that has been thought of as being in a boundary, presumably representing some border—and what the border is has never been exactly clear. Initially, this category represented patients who were marginally able to be treated with psychoanalysis. Over time, the category came to be synonymous with the boundary between neurosis and psychosis, with a neurotic level of adaptation presumably reflecting problems characterized primarily by difficulties with anxiety, and psychosis reflecting more primitive issues involving breaks with reality. In this framework, individuals with borderline personalities fell somewhere in the middle. It was thought that much of the time, the person with a borderline personality would superficially appear to be at a neurotic level of adaptation but that under stress and particularly in more unstructured situations, he or she would deteriorate and appear psychotic.

Over the years a number of investigators have examined the borderline construct using factor-analytic or cluster-analytic studies, including Grinker, Werble, and Drye (1968); Hurt and Clarkin (1990); and Morey (1989). These studies have provided convergence in identifying the major facets of the borderline construct, and each represents a theoretically important etiological mechanism. The four PAI BOR subscales were designed to reflect these facets.

A number of studies have demonstrated the construct validity of the BOR scale. For example, Bell-Pringle, Pate, and Brown (1997) examined the classification accuracy of the PAI among female inpatients diagnosed with borderline personality disorder (BPD) and a matched control group of female college students. Results indicated that a *t* score ≥ 70 accurately classified 81.8% (18 of 22) of the BPD patients and 77.3% (17 of 22) of the female students. Similarly, Trull (1995) administered a battery of self-report tests and a semistructured interview used to assess personality disorder symptoms to a sample of college students to compare the clinical features of participants scoring in a clinically significant range on BOR (raw score ≥ 38) to participants below this threshold. Results demonstrated that participants scoring in the clinically significant range on BOR differed on measures of mood and affect, personality, coping styles, and general psychopathology, and they exhibited more features of BPD. These BOR scale classifications were also found to be predictive of 2-year outcome on academic indexes in college students, even controlling for academic potential and diagnoses of substance abuse (Trull, Useda, Conforti, & Doan, 1997).

The full-scale score for BOR is probably best considered in line with Kernberg's (1975) view of borderline personality as a level of personality organization or adaptation that ranges somewhere between neurosis and psychosis. Thus, low scorers will tend to be fairly healthy with respect to personality issues, whereas high scorers will present with fairly primitive concerns, perhaps across many different *DSM* variants of personality disorder. Diagnostically, if the full BOR scale is elevated, problems in the personality realm are likely. Then, the configuration of the subscales can confirm whether the problems are classically borderline (i.e., elevations on three or four subscales) or circumscribed problems associated with other issues (e.g., single-subscale elevations, such as BOR-N reflecting relationship problems stemming from posttraumatic stress disorder).

Average scores on BOR (below 60*t*) reflect a person who reports being emotionally stable and who also has stable relationships. Scores between 60*t* and 70*t* are indicative of a person who may be seen as moody, sensitive, and having some uncertainty about life goals; scores in this range are not uncommon in young adults. Toward the upper end of this range, such individuals may be increasingly angry and dissatisfied with their interpersonal relationships. With scores above 70*t*, respondents are likely to be impulsive and emotionally labile; they tend to feel misunderstood by others (who often perceive them as egocentric) and find it difficult to sustain close relationships. They tend to be angry and suspicious while at the same time being anxious and needy, making them ambivalent about interactions with others. However, scores in this range do not necessarily suggest a diagnosis of borderline personality disorder unless there are prominent elevations on each of the four BOR subscales, because individual features are common to other disorders.

BOR scores that are markedly elevated (above 90t) are typically associated with personality functioning within the borderline range. These individuals typically present in a state of crisis, often regarding difficulties in their relationships. With elevations in this range, clients are invariably hostile and feel angry and betrayed by the people around them. Symptomatically, they often report being very depressed and anxious in response to their circumstances. They are impulsive and will act in ways that appear to others to be self-destructive; for example, they seem to sabotage their own best intentions with acting-out behaviors. These behaviors can include alcohol or drug abuse, suicidal gestures, or aggressive outbursts; scores on ALC, DRG, SUI, and AGG should be consulted to identify potential problem areas of this type.

Subscale Structure

The BOR scale is comprised of four subscales, shown in Rapid Reference 6.8, designed to measure distinct facets of personality immaturity: Affective Instability, Identity Problems, Negative Relationships, and Self-Harm.

≣ *Rapid Reference 6.8*

Subscales for Borderline Features (BOR)

Affective Instability (BOR-A): Focuses on emotional responsiveness, rapid mood changes, and poor emotional control.

Identity Problems (BOR-I): Focuses on uncertainty about major life issues and feelings of emptiness, lack of fulfillment, and an absence of purpose.

Negative Relationships (BOR-N): Focuses on a history of ambivalent, intense relationships in which one has felt exploited and betrayed.

Self-Harm (BOR-S): Focuses on impulsivity in areas that have high potential for negative consequences.

BOR-A: *Affective Instability*

Individuals with borderline personality disorder present with emotions that fluctuate impressively, leading some theorists to propose that the disorder may represent a variant of bipolar affective disorder (e.g., Akiskal, Yerevanian, & Davis, 1985). These affects are not a polarity between happiness and sadness, however. Rather, for persons with borderline personality disorder, it involves a propensity to alternate rapidly between various negative affects—for example, to become anxious, angry, depressed, and then irritable in rapid succession. The BOR-A subscale reflects this rapidity of mood shift. Elevations could, for example, represent an individual with a bad temper (which can be confirmed by an examination of the AGG-A subscale), or they might indicate a person who becomes anxious easily (a conclusion that might be supported from inspecting the ANX-A or ARD-P subscales). The unique contribution of the BOR-A subscale is in ascertaining the suddenness of the affective change.

Thus, high scorers on BOR-A are highly responsive emotionally, typically manifesting rapid and extreme mood swings rather than more cyclic mood changes as seen in affective disorders. In the highest ranges (roughly above 80t), all affects are probably involved, including episodes of poorly controlled anger. In the range from 70t to 80t, a propensity to experience a particular negative affect may be responsible, and investigation of other scales may determine whether anxiety (ANX-A or ARD-P), depression (DEP-A), or anger (AGG-A) is the typical response. On the other hand, unusually low scores (below 40t) reflect a person who describes him- or herself as fairly unresponsive emotionally and who may appear to others as affectively constricted.

BOR-I: *Identity Problems*

Theoretically, the notion of issues surrounding identity is central to Kernberg's (1975) view of borderline personality. Kernberg describes this facet as "identity diffusion," meaning that persons with borderline personality disorder have a difficult time maintaining a constant representation of who they are, where they are headed in life, and what they value. As a result of this diffuse sense of self, these individuals tend to rely on others to help them formulate an identity, thus defining themselves primarily in relationship to other people. Theoretically, this characteristic involves a developmental failure to establish an autonomous identity independent of the primary caregivers, leading to similar difficulties in adulthood. In a sense, it involves being dependent on others, as illustrated in *DSM* criteria such as fears of abandonment. Although there is certainly substantial diagnostic overlap between borderline and dependent personality disorders (Morey, 1988), there is a qualitative difference in the nature of these behaviors. Persons with borderline personality disorder do not really want the assistance of others; rather, they have a profound need for others to help provide a self-definition. In the absence of these important others, individuals with the disorder may initiate desperate and frantic efforts to try to reestablish this needed contact—not out of fear that they will be unable to perform a task competently, but because they are afraid they will cease to exist. In the absence of these others, the self-concept is unstable and inconsistent. No matter how deep an attachment to some particular course of action may appear, within a short period of time a design of equal intensity may emerge in an entirely different direction. Individuals with elevations on BOR-I are likely to be prone to these sudden shifts in ambitions and goals.

In sum, scores above 70*t* represent uncertainty about major life issues and difficulties in developing and maintaining a sense of purpose. Such uncertainty is more common in younger adults, and BOR-I is correlated with age: The average score for persons 18–29 years is 55*t*, whereas for those above age 60 it is 46*t*. Nonetheless, scores above 70*t* are reflective of identity issues beyond what is expected during adulthood, regardless of age. With more extreme scores (i.e., above 80*t*), such elevations may involve sudden and unpredictable reversals in life plans and directions; more modest elevations suggest feelings of emptiness, lack of fulfillment, and boredom. Elevations also suggest a fair degree of anxiety surrounding identity issues, and disruption or dysfunction within the family of origin is a possibility to be explored. Scores at the low end of BOR-I (i.e., below 45*t*) suggest a more stable and fixed self-concept, which in many cases represents a strength but can also involve a therapeutic challenge if there are strongly fixed negative elements to the person's identity.

BOR-N: Negative Relationships

The concept of negative relationships involves the interpersonal presentation of borderline personality—a tendency to become involved in relationships that are very intense and chaotic. High scores on BOR-A are an indication that the person's closest attachment relationships are likely to be stormy; these relationships might include one's family, spouse or partner, or therapist. Part of the storminess revolves around these individuals' experience that important other people have not met their needs. They approach such relationships with a great deal of longing and hope but invariably eventually come away feeling not only disappointed but also betrayed and exploited. To some extent, this pattern may stem from the general affective reactivity of the borderline personality described earlier, but the research literature does indicate that patients with this disorder report extremely high rates of physical and sexual abuse during childhood (Herman, Perry, & Van der Kolk, 1989). With this background in mind, it is easy to understand borderline individuals' fear that the people who are closest to them are likely to exploit them. The BOR-N items tap this perception of betrayal in past relationships as well as a distrust and pessimism surrounding future ones.

Considered in isolation, the BOR-N scale reflects a history of involvement in ambivalent, intense, and unstable relationships. At extreme scores (e.g., above 80*t*), respondents are bitter and resentful about the way past relationships have gone, feeling betrayed by the people who were once closest to them and preoccupied with fears of abandonment or rejection by those currently important to them. Scores between 70*t* and 80*t* suggest numerous problems and failures in past attachment relationships, although intense feelings of past exploitation are less likely in this range than they are for higher scorers.

BOR-S: Self-Harm

The final borderline subscale reflects a tendency to act impulsively, without much attention paid to the consequences of the acts. These acts will thus be viewed by others as self-damaging or self-destructive—for example, involving substance abuse, sexual recklessness, or sudden abandonment of a job with no prospects for the future. BOR-S is sometimes mistaken for a direct indicator of suicidal behaviors or self-mutilation. Although a person who scores high on BOR-S would be expected to be more at risk for such behaviors than would someone who scores low, the scale is more directly reflective of impulsivity than of either suicide risk or self-mutilation. Although a sample of self-mutilators did yield elevated BOR-S scores (Morey, 1991), certainly not all elevations on BOR-S will involve self-mutilation. Similarly, although persons currently on suicide precautions score above the mean on BOR-S, their average score was only around 60*t* (Morey, 1991). Because many completed suicides are premeditated and are not impulsive acts, BOR-S is probably neither sensitive nor specific if used in isolation as a suicide indicator.

Elevations on BOR-S reflect levels of impulsivity and recklessness that become more hazardous as scores increase. These clients are impulsive in areas that have high potential for negative consequences, such as in spending, sex, and substance abuse. Such behavior has typically interfered repeatedly with effective social and occupational performance. High scorers may also be at increased risk for self-mutilation and suicidal behavior, and accompanying SUI elevations may indicate a risk for impulsive suicide gestures.

Noteworthy Subscale Configurations

The combination of BOR-N and BOR-I represents the splitting dynamic of interpersonal need (represented by BOR-I) and interpersonal conflict and distrust (represented by BOR-N). Individuals with this combination tend to have a very unstable sense of what they desire from their relationships, leading to a pattern of involvement in intense, needy, and short-lived relationships and to a preoccupation with fears of being abandoned or rejected in these relationships. The combination of BOR-A and BOR-S indicates a marked overreactivity to the external world, leading to a pattern of rapid and extreme mood swings and episodes of poorly controlled and impulsively expressed anger. However, rather than being directed at others, the anger may be self-directed, resulting in behaviors likely to be self-harmful or self-destructive, such as irresponsible spending, sex, and substance abuse. Any angry gestures that are outwardly directed may be followed by considerable guilt, and their contrition may serve to sustain relationships that would otherwise suffer. Such individuals may be at increased risk for self-mutilation or suicidal behavior during times of affective turmoil, and the score on SUI should be examined.

Diagnostic Considerations

Although an elevation on the full-scale score of BOR does not necessarily indicate that the respondent will meet criteria for borderline personality disorder, it does greatly increase the probability of personality disorder involvement in the clinical picture. Nearly any personality disorder diagnosis may be involved, and the configuration of other PAI scales can be examined to provide hypotheses about particular Axis II diagnoses. BOR elevations can be associated with numerous Axis I diagnoses as well. Rather than suggesting any particular Axis I diagnosis, however, a BOR elevation suggests that any concurrent Axis I diagnosis is likely to be relatively chronic and long-standing in nature.

When three or four of the BOR subscales are all elevated above 70t, the probability of a categorical diagnosis of borderline personality disorder increases. When a single subscale primarily drives a full-scale BOR elevation, this pattern may reflect the presence of other diagnoses, but there is still likely to be a considerable personality component. Such additional diagnoses vary according to the subscale in question. For example, BOR-A elevations indicate a degree of affective responsivity that may point to histrionic personality disorder or bipolar disorders; low scores on this subscale may indicate affective constriction typical of schizoid or obsessive-compulsive personality disorders. Identity issues suggested by BOR-I can indicate problems that are dissociative in nature. BOR-N elevations often suggest relational conflict, and these conflicts may be pivotal expressions of impairment in disorders such as substance abuse or somatization disorder.

Treatment Considerations

Elevations on the BOR scale tend to be a troublesome sign for nearly all forms of intervention. These clients tend to present in a state of crisis, with their initial apparent motivation arising out of a sense of desperation for ameliorating their situation. The commitment to change may vanish as soon as the presenting crisis resolves. Such clients tend to be hypersensitive to any signs of rejection and may rapidly attempt to test the therapist's commitment or trustworthiness. The impulsive nature of these clients may lead them to flit from one caregiver to the next, convinced that the next intervention will hold the answers and disparaging any previous efforts at providing treatment. When multiple modes of treatment are involved (such as individual and group, or psychotherapy and pharmacotherapy), close coordination between caregivers will be particularly important because one provider may be played against the other.

ANT: ANTISOCIAL FEATURES

The ANT scale is the second of the two scales (BOR being the other) that specifically assess character pathology. These two constructs were selected for the PAI because together they account for the majority of empirical research that has been conducted on personality disorders. However, it is important to note that the representation of antisocial personality on ANT departs more from the *DSM* conceptualization of the disorder more than does the BOR scale. The underpinnings of the PAI representation of antisocial personality date back to the notion of the psychopath as classically described by Cleckley (1941) and refined in a number of empirical investigations by Hare (e.g., 1985). This approach makes explicit the personological features that set the psychopathic personality apart from criminality. For example, among the features that Cleckley stressed as pathognomonic of this personality constellation were a lack of guilt, a general absence of anxiety or depression, and a seeming inability to learn from experience. In contrast, beginning most notably with the *DSM-III,* the conceptualization of antisocial personality disorder represented a substantial departure from the notion of psychopathy. The *DSM* definition was based extensively on a history of delinquent or antisocial behavior in contrast to the personality elements described by Cleckley and others. These criteria seem to tap a somewhat different population than did the older psychopathic personality concept.

One difficulty with the *DSM* representation of this construct is that in failing to include the more personological elements of the construct, it misses critical motivational differences for antisocial behavior. Some have criticized the *DSM* definition as practically being synonymous with criminal behavior; for example, at least half of (if not more) inmates will meet such criteria for the disorder (Hart & Hare, 1989). Others have expressed the concern that the *DSM*'s focus on delinquent behaviors leads to the overapplication of the diagnosis to lower socioeconomic groups, missing white-collar variants of the disorder. Finally, there is some support for the conclusion that the concept of psychopathy may be more valid than the *DSM* representation of this disorder. For example, studies indicate that psychopathy ratings are more useful than the *DSM* concept of antisocial personality in predicting recidivism in prisoners (Hart, Kropp, & Hare, 1988; Serin, Peters, & Barbaree, 1990).

Hare's approach to the representation of psychopathy has been found to have two different components or factors. One of these is a behavioral component that involves a variety of antisocial acts; this factor corresponds reasonably closely to the *DSM* conceptualization. However, the second factor involves a component of psychopathy that incorporates personality traits, such as tendencies to be unempathic, callous, or egocentric. The inclusion of such traits in the conceptualization of the disorder increases predictive validity; therefore, the PAI was constructed to assure that these trait elements were built into the scale.

Validity evidence for the use of ANT has been promising. Salekin, Rogers, and Sewell (1997) examined the relationship between ANT and psychopathy in a sample of female offenders and found that elevations on ANT among this population were primarily the result of endorsements on ANT-A. Also, support was found for the convergent validity of ANT with other measures of psychopathy including the Psychopathy Checklist–Revised (PCL-R) total score ($r = 0.53$) and the Personality Disorder Examination (Loranger, Susman, Oldham, & Russakoff, 1987) Antisocial scale ($r = 0.78$). In a similar study, Edens et al. (2000) examined the relationship of the ANT scale to the screening version of the Psychopathy Checklist (PCL:SV; Hart, Cox, & Hare, 1995) and the PCL-R (Hare et al., 1990). Moderately strong correlations were found between ANT and the PCL:SV and the PCL-R total score, with the highest correlations with these measures being found for the PAI Antisocial Behaviors subscale. Finally, a study by Salekin, Rogers, Ustad, and Sewell (1998) investigated the ability of the ANT and the Aggression (AGG) scales of the PAI to predict recidivism among female inmates over a 14-month follow-up interval. Findings indicated that the ANT scale was significantly related to recidivism, as was the AGG scale; at the subscale level, ANT-E, AGG-V, and AGG-A were most highly related to recidivism.

At the full-scale level, the ANT scale provides an assessment of personality and behavioral features relevant to the constructs of antisocial personality and psychopathy. As noted earlier, the item content ranges from indicators of egocentricity, adventuresomeness, and poor empathy to items addressing antisocial attitudes and behaviors, and as a result individuals with average to moderate elevations can have very different constellations of features. It is the conjunction of elevations on the three subscales that is suggestive of the psychopath; however, a person with antisocial behaviors without psychopathic personality features may achieve a full-scale elevation on ANT solely through the elevated ANT-A.

Average scores on ANT (below 60*t*) reflect a person who reports being considerate and warm in relationships with others; these individuals also typically exhibit reasonable control over impulses and behavior. Scores between 60*t* and 70*t* are indicative of a person who may be seen as somewhat impulsive and risk taking. Moderately elevated scores are fairly common in young adults, particularly in young men, in whom the average *t* score approaches 60*t*. Toward the upper end of this range, respondents may be increasingly self-centered, disinhibited, skeptical of other's intentions, and unsentimental in their interpersonal relationships. With scores above 70*t*, the respondent is likely to be impulsive and hostile, and there may be a history of reckless or antisocial acts. Others may see such individuals as callous in their relationships, and long-lasting friendships tend to be the exception to the rule.

When ANT scores are markedly elevated (above 82*t*), respondents typically display most of the prominent features of antisocial personality disorder. They are likely to be unreliable and irresponsible and have probably had little sustained success in either social or occupational realms. They tend to have a coldly pragmatic approach to relationships and will exploit such interactions to suit their own needs. Such people tend to be impulsive in their approach to life and have a history of conflicts with authority figures.

Subscale Structure

As shown in Rapid Reference 6.9, the ANT scale is composed of three subscales designed to measure both personological and behavioral elements of

≡ Rapid Reference 6.9

Subscales for Antisocial Features (ANT)

Antisocial Behaviors (ANT-A): Focuses on a history of antisocial acts and involvement in illegal activities.

Egocentricity (ANT-E): Focuses on a lack of empathy or remorse and a generally exploitative approach to interpersonal relationships.

Stimulus-Seeking (ANT-S): Focuses on a craving for excitement and sensation, a low tolerance for boredom, and a tendency to be reckless and risk-taking.

the antisocial individual: Antisocial Behavior, Egocentricity, and Stimulus-Seeking.

ANT-A: Antisocial Behaviors

The items comprising the ANT-A subscale inquire about antisocial acts committed both during adolescence and during adulthood. High scorers are likely to have manifested a conduct disorder during adolescence, and during adulthood they may have been involved in illegal occupations and may have engaged in criminal acts involving theft, destruction of property, and physical aggression toward others. This subscale of ANT is the one that corresponds most closely to the more behavioral definition of the disorder because it reflects an individual who commits antisocial acts. The subscale in isolation does not, however, indicate psychological attributes underlying these acts. These behaviors could arise from impulsivity, from egocentricity or entitlement, from environmental presses, or from anger management problems. Inspection of other PAI scales and subscales can shed light on each of these potential sources.

Scores above 70*t* on ANT-A represent a history of difficulties with authority and with social convention. A pattern of antisocial behavior was probably first evident in adolescence, and with scores in this range it is likely that the pattern has continued into adulthood. Scores in the moderate range (60–69*t*) may be more likely to reflect historical problems than are more elevated scores. However, because many of the questions on the subscale are historical in nature, a past history of such acts can lead to elevations that may not reflect current functioning. For example, the item *I've done some things that weren't exactly legal* might be referring to behaviors that occurred 30 years previously. Scores that are very low (i.e., 40*t* or below) could indicate a very conforming, perhaps moralistic individual, or perhaps a person motivated to deny any history of mischievous behavior whatsoever.

ANT-E: Egocentricity

The items forming the ANT-E subscale tap a callousness and lack of empathy in interactions with others. It is this personological component that is probably closest to the classic definition of the psychopath, yet in isolation this scale does not imply psychopathy—rather, it suggests a certain self-centeredness that could also be suggestive of a histrionic or narcissistic personality pattern as well. However, in combination with acting-out behavior

(ANT-A) and anger management problems (AGG), the likelihood of psy-chopathy as opposed to other issues increases considerably. It should also be recognized that higher scores are obtained in younger people; the average score for those 18–29 years is 56t.

High scorers on ANT-E (70t and above) tend to be seen as egocentric, with little regard for others or for the opinions of the society around them. In their desire to satisfy their own goals and impulses, they may take advantage of oth-ers—even those who are most close to them. They feel little responsibility for the welfare of others and have little loyalty to their acquaintances. Such indi-viduals would be expected to place little importance in their social role oblig-ations as a spouse, parent, or employee. Although they may describe feelings of guilt over past transgressions, they are not likely to feel much remorse of any lasting nature because their inflated sense of self and their feelings of en-titlement would make them unlikely to believe that they were in the wrong. Such people may be perceived by others as hostile, but aside from irritability there may be little affective involvement in their interactions with others. More marked anger and hostility, if present, will be identified by elevations on AGG and PAR rather than ANT-E.

Moderate elevations on ANT-E (60–69t) suggest a person who tends to be self-centered and pragmatic in interactions with others. Such people feel relatively little social anxiety or guilt; consequently, they may be effective in superficial social contacts. However, long-lasting relationships are unlikely because these individuals rarely will place others' needs before their own. In contrast, scores that are very low (40t or below) suggest persons who may re-peatedly place the needs of others ahead of their own and consequently have difficulty getting their own needs met. In combination with below-average scores on MAN-G, this pattern suggests a humility that is driven by low self-esteem.

ANT-S: Stimulus Seeking

The ANT-S items tap a personality component associated with a willingness to take risks and a desire for novelty. Although individuals with antisocial per-sonality disorder score considerably above average on most sensation-seeking scales, this trait is not specific to this diagnostic group, nor is it in isolation a pathological or even undesirable characteristic. However, in combination with other traits (such as a lack of empathy, poor impulse control, or anger management problems), this characteristic can lead to a variety of problem behaviors because the inhibiting effects of anxiety are minimized. Thus, in relation to other PAI scales, ANT-S has a disinhibition component that might heighten the impact of elevations beyond what might be expected otherwise. Like the other ANT subscales, ANT-S tends to be higher in younger individuals (the average score is 56*t* in 18- to 29-year-olds), perhaps lending empirical support to the notion of "the recklessness of youth."

High scorers on ANT-S (70*t* or above) are likely to manifest behavior that is reckless and potentially dangerous to themselves or to those around them. They crave novelty and stimulation; easily bored by routine and convention, they may act impulsively in an effort to stir up excitement. Their desire for new experiences may lead to periods of nomadic wandering and make any long-term commitments unlikely. They also tend to be less anxious than most people are, even when they end up in a situation (e.g., in a forensic situation) in which some anxiety would be expected. More moderate elevations (60–69*t*) suggest a more controlled but still potentially reckless individual. In this range, however, the trait may not have led to difficulties and may simply reflect an adventurous individual who enjoys new challenges. However, accompanying elevations on ANT-A, AGG, BOR-S, ALC, or DRG are all signs that this novelty is being sought in self-destructive, acting-out ways.

Very low scores on ANT-S (40*t* and below) suggest a person who is very timid and avoiding of novelty. These people are likely to feel uneasy over disruptions in routine, and persons scoring high in ARD-P and low in DOM and WRM may show phobic avoidance behaviors or interpersonal submission.

Noteworthy Subscale Configurations

As noted previously, the ANT subscales can be divided into the personological (ANT-E and ANT-S) and the behavioral (ANT-A) elements of antisociality and psychopathic features. The typical subscale patterns of ANT tend to reflect this grouping. When ANT-A is elevated in isolation, the respondent is likely to present with a history of behavioral troubles, but these behaviors may not be a consequence of a classic psychopathic orientation. Rather, such problems may arise from a variety of sources, including impulse control problems, anger management issues, substance abuse, or impaired judgment. Conversely, when ANT-E and ANT-S are elevated but ANT-A is within normal limits, this configuration suggests an individual who may appear successful and effective but is ultimately likely to be self-centered and irresponsible in dealing with social and vocational obligations. Although such persons are perhaps able to conform to social convention to avoid negative consequences, this pattern reflects a lack of empathy or respect for others. Dangerous risks—resulting from the desire for personal gain as well as the sheer excitement of the danger—may be taken, and such people may not hesitate to expose others to similar risks.

Diagnostic Considerations

Full-scale elevations on ANT are suggestive of antisocial personality disorder, particularly with a significant involvement from ANT-A. Other personality disorders that fall within a similar cluster, such as borderline or narcissistic personality disorder, are also possibilities. On Axis I, the most common diagnostic correlates of ANT elevations appear to be substance abuse and bipolar disorder; confirmation of these diagnostic possibilities should begin with an examination of the PAI scales DRG and MAN, respectively.

Treatment Considerations

ANT elevations generally suggest a poor prognosis for most forms of treatment, although the degree of pessimism tends to vary as a function of the subscale configuration. Patients with ANT-A elevated but with the other ANT subscales falling within normal limits may be amenable to treatment when appropriate remorse is apparent (often reflected in DEP elevations) and when the client has maintained some relations with the social support network (i.e., NON scores within normal limits), such as in family, friends, or work relationships. Prominent ANT-E elevations are likely to point to poor prognosis in most forms of treatment because responsibility for life disruptions is projected outwards and there will be limited capacity or interest in forming any sort of alliance with a mental health professional unless some instrumental gain is involved. Group therapy with similar individuals is sometimes recommended for such patients because it is thought that this setting allows such clients, who typically have little capacity or tolerance for self-examination, to scrutinize the often similar motivations and their consequences in other group members. Finally, significant ANT-S involvement suggests a greater

need for structure and focus in treatment, with short-term, behaviorally focused goals and techniques (such as contingency management) having potential utility.

SUBSTANCE ABUSE SCALES: ALCOHOL PROBLEMS (ALC) AND DRUG PROBLEMS (DRG)

The PAI includes two scales pertinent to substance abuse—one measuring
alcohol problems (ALC) and one related to drug use and abuse (DRG). The
ALC and DRG scales share certain features that merit consideration before
interpreting scores on these scales. First, a good deal of the information gathered on these scales is historical, meaning that inquiries are made about events
that may have happened in the past. These historical items reflect major mile-
stones or major markers that exist in the development of a substance abuse
career (e.g., Jellinek, 1960), and it is these markers that are critical in assigning
diagnoses under most widely used diagnostic systems (including the *DSM*).
For this reason, ALC and DRG can be elevated in people with a history of
problems with drugs or alcohol but who are not currently drinking or using
drugs. In individuals with a prominent current substance abuse problem, this
is generally not an issue because most such individuals will tend to have ALC
and DRG scores that are markedly elevated—typically above 80*t*. However, a
more modest elevation, such as 70*t*, could reflect a current (but relatively
mild) problem, or it could be a reflection of historical information. As an
example of the latter instance, a recovering alcoholic who has been abstinent
for 10 years might still obtain an elevated score on ALC if he or she had lost
jobs or had experienced withdrawal symptoms during past episodes of heavy
drinking. An examination of individual ALC and DRG items can be useful as
a first step in evaluating these moderate elevations because some items inquire about current circumstances, whereas others assess historical information. Also, current impairment resulting from moderate abuse is likely to
result in subjective distress that could appear in the form of ANX or DEP
elevations; such distress would not be necessarily present if substance use
were entirely historical. Finally, moderate elevations should receive further
follow-up with some inquiry about current or recent substance consumption
patterns.

Another issue that figures prominently in the interpretation of ALC and

DRG involves the possibility of denial of substance abuse or use. As with positive distortion in general, the form of denial in substance abuse can involve both self-deception and other-deception. The self-deceptive form of denial in substance use involves a minimization of problems and a refusal to recognize that the use of alcohol or drugs is having adverse consequences. For example, the clinical lore surrounding alcoholism is that alcoholics fail to recognize the problematic nature of their drinking until they "hit bottom" (Alcoholics Anonymous, 1937). The second form of denial involves an overt attempt to deceive others concerning the extent of substance use or misuse. Such efforts are likely to be strongly influenced by assessment context. For example, a person receiving a mental health assessment following an arrest is likely to deny use of illicit drugs because such acknowledgment would be tantamount to confessing to a crime. Similarly, parents in a custody evaluation may be reluctant to acknowledge problems in general and substance misuse in particular.

For either type of denial, underreporting of substance-related impairment should be considered when the PIM score is elevated. A study by Fals-Stewart (1996) examined substance abuse underreporting in two groups—the first was a group of substance abusers instructed to avoid detection of substance problems, and the second was a group of individuals in forensic settings who had denied substance involvement but who tested positive for substances at the time of arrest. Fals-Stewart found that a cutting score of >56t on PIM successfully distinguished 88% of these dissimulators from a group of substance abusers responding under standard instruction conditions. Fals-Stewart also derived a discriminant function to separate the underreporting from the standard group; however, this function performed less well in a subsequent cross-validation sample (Fals-Stewart & Lucente, 1997).

A second strategy for identifying underreporting related to substance abuse (Morey, 1996) involves the use of regression estimates of the ALC and DRG scores from personality predictors that—unlike ALC and DRG—do not inquire directly about substance use and misuse. The procedures for determining this estimate as well as the Fals-Stewart (1996) functions are pro-

DON'T FORGET

Among other things, a PIM elevation can signify that an individual is underreporting problems with alcohol or drugs.

vided in chapter 5. The regression procedure seeks to determine whether the reported level of alcohol or drug involvement is substantially less than would be anticipated from salient personality characteristics typically associated with substance misuse. The procedure uses the sum of the t scores from the five largest correlates of the ALC and DRG scales to produce an estimated score on these scales that can be compared to the scores that were actually reported by the client.

Using this procedure to estimate ALC and DRG scores for the defensive-responding groups in the Fals-Stewart (1996) study described previously yielded estimated scores that were on average roughly 10–15t score points above the actual scores obtained by these individuals (Morey, 1996). Thus, a useful rule of thumb for using these estimates is to consider the possibility of alcohol- or drug-related underreporting when the discrepancy between these two scores is 10t or greater, with estimated exceeding observed. However, there has been little confirmatory research on this procedure aside from the data presented in Fals-Stewart (1996); therefore, this estimate should be used with caution. In particular, two variables reflect potential moderators of the efficiency of this procedure: the client's age and the client's score on PIM. With respect to age, many of the predictor scales used to derive the estimated substance abuse scale scores have relatively strong age associations, with younger clients tending to obtain higher scores than do older respondents. Although substance misuse (and the DRG scale in particular) also displays a similar age relationship, the estimation procedure may be more likely to lead to overestimates in younger clients. One interesting hypothesis that remains untested is that such discrepancies in younger adults, such as those ages 18–21, may reflect a propensity to develop alcohol- or drug-related problems rather than an underreporting of these problems.

The second potential moderator of the efficiency of this procedure involves the elevation of the profile on the PIM scale. PIM elevations tend to have a suppressive effect on most of the PAI scales, and this tendency includes all five of the predictive elements included in the substance abuse estimation procedure. Because PIM has itself been found to be associated with substance abuse dissimulation (Fals-Stewart, 1996), it will probably have a suppressive effect on the substance abuse predictors as well as on the substance abuse scales themselves. Thus, when the PIM score displays some elevation (e.g., 57t or above), particular attention should be paid to the discrepancy of the estimated and observed substance abuse scores rather than to the absolute elevation of the estimated score itself. In such instances, the estimated score will itself probably be an underestimate of the score that might have been obtained in a fully candid profile. When PIM is elevated, discrepancies in the significant direction are noteworthy even when they fall within the normative range. For example, an estimated DRG score of 58*t* contrasted with an observed DRG score of 45*t* may be an indication of underreporting of substance abuse in the presence of an elevated PIM score. Indeed, discrepancies of that nature were typical in the Fals-Stewart (1996) dissimulation samples, in which 88% of the sample displayed PIM elevations. When the PIM score suggests candid responding, the substance abuse estimates are more likely to yield a useful estimate of where the scores might be expected to fall.

In some instances, respondents may be hesitant to answer particular ALC and DRG items, feeling that the items are not relevant because they do not use alcohol or drugs. This reaction has been most commonly observed in individuals who approach the test in a cautious or legalistic manner. For instance, such responses are sometimes found among preemployment screening applications of the test. For example, such people will not answer an item such as *My drug use has never caused problems for me* because they feel that responding to this item would be admitting to using drugs. In such instances, it is recommended that the respondent consider all types of drugs—not only illegal or street drugs, but also prescription medication, over the counter preparations, and so forth. Such a response to these items is most likely not an indicator of hidden substance abuse, but it is a suggestion that the test is being approached in a very careful and guarded manner that itself may be of use in evaluating the test results.

ALC: Alcohol Problems

The ALC scale provides an assessment of behaviors and consequences related to alcohol use, abuse, and dependence. The item content ranges from statements of total abstinence through frequent use to severe consequences of drinking, loss of control, and alcohol-related cravings. Questions inquire directly about the use of alcohol, and thus prominent denial of alcohol problems can suppress scores on the scale; if ALC raw scores are very low and there are elevated scores on the five predictor scales mentioned previously, some follow-up inquiry about alcohol use might be merited. However, in general a direct inquiry about alcohol use will usually provide more accurate data than do inferences from indirect sources.

Average scores on ALC (below 60*t*) reflect a person who reports a moderate alcohol intake and few adverse consequences related to drinking. Scores between 60*t* and 70*t* are indicative of a person who may drink regularly and may have experienced some adverse consequences as a result. Toward the upper end of this range, there is increasing likelihood that alcohol has caused or is causing problems for the person. With scores above 70*t*, the client is likely to meet criteria for alcohol abuse. Such a score indicates that use of alcohol has had a negative impact on the respondent's life. Alcohol-related problems are likely, including difficulties in interpersonal relationships, difficulties on the job, and possible health complications, and the respondent's current functioning is probably compromised.

ALC scores that are markedly elevated (above 84*t*, which is the average score for individuals in alcoholism treatment centers) are typically associated with severe alcohol dependence. Such a score indicates that the use of alcohol has had a number of adverse consequences. Numerous alcohol-related problems are probable, including difficulties in interpersonal relationships, difficulties on the job, and possible health complications. These individuals are likely to be unable to cut down on their drinking despite repeated attempts at sobriety. They typically feel guilty about their drinking but report little ability to control the effect it has on their lives. They are likely to have a history of social and occupational failures that were related to drinking and have had episodes in which they were intoxicated for prolonged periods. Blackouts and physiological signs of dependence and withdrawal are probable with scores in this range.

Diagnostic Considerations

Because ALC items inquire directly about alcohol misuse and its consequences, the scale is most directly pertinent to the diagnosis of alcohol abuse and dependence. The distinction between these diagnostic hypotheses is most informed by the elevation on the scale. In the absence of significant denial, alcohol dependence will result in scores that are markedly elevated—the average score for individuals in alcohol treatment centers is approximately

84*t*. Scores that fall within the 70–80*t* range may reflect alcohol abuse, although they may also suggest historical problems with alcohol that involved dependency symptoms that are no longer manifested. The distinction between these diagnoses can also be aided by the examination of other scales in the profile. For example, prolonged alcohol dependence can lead to peripheral neuropathy that can sometimes be reflected in an elevation on SOM-C. Alcohol dependence invariably leads to significant psychosocial disruption that would elevate STR, and the associated disinhibition can lead to physical confrontations manifested on AGG-P. Finally, historical alcohol withdrawal symptoms may be reflected in ANX-P elevations, whereas concurrent detoxification can elevate scores on NIM and SCZ.

Treatment Considerations

Alcohol problems tend to be difficult to treat, and the course of these difficulties tends to involve a chronic cycle involving periods of remission followed by relapses. ALC scores that are markedly elevated may be particularly suggestive of this more chronic course. On the other hand, elevated ALC scores may also reflect a favorable prognostic sign in some instances because it represents an acknowledgement of the severity of the consequences that alcohol misuse has created. The severity of these consequences is often cited as a powerful motivating factor that can support the client's readiness for change.

DRG: Drug Problems

The DRG scale provides an assessment of behaviors and consequences related to drug use, abuse, and dependence. The item content ranges from statements of total abstinence through frequent use to severe consequences of drug use. Questions inquire directly about the use of drugs (both prescription and illicit), and thus prominent denial of drug use can suppress scores on the scale. As with ALC, if DRG raw scores are very low and there are elevated scores on the five predictor scales described previously, some follow-up inquiry about drug use might be merited. Because some of the DRG items may involve acknowledging activities that are illegal, effortful underreporting is probably a greater issue for DRG than for ALC (particularly in forensic as opposed to voluntary treatment contexts), and the DRG estimation procedure described in chapter 5 may be particularly helpful with this issue.

Average scores on DRG (below 60*t*) reflect a person who reports using drugs infrequently if at all. Scores between 60*t* and 70*t* are indicative of a person who may use drugs on a fairly regular basis and may have experienced some adverse consequences as a result. As with ALC, one should consider the possibility that the drug misuse is historical rather than current, and an examination of individual item responses may be helpful in this regard. Toward the upper end of this range, there is increasing likelihood that drug use has caused or is causing problems for the person. Respondents with scores above 70*t* are likely to meet criteria for drug abuse. It is likely that their drug use has caused difficulties in interpersonal relationships or in work performance, and their current functioning is probably compromised.

DRG scores that are markedly elevated (above 80*t*, the average score for individuals in treatment for drug abuse) are typically associated with drug dependence. These individuals are likely to be unable to cut down on drug use despite repeated attempts and have little ability to control the effect that the desire for drugs has on their lives. They are likely to have a history of social and occupational failures that were related to drug use. Depending on the primary substance of abuse, physiological signs of dependence and withdrawal are probable with scores in this range.

Diagnostic Considerations
The DRG scale is most relevant to the diagnosis of drug abuse and dependence, with the distinction between the two made primarily by the elevation on the scale. Scores that fall within the 70–80*t* range are more likely to reflect abuse, although they may also suggest historical dependency symptoms that are no longer manifested. Examining other scales in the profile may also aid in making this distinction; for example, the substance-dependent individual typically experiences severe life disruption (evident on STR) and problems with disinhibition (AGG-P). These individuals also tend to have very little regard for their health, leading to relatively low SOM-H scores. Finally, elevated DRG scores were frequently associated with a diagnosis of antisocial personality disorder in the PAI clinical standardization sample.

Treatment Considerations
When DRG is markedly elevated, it is possible that the respondent may be physically dependent and may require medical detoxification as part of treat-

ment. Signs of confusion or psychosis (examine NIM, SCZ-P, PAR-P) in the presence of very high DRG scales point to the need for evaluation of this issue. Because DRG items require the acknowledgement that substance abuse issues are leading to life disruption, an elevation may also reflect a readiness for change that can make the prognosis more positive. In contrast, when the estimated DRG score (calculated from the procedure described previously) is substantially higher than the observed score, accompanied by an RXR that approaches or exceeds 50*t*, the respondent is very unlikely to follow through with substance abuse treatment. Group-based treatments are often used to confront the denial that is characterized by this pattern.

AGG: AGGRESSION

The AGG scale is a treatment consideration scale, and it has no direct correspondence to any *DSM* diagnostic category; rather, it taps fundamental affects and behaviors involved in many categories. Indeed, the *DSM* has been criticized for failing to include any reasonable classification of problems related to anger, aggression, and their management (Deffenbacher, 1992). There are a variety of diagnostic groups for whom anger control is central. Many of these are personality disorders; antisocial, borderline, and passive-aggressive diagnoses all have significant issues surrounding anger management. Intermittent explosive disorder is classified as an impulse control disorder, but failure to control anger is central. Physical abuse of adults or children is another condition that may be a focus of clinical attention when anger management problems are involved. Because anger control issues are a prominent part of many diagnoses, the AGG scale provides useful information for a wide array of such diagnoses, but it also has important applications for treatment planning and decision making.

The AGG scale of the PAI was assembled to assess three different elements of aggression that have emerged from factorial studies of this topic (Riley & Treiber, 1989). These elements include a general assessment of temperamental anger and hostility as well as a determination of the typical modes through which this anger and hostility are expressed. These different aspects can vary substantially among people with anger control issues. For example, strong inhibition and suppression of anger (as with an individual who turns anger inward) might be reflected in positive indications of the experience of anger but suppression of scales suggesting that this anger might somehow be expressed.

As a full scale, AGG provides a global assessment of attitudinal and behavioral features relevant to aggression, anger, and hostility. The item content ranges from indicators of verbal assertiveness and poor anger control to violent and assaultive behaviors. The scale has a relatively soft floor, and low scores can be indicative of problems; such scores suggest very meek and unassertive persons who may have difficulty standing up for themselves, even when assertiveness is called for. Average scores on AGG (below 60*t*) reflect a reasonable control over the expression of anger and hostility. Scores between 60*t* and 70*t* are indicative of a person who may be seen as impatient, irritable, and quick-tempered when frustrated or crossed. Toward the upper end of this range, such persons may be increasingly angry and easily provoked by the actions of others around them.

With scores above 70*t*, clients are likely to be chronically angry and are increasingly likely to express their anger and hostility; the subscale configuration should be consulted to determine the typical modality (e.g., verbal or physical) through which the anger is expressed. When AGG scores are markedly elevated (above 82*t*), there is usually considerable anger and potential for aggression. Such individuals are easily provoked and they may explode when frustrated, leading the people around them to be afraid of these clients' temper. There is probably a history of episodes in which anger has clouded the client's judgment, often leading to legal or occupational difficulties. Aggressive behaviors are likely to play a prominent role in the clinical picture; such behaviors represent a potential treatment complication that should receive careful attention in treatment planning. In such instances, other indicators of the potential for violence (both from the PAI and from other sources of data) should be considered carefully; this issue is discussed further in chapter 9.

Subscale Structure

The AGG scale is comprised of three subscales—one indicative of the global degree of anger and hostility in the clinical picture and the remaining two providing information about the typical mode through which anger is expressed.

≡Rapid Reference 6.10

Subscales for Aggression (AGG)

Aggressive Attitude (AGG-A): Focuses on hostility, poor control over anger expression, and a belief in the instrumental utility of aggression.

Verbal Aggression (AGG-V): Focuses on verbal expressions of anger ranging from assertiveness to abusiveness and on a readiness to express anger to others.

Physical Aggression (AGG-P): Focuses on a tendency to have physical displays of anger, including damage to property, physical fights, and threats of violence.

These subscales, as shown in Rapid Reference 6.10, are Aggressive Attitude, Verbal Aggression, and Physical Aggression.

AGG-A: Aggressive Attitude

The Aggressive Attitude subscale was conceptualized to include general affects and attitudes conducive to aggressive behavior. Individuals scoring high on this scale may perceive themselves as easily angered and may believe that an aggressive approach to life has a greater likelihood of yielding favorable results than does a more passive approach. However, the concept is distinct from the expression of anger in that individuals can be angry and yet not express it, instead suppressing it or perhaps turning it inward. The concept instead resembles one of anger proneness—the tendency to become easily frustrated or irritated, to experience anger or hostility when criticized or treated poorly by others.

Low scorers on AGG-A would be described as calm and placid individuals who are very slow to anger and are tolerant and forgiving of others. Moderate elevations (between 60*t* and 70*t*) suggest an individual who is easily angered and frustrated. Others may perceive such individuals as hostile and readily provoked. Scores exceeding 70*t* suggest persons who are very prone to anger, often losing their temper with little provocation. Such people may use anger to intimidate or control others and become furious when others criticize or obstruct them in some way. However, such anger may not be readily expressed if the remaining subscales are suppressed.

AGG-V: Verbal Aggression

The Verbal Aggression subscale reflects a readiness to display anger through verbal interactions with others. In its milder form, this characteristic may be manifested as sarcasm or a hypercritical style; more extreme manifestations may take the form of yelling or verbal abuse. The distinguishing characteristic of the verbal mode of anger expression is its visibility; high scorers will display their anger readily when it is experienced rather than making an attempt to suppress or hide it. AGG-V is inversely related to efforts to control anger; low scorers often make an effort to hide their anger from others, whereas high scorers make little or no effort to control their outward expression of anger. Thus, this subscale is particularly useful in determining how readily apparent experienced anger will be to the outside observer.

Low scores on AGG-V suggest a person who prefers not to express his or her anger when it is experienced; rather, such people tend to overcontrol their anger, keeping it in to the best of their ability. Although control of anger is desirable, excessive control can lead to passivity and withdrawal (look for low DOM scores), intro-punitive attitudes (suggested by DEP-C elevations or MAN-G suppression), or episodic, poorly controlled outbursts of anger when it is released (suggested if AGG-P is elevated). Scores on AGG-V that are moderately elevated (between 60t and 70t) reflect a person who is assertive and not intimidated by confrontation; toward the upper end of this range, such individuals may be verbally aggressive (e.g., critical, insulting, or verbally threatening) with little provocation. Elevations above 70t suggest that these verbal outbursts are likely to be abusive; such people are generally not well-liked and are viewed as hostile. It is likely that others perceive such people as being considerably more hostile than the persons themselves acknowledge.

AGG-P: Physical Aggression

The Physical Aggression subscale inquires about past history and present attitudes toward physically aggressive behavior. The questions inquire about a history of fighting and physical violence during adulthood; it is unlikely that significant elevations would result from conduct problems during adolescence in the absence of problems during adulthood. This scale has a relatively hard floor, meaning that community adults typically obtain low raw scores. However, elevations in clinical samples are relatively common.

Average scores on AGG-A indicate a person who reports being generally in control of angry feelings and impulses and who rarely expresses an angry outburst. Moderate elevations suggest that losses of temper are more common and that the person is prone to more physical displays of anger, perhaps breaking objects or engaging in physical confrontations; such people probably attempt to maintain close control over their anger, preferring to brood rather than risk expressing it in potentially destructive ways. As scores elevate above 70*t*, this control often lapses, resulting in more extreme displays including damage to property and threats to assault others. Some of these displays may be sudden and unexpected because such persons may not display their anger readily when it is experienced, particularly if AGG-V is below the mean. It is likely that those around such people are intimidated by their temper and the potential for physical violence and that they go to great lengths to avoid provoking such individuals.

Noteworthy Subscale Configurations
The particular configuration of subscales that drive AGG elevations are very informative in determining the nature and severity of any aggressive behaviors that may occur. In general, AGG-A will be expected to elevate in most individuals with anger control difficulties. However, AGG-V and AGG-P can display different patterns of elevation in such people. When AGG-V is elevated and AGG-P is average or lower, the person is likely to display anger immediately when it is experienced rather than brood or otherwise suppress it. This pattern suggests persons whose bark is worse than their bite, so to speak; it is possible that the more frequent venting of anger suggested by this pattern serves to prevent a more dramatic and overwhelming loss of control of their temper. In contrast, when AGG-P is elevated and AGG-V is relatively low (often well below the community norm), this pattern reflects a person who struggles to maintain control over his or her temper but who tends to lose this control easily. When this happens, the person is likely to respond with more extreme displays of anger; these displays may be sudden and unexpected because anger may not be displayed readily when it is experienced. It is likely that those around such people are afraid of their unpredictability, their potentially explosive temper, and the potential for physical violence. In rare instances, AGG-A may be prominently elevated but AGG-V and AGG-P both lie at or below the mean. This pattern suggests that the individual is exerting consid-

erable effort to suppress any expression of anger (look for low scores on DOM) and instead may be turning it inward (suggested with DEP-C elevated and MAN-G low).

Diagnostic Considerations

A variety of diagnostic groups display difficulties with anger management that can be reflected in an AGG elevation. The diagnosis of intermittent explosive disorder is probably the *DSM* diagnosis that bears most directly on anger issues; the overcontrolled AGG-P, AGG-A > AGG-V configuration of subscales previously noted maps onto the behavioral pattern of alternating suppression and outbursts that characterize this disorder. Prominent anger and hostility are also a part of many personality disorders such as antisocial, borderline, or paranoid personality disorder. Individuals with alcohol or drug abuse problems sometimes manifest AGG-P elevations because their aggression may become overt when disinhibited by substance use. Persons with posttraumatic stress disorder often have marked anger and resentment that can manifest as an AGG elevation. Finally, some disorders are associated with low AGG scores. Dependent individuals may be unassertive and have very low AGG scores across the board, particularly on AGG-V. Individuals with conversion or histrionic concerns often strongly deny any involvement of anger in their experience, leading to AGG scores that are below average. Finally, persons with a passive-aggressive personality style may experience considerable anger (leading to an above-average score on AGG-A) but make great efforts to avoid any overt display of anger (i.e., below-average scores on both AGG-V and AGG-P).

Treatment Considerations

The AGG scale can have important implications for treatment with both high scores and low scores. Scores on AGG that are markedly elevated suggest that it will be critical for treatment to address anger management issues, regardless of the specific diagnosis. When AGG-P is markedly elevated, the need for more intensive and highly structured treatment increases; a careful evaluation of the client's potential dangerousness to others will be necessary (this issue is discussed in more detail in chapter 9). Anger control will reflect a high priority in the treatment of these individuals, and strategies for anger management (such as relaxation, cognitive restructuring, or working on problem-solving skills) will need to be implemented in the earliest stages of treatment.

Low scores on AGG can signal assertiveness problems that may represent a target for treatment in itself or can signal self-esteem issues associated with various diagnoses. Even with the AGG full score within normal limits, when the AGG subscales display the overcontrolled configuration noted previously (when AGG-V score is substantially below scores on AGG-P and AGG-A), this configuration can reflect a more general pattern of affect suppression that may be difficult to get past in treatment. Such people may censor any discussion of their feelings on various topics, and the affective impact of the material may be more evident in their behavior than in their words.

SUI: SUICIDAL IDEATION

The SUI scale is the starting point on the PAI for evaluating suicide potential. As with the other scales of the PAI, SUI includes items that range in severity from thinking about death, to ever having contemplated suicide, to a current serious consideration of suicide. The latter item is placed near the end of the test as a final opportunity to alert caregivers to the desperateness of the person's need for help. Like other scales on the PAI, the content of the SUI items is directly related to thoughts of suicide and related behaviors, and individuals who wish to disguise suicidal intents can do so easily. However, the large majority of completed suicides occurred in persons who communicated their intent (Shneidman, 1985), and the SUI scale offers an in-depth probing of any such intention. The SUI scale has been found to correlate with suicide precaution status in clinical patients and with other self-report measures of suicidal ideation (Morey, 1991). Similarly, a study by Rogers et al. (1998) using a sample of correctional emergency referrals found correlations between the PAI SUI scale and suicidal symptoms as assessed via structured clinical interview.

It must be kept in mind that SUI is a suicidal ideation scale rather than a suicide prediction scale. Therefore, high scores indicate that a person has thought and is thinking about suicide—such scores do not necessarily mean that the person will actually commit suicide or even attempt it. *Ideation* (in contrast to completion) is fairly common in clinical settings, and in fact the raw score in the general population is not 0, implying that the average individual in the community is likely to have at one time thought about suicide. Nonetheless, because suicide rates are fairly low, it is clear that thinking about suicide and actually committing suicide are different matters. There are obviously a host of other factors in addition to ideation that determine whether a person will commit suicide. However, ideation still has a central role because it is a necessary but usually not sufficient condition for a completed suicide.

Scores on SUI in the average range are those below 60t, and these scores indicate that the respondent is not reporting being disturbed by thoughts of self-harm. It is fairly unusual for individuals in clinical settings to score below 45t. If such scores are accompanied by other risk factors described later in this chapter, the possibility of denial and masked ideation should be considered. Scores from 60t to 69t are typical of clinical patients. Scores in this range suggest that the person is experiencing periodic and perhaps transient thoughts of self-harm. Such people are pessimistic and unhappy about their prospects for the future. Although such scores are common in clinical settings, specific follow-up regarding the details of any suicidal thoughts and the potential for suicidal behavior is warranted.

SUI scores from 70t to 84t suggest recurrent thoughts related to suicide. Although only a small percentage of individuals who entertain suicidal thoughts actually act on them, a score in this range should be considered a significant warning sign of the potential for suicide. The presence of additional risk factors is of particular concern for scores in this range because such scores still reflect significant ambivalence about suicide. For such individuals, an evaluation of their life circumstances and available support systems is critical. As scores get higher, in the range from 85t to 99t, this ambivalence lessens and the thoughts of suicide are intense and recurrent. Such scores are typical of individuals placed on suicide precautions. As SUI scores become extreme (e.g., above 100t), the person is likely to be morbidly preoccupied with death and suicide, and many of the steps toward suicide (giving away belongings, writing a note, formulating a specific plan) are likely to have been completed. In such cases the potential for suicide should be evaluated immediately, and appropriate interventions should be implemented without delay. Scores at these levels must be considered a significant warning sign of the potential for suicide, regardless of the levels of elevation on other scales.

Diagnostic Considerations

Increased suicidal ideation and risk are associated with virtually every diagnostic category in mental health. As such, the SUI scale is unlikely to be a specific diagnostic indicator for any particular diagnosis. However, the elevation of SUI can sometimes be useful in distinguishing among different diagnoses within the same general class. For example, individuals in a major depressive episode will tend to have markedly elevated SUI scores, whereas those with a more chronic but milder form of depression, such as dysthymic disorder, may have less prominent elevations on SUI. Similarly, individuals with borderline personality disorder often have more marked SUI elevations than do individuals with related personality disorders (such as antisocial, paranoid, or dependent personality disorders).

Treatment Considerations

An elevation on SUI clearly suggests that a careful assessment of suicidality will be required in the earliest stages of treatment. Although the SUI scale provides a useful indication of the extent and pervasiveness of suicidal ideation, many other PAI scales provide additional information to help gauge other risk factors for suicide, such as depression, alcohol abuse, poor social supports, or impulsivity. Assessing these risk factors is described in more detail in chapter 9. The suicidality assessment will also need to determine a variety of other important information that cannot be determined by the PAI, such as the respondent's specific plans for suicide, if any; his or her access to lethal means of self-harm; his or her specific living arrangements; and the quality of his or her capacity for judgment. When suicidal ideation is marked and many such risk factors exist, hospitalization may be required. When the risk of self-harm appears less imminent, intensive outpatient treatments may be possible. One technique that is often used in conjunction with outpatient treatments involves asking the patient to sign a no-harm contract, in which the patient agrees not to harm him- or herself for a specific time period during which the patient will contact the therapist if the risk of suicide seems to worsen. Such contracts are accompanied by frequent follow-up and are renewed as long as the risk appears tangible. Ideally, the patient's social support system should also be involved in the implementation of the contract, and the absence of such a support system constitutes a further risk for self-harm.

ASSESSMENT OF PERCEPTION OF ENVIRONMENT: STRESS (STR) AND NONSUPPORT (NON)

Although personality assessment instruments have typically focused on the contributions of individual differences to behavior, it is clear that situational elements can also be a powerful determinant of behavior. To provide some insight into these influences, the PAI includes two scales assessing characteristics of the environment. One of these scales addresses the predictability, organization, and structure of the person's surroundings, ranging from fairly predictable environments to highly changeable and very stressful kinds of environments. The second aspect involves the availability and quality of supports in the environment. In both instances, it must be remembered that scores on these scales reflect the perceptions of the respondent rather than any objective appraisal of the environment, and thus these assessments are themselves filtered through the lens of individual differences. However, as is noted later in this chapter, a comparison with other scales on the instrument can help distinguish a global personality style from a specific environmental influence. The following sections provide a description of these two scales individually, followed by a consideration of the scales in combination for the assessment of the respondent's view of their environment.

STR: Stress

The STR scale provides an assessment of life stressors that the client is currently experiencing or has recently experienced. Item content includes problems in family relationships, financial hardships, difficulties related to the nature or status of employment, or major changes that have recently occurred or are about to occur in the client's life. The stress scale correlates moderately well with life events checklists. However, unlike these checklists, the items are not specific about the precise nature of the stressors; they merely indicate the presence of many changes and that day-to-day circumstances are not predictable. Although item content is not specific, it appears that the majority of these changes have not been perceived as being for the better because corre-lations between STR and most indicators of depression are high.

Average scores on STR (below 60*t*) reflect a person who reports his or her life as stable, predictable, and uneventful. Scores between 60*t* and 70*t* are in-dicative of a person who may be experiencing a moderate degree of stress as a result of difficulties in some major life area. With scores above 70*t*, these dif-ficulties are likely to be having a significant impact on the client; a review of their current work situation, family and close relationships, or financial status will probably reveal circumstances that are a source of worry, rumination, and unhappiness. These individuals are at risk for development of a number of ad-justment or reactive disorders; scores on the clinical scales should be reviewed to determine the severity and nature of any such symptomatology.

STR scores that are markedly elevated (above 85*t*) indicate that the client perceives him- or herself as surrounded by crises; nearly all major life areas are reported to be in turmoil. Such individuals feel that they are powerless to con-trol a series of undesirable events that are happening to them. They see them-selves as ineffectual, dependent, and at the mercy of those around them—a situation that may lead to some bitterness. Levels of stress in this range make the client vulnerable to many different clinical disorders, and scores on the clinical scales should be examined to determine the precise nature of the in-dividual's reactions to stresses of this magnitude.

NON: Nonsupport

The NON scale provides a measure of a perceived lack of social support, tap-ping both the availability and quality of the client's social relationships. Item content addresses the level and nature of interactions with acquaintances, friends, and family members. The scaling of NON is such that low scores re-flect high perceived social support, whereas elevations indicate a perception of the social environment as unsupportive. The scale is a measure of the per-ception of social support rather than an objective measure (such as a count of frequency of contact with family members) because perception tends to be more important than the actual amount of support received when the impact of social support as a moderator of stress is examined.

Average scores on NON (below 60*t*) reflect a person who reports close, generally supportive connections with family and friends. Scores between 60*t* and 70*t* are indicative of a person who may have few close interpersonal relationships or is perhaps dissatisfied with the nature of these relationships. With scores above 70*t,* respondents are reporting that their social relationships offer them little support; family relationships may be either distant or combative, whereas friends are generally seen as unavailable or not helpful when needed.

NON scores that are markedly elevated (above 88*t*) indicate clients who perceive that they have little or no social support system to help them through significant events in their lives. They tend to be highly critical of themselves as well as of other people, whom they perceive as uncaring and rejecting. These individuals have few emotional resources for dealing with crises and are particularly prone to severe reactions to stress.

Configurations of STR and NON

The STR and NON scales tend to display a moderate positive correlation, and both scales tend to be somewhat elevated when the PAI is used in clinical settings; the average scale scores were 64*t* for STR and 60*t* for NON in the clinical standardization sample. When both scores fall below these means, the combination of a stable and relatively stress-free environment with the extensive social support system suggests a favorable prognostic sign for future adjustment. However, when lower scores are accompanied by elevations on the clinical scales (particularly on DEP or ANX), this pattern may suggest a person with a strong tendency to internalize blame for problems. In contrast, when both scores fall above these means, the respondent is likely to be experiencing notable stress, chaos, and turmoil in a number of major life areas. A primary source of stress may involve relationship issues because social relationships are described as unsupportive; family relationships may be somewhat distant or ridden with conflict, and friends are not seen as available when they are needed.

When the STR and NON scales demonstrate noteworthy discrepancies, the interpretation becomes more specific. When STR exceeds NON by a considerable margin (e.g., more than 10*t* points), the clinical picture is likely to focus on stress and turmoil, perhaps related to external features such as the current employment situation or financial status, in a number of major life areas.

The difficulties observed on the clinical scales (particularly DEP and ANX) are likely to be related to situational presses rather than to a more enduring pattern, and the relatively lower NON score suggests the presence of supportive relationships that may serve as a buffer against the effects of this stress. In contrast, when NON exceeds STR by a significant margin, it appears that the support system is the origin of most stressors from the environment. Such individuals view important others as rejecting and uncaring and believe that there is hardly anyone in their environment to whom they can turn for help. These relationship issues appear to be a major source of stress and concern. Accompanying elevations on PAR or BOR-N could suggest that this dissatisfaction with social relationships may be chronic and related to personality problems as opposed to a specific environmental circumstance.

Diagnostic Considerations

Although neither the STR nor the NON scales bear directly upon diagnostic constructs, both can be of use in differential diagnosis. The STR scale is particularly helpful for identifying situational adjustment disorders; in such instances the STR score should be expected to be among the highest elevations on the profile, typically accompanied by comparable scores on DEP, ANX, or both. Family or marital problems are often reflected by a NON elevation that exceeds the scores of most of the clinical scales. In somatization disorders, it is not uncommon for NON to be elevated, because such individuals sometimes feel that their physical problems are not understood or accommodated for by those close to them.

Treatment Considerations

A STR scale that is markedly elevated relative to the rest of the profile suggests the presence of a situational crisis that is likely to present as the focus of treatment. Support and problem solving will probably be indicated in addressing this crisis; however, with additional scale elevations (BOR in particular), the current crises may simply be the latest in a long series, and the focus of treatment may then need to shift to the origins of this pattern. With the NON scale displaying a prominent elevation, one important function of treatment may be to provide a source of support that seems to be lacking in the respondent's environment. Within this supportive context, it will be important to explore the interpersonal patterns of the client that might have contributed to the problems in the support system. If NON represents the high point of the profile, this configuration may signify familial difficulties that might profitably be addressed in family or marital therapy.

RXR: TREATMENT REJECTION

RXR items were written to indicate attitudes that could pose potential problems with motivation for treatment. An individual who is motivated for treatment presents with a number of characteristic attitudes, including a willingness to participate actively, honesty in self-description, ability to recognize problems when they exist and an acceptance of some degree of responsibility for these problems and their solutions, psychological mindedness, openness to new ideas, and an interest in personal improvement. High scorers on RXR *lack* these characteristics, suggesting that they will be at risk for treatment noncompliance and early termination. The scale was designed to be applicable across different therapeutic modalities—for example, pharmacotherapy or self-help approaches as well as traditional psychotherapy. Broad content areas that were sampled included a refusal to acknowledge problems, a lack of introspectiveness, an unwillingness to participate actively in treatment, and an unwillingness to accept responsibility for change in one's life. The RXR scale clearly differentiates patients in treatment from individuals not in treatment (e.g., Alterman et al., 1995; Boyle & Lennon, 1994; Cherepon & Prinzehorn, 1994); average scores on RXR among individuals presenting for treatment are typically 1–2 standard deviations below the mean for adults in the community.

In interpreting scores on RXR, it is critical to keep in mind that the *t* scores were referenced against a community sample, not a treatment sample. As a result, average scores, although they are typical of normally functioning individuals, actually represent little motivation for treatment. Thus, even *t* scores that appear to be within the average range can have negative implications for treatment motivation when they are obtained within a clinical setting. In other, nonclinical settings (e.g., a preemployment screening) scores of 50*t* or higher may well be typical, but they should not be expected from clinical populations. In the standardization clinical sample, the mean score on RXR was 40*t*.

Another aspect of RXR that is important in its interpretation is that it is related to treatment motivation, not prognosis. Motivation may constitute a necessary but not sufficient condition for successful treatment because recognizing that changes need to be made does not assure that those changes will be accomplished. In fact, very low scores on RXR are often sort of an indication of a cry for help, indicative of overwhelming distress and perhaps unrealistic expectations for an immediate alleviation of suffering. For example,

> **DON'T FORGET**
>
> A score of 50t on RXR in the presence of clinical difficulties represents a problematic level of treatment motivation, even though it reflects an average score in the general population.

individuals with borderline personality disorder who are in acute distress will often score extremely low on this scale, indicating high motivation for treatment that reflects that they truly do desperately want their lives to change. However, because such patients are extremely difficult to work with for other reasons, the prognosis for treatment is not necessarily favorable.

The scaling of RXR is such that low scores reflect high motivation for treatment, whereas elevations indicate little motivation for treatment. In clinical settings, scores below 40t indicate an acknowledgement of significant difficulties in functioning and the perception that help is needed in dealing with these problems. However, scores below 20t indicate a desperate quality to these needs that does not augur well for treatment prognosis. Scores on RXR between 40t and 50t reflect a person who acknowledges the need to make some changes, has a positive attitude toward the possibility of personal change, and accepts the importance of personal responsibility. However, scores in the upper portion of this range sometimes are higher than expected in respondents about whom available information (such as from the history or from other scales of the PAI) suggests some impairment; in such circumstances, the possibility of defensiveness, rigidity, or lack of insight must be considered. Scores between 50t and 60t are indicative of persons who are generally satisfied with themselves as they are and who see little need for major changes in their behavior. Individuals scoring in this range would generally have little personal motivation to enter into psychotherapy, and if they are presenting in a treatment setting, it is typically at the insistence of others. Such patients might be at risk for early termination if they do enter treatment. RXR scores above 60t reflect a person who admits to few difficulties and will rigidly resist efforts to change the status quo. Such individuals are not likely to seek therapy on their own initiative and are likely to be resistant if they do begin treatment; they will probably dispute the value of therapy and have little (if any) involvement in any therapeutic attempts. RXR elevations are commonly obtained in profiles of individuals who are making overt efforts to present a favorable impression.

Diagnostic Considerations

RXR has little specificity for assisting with particular diagnostic decisions because it is primarily oriented to treatment planning. It has been observed that individuals with borderline personality disorder can sometimes present with very low scores on the scale. Scores of 50*t* and above are often obtained in persons who have been mandated to receive treatment—for example, in forensic settings.

Treatment Considerations

As noted previously, high scorers on RXR are likely to be difficult to engage in nearly any form of treatment. However, RXR is a reflection of a willingness to be involved in efforts to achieve personal change; it is not a prediction of the likelihood of achieving such change. Strategies for identifying features that may be effective in making such predictions are described in more detail in chapter 9.

INTERPERSONAL STYLE: DOMINANCE (DOM) AND WARMTH (WRM)

The two interpersonal scales, DOM and WRM, represent the core of the assessment of interpersonal style with the PAI. The selection of these two dimensions was based on the interpersonal circumplex model originally formulated by Leary (1957) and elaborated on by many others. An individual's interpersonal style constitutes a significant portion of his or her personality. The way that a person relates to others is certainly associated with overall adjustment; however, there are a variety of ways in which people interact with one another, and there is no one healthy style that is necessary for personal effectiveness. Nonetheless, the interpersonal style can mediate a number of clinical concerns.

The DOM and WRM scales have nearly identical distributions in clinical and normal subjects. This supports the conclusions that the two scales capture variation across a normal personality trait and that variability on these dimensions exists as widely within normally functioning individuals as it does within individuals presenting for treatment. On these scales, high scores may be problematic, and low scores may also reflect problems; the interpersonal scales are probably the most bipolar of all PAI in that the low and high extremes are equally interpretable and have equal potential for problems.

DOM: Dominance

The DOM scale captures the degree to which a person desires control in interpersonal relationships. Low scorers on DOM (below 40t) seek to relinquish control in relationships, preferring to approach these relationships in a passive manner. Such people are often self-effacing and lack confidence in social interactions. These characteristics make it difficult for such people to get their needs met in personal relationships; instead, they tend to subordinate their own interests to those of others in a manner that may seem self-punitive as the scores approach 30t. The lack of assertiveness may open the possibility for mistreatment or exploitation by others.

In contrast, high scores on DOM (above 60t) suggest a person who is self-assured, confident, and dominant. Such people are likely to be described by others as ambitious and having a leader-like demeanor. Although they are comfortable in social settings, they are not likely to mix indiscriminately, preferring to interact with others in situations over which they can exercise some measure of control. As scores approach 70t, the person may be viewed by others as domineering and overcontrolling. In this range, there will be strong needs to control others and the expectation of respect and admiration in return. Individuals scoring in this range may be driven to appear competent and authoritative and are likely to have little tolerance for those who disagree with their plans and desires.

WRM: Warmth

The WRM score indicates the degree to which a person is interested in and comfortable with attachment relationships. Although WRM scores are normally distributed in the general population, in many instances it appears that higher scores on WRM are preferable to low scores because this scale is typically positively related to indicators of favorable adjustment. However, this is not always the case because high scores on WRM could reflect a person who is sacrificing too much to maintain attachment relationships and is thus ineffective in interpersonal relationships in many ways.

Low scores on WRM (below 40*t*) suggest a person who may be somewhat distant in personal relationships. Such people may not appear to place a high premium on close, lasting relationships, and they may well view most social interactions without much enthusiasm. Others may view these individuals as reserved and possibly aloof and unsympathetic. However, low scorers on this scale may view themselves as independent, practical, and less preoccupied with the opinions of others than are most people. As scores approach 30*t* and below, the person is increasingly likely to be perceived as being cold and unfeeling. Such people appear stern, impersonal, and unable to display affection or make a commitment to personal relationships. Examining other PAI scales can help shed some light on the nature of the interpersonal withdrawal, which can alternatively reflect social disinterest (SCZ-S), social anxiety (ARD-P), limited capacity for empathy (ANT-E), a pattern of interpersonal instability (BOR-N), interpersonal bitterness (PAR-R), or suspiciousness and touchiness (PAR-P).

In contrast, high scorers on WRM (above 60*t*) can be characterized as being warm, friendly, and sympathetic. These individuals particularly value harmonious relationships and derive a great deal of satisfaction from these relationships. Because of the premium placed upon harmony, they may be uncomfortable with interpersonal confrontation or conflict and will tend to shun controversy. Such people are probably quick to forgive others and will readily give others a second chance. As scores approach 70*t*, the interpersonal style is characterized by an exceptionally strong need to be accepted by others. This need for acceptance probably dominates the interactions of such people. Others may see them as being too caring, trusting, and supportive for their own good. They are at risk for being so committed to acceptance that they lose all individuality or creativity. Such people attempt to avoid any conflict in relationships, and they are reluctant to accept any hint of hostility in themselves, particularly if AGG-V and MAN-I are below average. Others are likely to take advantage of this strong need to be liked, which may be seen as an invitation to exploit the respondent's trust.

Configurations of DOM and WRM

The basic circumplex model of interpersonal behavior, dating back to Leary (1957), involves combining the two dimensions of dominance and warmth into a structure that characterizes one's preferred manner of interacting with others. A particularly interesting aspect of the theory surrounding the interpersonal circumplex is the principle of *complementarity*. This principle governs the expected nature of interpersonal transactions within the circumplex; every interpersonal behavior has a complement, which is the natural interpersonal reaction to a given event or transaction. Complementary behaviors are the same on the warmth dimension and on the opposing end in the dominance dimension. For example, if a person controls people (dominance) in a friendly (warmth) way, as in a parenting relationship, the complementary reaction is for people to submit in a friendly way. On the other hand, if a person controls others in a hostile and uncaring way, the complementary reaction is to submit but in a hostile manner. This property of the interpersonal dimensions is useful in allowing one to predict the types of interpersonal behaviors a person is likely to evoke in others.

Combining these two scales forms four quadrants: a warm, dominating quadrant; a cold, dominating quadrant; a cold, submitting quadrant; and a warm, submitting quadrant. For each of the quadrants, stereotypical behaviors can be described. A prototype for the friendly control (high DOM, high WRM) quadrant would be parenting behavior—an example of controlling others while being interested in maintaining the attachment relationship. Such people tend to be eager to be seen by others as popular and socially effective. As the two scores get increasingly high, strong needs for attention become prominent, perhaps leading the person to attempt to control or interfere with others' social interactions to meet the respondent's own needs.

An impersonal, superordinate-subordinate relationship characterizes the hostile control (high DOM, low WRM) quadrant. Such people tend to have a pragmatic and independent interpersonal style. Others will probably view such a person as being shrewd, competitive, and self-confident. As the two scores become more extreme, the person is likely to be egocentric and suspicious. Such people are likely to demand more from relationships than they are willing to give, perhaps using relationships in an exploitative fashion for self-enhancement.

The hostile submission (low DOM, low WRM) pattern characterizes a person who habitually submits to others unwillingly, perhaps in a passive-aggressive fashion. Such people tend to be withdrawn and introverted. They tend not to invite social interaction with others, make little special effort to appear friendly, and will be passive and distant in those relationships that are maintained. If PAR-R is also elevated, this passivity probably leads to feelings of resentment when others attempt to secure cooperation.

Finally, the prototype for the friendly submission style is dependency—a person who is very interested in maintaining the attachment relationship and willing to submit in the context of that relationship in order to maintain it. This type of individual is likely to be rather unassuming and conforming, preferring to avoid being the center of attention in social interactions. Given their rather unobtrusive stance in social interactions, such people often value their relationships more than is readily apparent to those around them. They are likely to be seen by others as someone who is fairly eager to please but at times overly sensitive in relating to others. As the scores become more extreme, there is increasing neediness and gullibility. Such people will have strong fears of rejection by others and as a result find it difficult to be assertive or to display any anger. Feeling helpless and overwhelmed under relatively mild pressure, they will dependently seek the assistance of others. An investigation of the self-esteem indicators often reveals a poor self-image.

Diagnostic Considerations

Although they are not diagnostic constructs in and of themselves, the interpersonal scales can be useful in differential diagnosis of conditions with a prominent interpersonal component, such as the personality disorders. Many of the personality disorders display interpersonal styles characterized by low WRM scores (such as schizotypal, schizoid, paranoid, or obsessive-compulsive personalities). Some of these disorders also show low DOM scores (avoidant, passive-aggressive). Narcissistic and antisocial personalities often display high DOM scores, reflecting the respondent's needs for attention and control. As noted earlier, a person with dependent personality disorder would be expected to be interested in maintaining relationships (high WRM) but would do so in a passive manner (low DOM). The interpersonal scales can also provide information that may be helpful but probably less specific for Axis I diagnosis. Low WRM scores can be associated with social anxiety or phobia as well as with the interpersonal detachment of schizophrenia. Individuals in a manic episode are often controlling and would be expected to yield above-average scores on DOM.

Treatment Considerations

Through the principle of complementarity, the interpersonal scales can be particularly helpful in anticipating the reaction of the therapist to a patient entering treatment. For example, the therapist may find him- or herself pulled to be controlling by a patient with a habitually submissive interpersonal style. On the attachment axis, the therapist may find him- or herself seeking distance from a patient with a detached style. Although such behaviors are natural reactions, they present the danger of propagating the interpersonal problems that may have led the patient to seek treatment. Thus, attending to the configuration of these scales can help the therapist anticipate likely countertransference reactions.

 TEST YOURSELF

1. **For which of the following scales would a t score of 50 indicate a troublesome course in psychotherapy?**
   (a) ICN
   (b) SOM
   (c) RXR
   (d) SUI

2. **Which of the following PAI scales has four subscales?**
   (a) BOR
   (b) DEP
   (c) AGG
   (d) SUI

3. **A moderate elevation on ALC can represent**
   (a) a moderate degree of current problems.
   (b) severe problems with alcohol that occurred in the past.
   (c) a failure to recognize some consequences of a severe drinking problem.
   (d) all of the above.

(continued)

4. **Which of the following scales is most difficult to interpret at the full-scale level?**
   (a) ANX
   (b) ARD
   (c) DEP
   (d) BOR

5. **Characteristics of the client's social environment can be determined by inspecting**
   (a) ICN and INF.
   (b) NON and STR.
   (c) ANT and PIM.
   (d) ALC and DRG.

6. **Clinical and community samples tend to obtain similar scores on the interpersonal scales.** True or False?

7. **Reckless behavior may be associated with very low scores on**
   (a) ANT-S.
   (b) BOR-S.
   (c) ARD-P.
   (d) AGG-P.

8. **The average score on DOM is much higher for normal individuals than it is for clinical patients.** True or False?

9. **What type of behavior will a person with high DOM and low WRM provoke from people?**

10. **What type of AGG subscale configuration can indicate the potential for unexpected aggressive behavior?**

Answers: 1. c; 2. a; 3. d; 4. b; 5. b; 6. True; 7. c; 8. False; 9. hostile submission; 10. high AGG-P and AGG-A with low AGG-V

Seven

INTERPRETING TWO-POINT CODE TYPES

As the interpreter moves beyond a consideration of individual scales in arriving at a formulation, the next step involves an examination of the profile configuration. The beginning point in this process involves a consideration of the implications of combining the two highest clinical scale scores (the *two-point code*) for the profile. The use of two-point codes in profile interpretation has become somewhat of a tradition in the assessment field. Although the use of two-point codes provides a starting point for the configural interpretation of the PAI profile, it should also be recognized that such a code provides a limited summary of the information contained in the profile. First, the two-point code ignores the wealth of information provided by the other scales on the test. Second, because of the subscale structure of the PAI scales, meaningful differences on even the two scales that comprise the code can be observed between persons with identical codes. Finally, the reliability of the small differences that can determine a two-point code on any psychological instrument is often suspect. For example, consider a profile in which DEP is at 75t, ANX is at 72t, and BOR is at 71t. Although this is nominally a DEP-ANX two-point code, the difference between ANX and BOR is considerably less than one standard error of measurement and the difference between the two is not likely to be a reliable one. Yet, the DEP-BOR two-point code has implications considerably different from those of the DEP-ANX code. Given these limitations, it is best to (a) consider the following descriptions of code types as a rough starting point for the configural interpretation of the PAI profile, and (b) examine all relevant descriptions (e.g., DEP-ANX, DEP-BOR, ANX-BOR for the example provided earlier) when scales determining the code type fall within 5t of each other, a value that reflects at least one standard error of measurement of the scales.

CAUTION

Distinctions between two-point code types in profiles with several elevated scales are often of low reliability. In such profiles it is important to examine the implications associated with code types involving all prominent elevations.

The following sections provide a capsule summary of the major features and interpretive significance of the 55 possible PAI two-point codes. Inclusion in one of these code types is based on the two highest scores on the 11 PAI clinical scales, with each of the two scales involving scores of at least 70t. No distinction is provided in these sections with respect to order of the scales within the code: for example, the SOM/ANX code type applies to all profiles for which SOM and ANX are the two highest clinical scales (regardless of which is higher), with both at least 70t. The code types are presented in the order provided in the individual scale descriptions in chapter 6 (corresponding to their ordering on the PAI profile form). Thus, the 10 combinations of code types involving SOM are presented first, then the remaining nine combinations of code types involving ANX, and so on for all 11 clinical scales. Rapid

≡Rapid Reference 7.1

Frequent and Infrequent PAI Code Types

Common code types	Frequency in Clinical Populations[a]
ALC-DRG	9.0%
SOM-DEP	2.8%
ARD-DEP	2.5%
DEP-BOR	2.5%
DEP-SCZ	2.4%
Uncommon code types	
SOM-ANT	0.0%
ANX-ANT	0.0%
ARD-MAN	0.0%
DEP-MAN	0.0%
SCZ-ANT	0.0%

[a]From Morey (1991).

Reference 7.1 summarizes these code types that are most and least frequently observed in clinical populations.

SOM/ANX

- Suggests marked distress, with particular concerns about physical functioning. Life is viewed as severely disrupted by a variety of physical problems, some of which may be stress-related. These problems render such individuals tense, unhappy, and probably impaired in their ability to concentrate on and perform important life tasks. The somatic concerns may have led to friction in close relationships, and other people often perceive these individuals as complaining and demanding.
- Secondary elevations on ARD and DEP are often observed with this code type. When such elevations are present, they may suggest that the somatic features may be part of a broader neurotic pattern, such as autonomic features of a panic attack or vegetative features of depression. The level of STR can be informative in ascertaining the degree of life disruption associated with the somatic concerns.
- Treatment: The elevated ANX may make the respondent more receptive to psychological interventions for health problems, as opposed to persons who view their problems as purely physiological in nature.
- A relatively common profile configuration, observed in 1.1% of clinical subjects.
- Common diagnostic correlates include somatoform disorders, posttraumatic stress, adjustment reactions, and major depression. It is interesting to note that this code type is also observed disproportionately in persons with schizophrenia, perhaps reflecting the onset of somatic delusions.

SOM/ARD

- Suggests a person who has ruminative concerns about physical functioning; life is viewed as disrupted by a variety of physical problems, some of which may be related to marked stressors. Problems have left the individual tense and worried, leading to particular disruption in close relationships.

- Relative elevations of ARD-T and STR may reveal whether such stressors involve recent (indicated by STR > ARD-T) or more long-term (ARD-T > STR) events.
- Secondary elevations on ANX and DEP often observed as part of a general neurotic pattern; elevations in other areas tend to be more unusual.
- Treatment: If ARD-O subscale is driving the ARD elevation, the pattern might suggest a rigid adherence to physiological explanations of problems and a potential resistance to psychosocial interventions.
- Pattern is observed in 0.9% of clinical subjects.
- More often seen in anxiety disorders (including posttraumatic stress disorder) than in more purely somatoform disorders.

SOM/DEP

- Suggests a person who is reporting significant distress and unhappiness, with particular concerns about physical functioning. Life is viewed as severely disrupted by a variety of physical problems, which have left the individual unhappy, with little energy or enthusiasm for concentrating on important life tasks and little hope for improvement in the future. Performance in important social roles has probably suffered as a result, and lack of success in these roles serves as an additional source of stress.
- Secondary elevations on ANX are frequent, although if this elevation is driven primarily by ANX-P, this pattern might simply be part of the somatic symptom pattern rather than a true involvement of anxiety. Also, SUI is often elevated with this pattern, suggesting that some probe of suicidal ideation is merited when this code type is observed, particularly if the somatic problems are chronic in nature.
- Treatment: Somatic complaints may reflect vegetative signs of depression (check DEP-P), warranting an evaluation for antidepressant medication.
- A relatively common profile, observed in 2.8% of clinical subjects.

- Diagnostic correlates include somatoform disorders, organic mental disorders, and major depression.

SOM/MAN

- Unusual configuration reflects unlikely combination of significant problems in physical functioning accompanied by potentially heightened energy and activity levels. Somatic concerns and emotionally labile style have probably led to friction in close relationships; others may view the respondent as complaining and demanding.
- Secondary elevations on ARD, BOR, and STR tend to be seen with this code type, suggesting that both situational (suggested by STR > BOR) and characterological (BOR > STR) factors should be considered in evaluating the somatic concerns. Inspection of DRG is also warranted because abuse of prescription drugs may be a risk for this type of individual.
- Treatment: Pattern suggests possible compliance problems with either psychosocial or medical interventions; either form of treatment may need to be monitored closely with persistent follow-through.
- An uncommon pattern, seen in only 0.2% of clinical subjects.
- Observed with some frequency in patients diagnosed with schizoaffective disorder.

SOM/PAR

- Unusual configuration suggests prominent hostility and suspiciousness accompanying significant problems in physical functioning. The mistrust suggested by PAR is likely to be expressed in the realm of health concerns. Others are likely to be perceived as unsympathetic to the respondent's somatic concerns and unsupportive of his or her perceived limitations. Hostility has probably led to some friction in close relationships; other people may view respondent as complaining and demanding. Respondent is more likely to attribute the source of these conflicts to poor health and to the poor treatment (interpersonal as well as medical) that he or she receives from others.

- Secondary elevations on NON are often observed with this code type, underscoring the resentment experienced toward the perceived lack of support received from family or friends with their health concerns.
- Treatment: Such clients are unlikely to be receptive to examining any psychological factors associated with physical complaints and will probably be resistant to psychological interventions.
- A rare configuration, with only 0.1% of patients in the standardization clinical sample displaying this pattern.
- Individuals with organic mental disorders were disproportionately represented in this code type.

SOM/SCZ

- Configuration suggests significant thinking and concentration problems accompanied by marked concerns about health and physical functioning. When the SCZ elevation is driven primarily by SCZ-P, these somatic complaints may be highly unusual; they could involve hypochondriacal preoccupations, or in extreme circumstances they might involve somatic delusions. On the other hand, if the SCZ elevation reflects a major contribution from SCZ-T, these symptoms may reflect a disruption in cognition and attention that are part of a general organic process. In either instance, the reported combination of physical limitations and social discomfort probably limits the extent of the respondent's social interactions; whatever few close relationships there are may revolve around somatic preoccupations.
- Secondary elevations on DEP are often observed; when these elevations are present, they raise the possibility that the somatic disruptions and concentration problems might be part of a major depressive episode. Also seen with some frequency are pronounced elevations on NIM, suggesting that the possibility of symptom exaggeration should be evaluated.
- Treatment: Combination of confusion and somatic preoccupation poses a considerable obstacle to insight-based approaches; biological interventions may be preferred by clients and may be warranted by symptomatology.

- Pattern observed in 0.6% of clinical subjects.
- Diagnostic correlates include schizophrenia and bipolar disorder, manic episode.

SOM/BOR

- Suggests significant problems in physical functioning, accompanied by hostility and emotional liability. Such people are likely to harbor some bitterness toward important others, who may be viewed as unsympathetic to the respondents' somatic concerns and unsupportive of their perceived limitations. This hostility and emotionality has probably been a particular source of friction in close relationships. Others are likely to view the respondent as complaining and demanding, and others may perceive the somatic complaints as a manipulative means through which the respondent can control relationships.
- Implications of the profile may vary according to whether the health problems are acute or chronic in nature; with chronic health problems, the BOR elevation might reflect a problematic adaptation to physical limitations that are perceived as intractable.
- Secondary elevations on DEP and SUI are often observed with this code type, underscoring the marked distress of such people, and the intensity of associated bitterness and anger is often revealed with elevations on PAR and AGG.
- Treatment: Course of treatment is likely to be difficult with either psychosocial or medical interventions. If both types of treatment are received, coordination of efforts will be particularly important because clients may play one treatment provider against the other.
- A relatively rare profile, observed in 0.3% of clinical subjects.
- Diagnostic correlates include somatoform disorders, posttraumatic stress disorder, and antisocial personality disorder.

SOM/ANT

- Unusual configuration suggests a person who is self-centered and preoccupied with somatic problems to the exclusion of concern or caring for other people. Such people are typically seen as complaining, self-centered, and demanding. Others may perceive the somatic complaints as a means through which the respondent can achieve some other form of secondary gain.

- Secondary elevations on ALC and particularly DRG should be examined to determine whether substance abuse may be contributing to the health issues; alternatively, the health issues may serve as a means to obtain prescription medication.
- Treatment: Course of treatment likely to be difficult; pattern suggests lack of receptiveness to examining psychological factors associated with the physical complaints and probable resistance to psychological interventions.
- Very uncommon profile pattern; it was never observed in the standardization clinical sample.

SOM/ALC

- Suggests a history of drinking problems accompanied by a number of physiological problems that may be partially related to alcohol consumption. Somatic problems could involve withdrawal symptoms (look for recent alcohol use or cognitive confusion that might lead to validity scale elevations), or they might be medical complications of alcohol abuse, such as problems associated with the central nervous system sequelae of alcoholism (rendered more likely by chronic, long-term misuse of alcohol; often evident on SOM-C). The combination of alcohol use and physical symptomatology is probably causing severe disruptions in relationships and work, and these difficulties are most likely serving as additional sources of stress.
- Secondary elevations on STR are often observed, and its items might help document the nature of functional disruptions.
- Treatment: Health problems may serve as an impetus for treatment of alcohol dependence in a previously resistant individual.
- Code type observed in 1.3% of clinical subjects.
- Common diagnostic correlates include alcohol dependence and organic mental disorders.

SOM/DRG

- Suggests a person with a history of drug abuse who is experiencing a number of physiological problems that may be partially related to his or her use of drugs. Somatic problems might involve withdrawal symptoms; look for recent use of substances with high physical dependence potential or cognitive confusion that might lead to ICN, INF, or NIM elevations. Somatic symptoms might also be medical complications of drug abuse, such as hepatitis or HIV. The combination of substance use and physical symptoms is probably causing severe disruptions in social role functioning, and these difficulties typically will serve as additional sources of stress.
- Secondary elevations on DEP are common and suggest that the drug abuse could reflect efforts at self-medication. Elevations on ANT and BOR may raise the possibility that the person is at risk for abusing prescription medication associated with the somatic condition.
- Treatment: The combination of health problems and drug abuse history will require careful management and monitoring of any prescribed medications.
- Pattern observed in 0.6% of clinical subjects, with somatoform disorders predominating.

ANX/ARD

- Suggests marked anxiety and tension; such people may be particularly uneasy and ruminative about problems in their personal relationships. These relationships may be an important source of current distress, and such people tend to respond to these circumstances by becoming socially withdrawn (look for low WRM scores) or passively dependent (suggested by low DOM scores). The disruptions in their life often leave them questioning their goals and priorities (which can be confirmed by examining BOR-I), and they may be tense and fearful about what the future may hold.
- Secondary elevations on DEP and SUI are often observed with this

code type; these elevations become prominent as the distress becomes more debilitating.

- Treatment: Level of subjective distress reflected in this pattern often serves as a strong motivator for treatment. Focal anxieties may be responsive to behavioral or cognitive interventions, which may need to be supplemented by psychopharmacological treatments in the presence of panic disorder or agoraphobia.
- A fairly common pattern, observed in 1.9% of clinical subjects.
- Common diagnostic correlates include various types of anxiety disorders as well as major depression.

ANX/DEP

- Suggests significant unhappiness, moodiness, and tension. Self-esteem is often low (look for low MAN-G), and these individuals view themselves as ineffectual and powerless to change the direction of their lives. Life disruptions, which are evident if this configuration is accompanied by elevations on STR, can leave such people uncertain about goals and priorities and uncertain and pessimistic about what the future may hold. There are likely to be difficulties in concentrating and making decisions, and the combination of hopelessness, agitation, confusion, and stress apparent in these scores may place such people at increased risk for self-harm.
- Secondary elevations on SUI are often observed with this code type, and the Suicide Potential index should be examined in such cases as part of an evaluation of potential for self-harm.
- Treatment: Although these individuals are distressed and acutely aware of their need for help, a low energy level, passivity, and withdrawal may make it difficult to engage the respondent in treatment. Biological interventions may assist in this process for patients with prominent vegetative symptoms. Treatment management should include a careful monitoring of suicidality; risk may increase as the depressive apathy resolves.
- Pattern is observed in 1.3% of clinical subjects.
- Commonly associated with diagnoses of dysthymic disorder, major depression, and borderline personality disorder.

ANX/MAN

- Unusual configuration suggests a person who is agitated, irritable, and affectively labile. A high activity level is likely to have left such individuals feeling stretched to their limits and hindered in their ability to perform any of their roles effectively. Such people are tensely preoccupied and feel overwhelmed by self-imposed demands. Close relationships may have suffered particular strain because individuals with this pattern are very self-focused and often lack the empathy required to recognize the impact that their moody and demanding presentation has on others.

- Secondary elevations on BOR and STR are often observed with this code type, which will accentuate the feelings of being overwhelmed and out of control. DOM is also often elevated, indicative of strong needs for control and suggesting that intense anxiety most likely ensues when this control is not possible or must be relinquished.

- Treatment: The subjective distress represented by ANX may indicate greater insight and a better prognosis for treatment than is typical for most individuals with a MAN elevation. However, motivation may rapidly wane as the immediate crisis that precipitated treatment resolves.

- This is an uncommon profile pattern, observed in only 0.2% of clinical subjects.

ANX/PAR

- A relatively unusual configuration that suggests prominent hostility and suspiciousness accompanied by acute anxiety and sensitivity. These individuals tend to demonstrate a touchiness in social interactions that probably serves as a formidable obstacle to the development of close relationships. Although such people may harbor considerable anger and resentment, the degree of anxiety may lessen the likelihood that this anger is expressed directly. The anxiety may also reflect a perception that the protection provided by the respondent's interpersonal caution is failing.

- Secondary elevations on ARD and BOR are often observed with this code type, with the latter particularly suggesting that these features may be part of a more general pattern of personality problems. SUI can also be elevated in these individuals, and any such ideation should be carefully evaluated given the extent of the hostility and anxiety suggested by the profile.
- Treatment: Establishing a treatment alliance may be difficult because such clients may be hesitant to disclose the degree of their distress and will particularly avoid any direct discussion of the therapy relationship and any feelings it may evoke.
- This pattern tends to be rare, observed in only 0.1% of clinical subjects.

ANX/SCZ

- Suggests significant thinking and concentration problems accompanied by prominent agitation and distress. Such individuals are likely to be withdrawn and isolated, having few (if any) close interpersonal relationships, and anxious and threatened by such relationships. Social judgment is probably fairly poor, and such people tend to have marked difficulty in making decisions (particularly when SCZ-T drives the SCZ elevation), even about matters of little apparent significance. When SCZ-P is prominent as part of the SCZ presentation, the possibility of an incipient psychotic deterioration should be considered.
- Secondary elevations on DEP are often observed with this code type; when such elevations are present, the configuration further underscores the extent of the distress and cognitive inefficiency.
- Treatment: At high elevations this profile suggests a need for close monitoring and appropriate crisis intervention. Biological interventions should be considered if the profile appears to represent an acute psychotic episode.
- Seen in 0.9% of clinical subjects.
- Pattern is most frequently associated with diagnoses of schizoaffective disorder, schizophrenia, and posttraumatic stress disorder.

ANX/BOR

- Suggests a person who is tense, angry, unhappy, and emotionally labile. Often represents a state of crisis and marked distress, commonly triggered by difficulties or rejection (perceived or actual) in interpersonal relationships. The current crisis may be part of a more general pattern of anxious ambivalence in close relationships, marked by bitterness and resentment on one hand and dependency, intense anxiety, and fear of possible rejection or abandonment on the other.
- Secondary elevations are often observed on DEP, accompanying ANX in suggesting the extent of the distress, and both are likely to be recurrent rather than isolated incidents. Also noted with some frequency are AGG elevations, pointing to significant underlying anger when present and perhaps alternating with anxiety over the consequences of angry outbursts.
- Treatment: Despite motivating properties of the anxiety, such individuals may become quickly disillusioned with treatment if it does not yield immediate results, suggesting need for careful alliance building and addressing goals and expectations in early stages of treatment.
- This profile is observed in 0.9% of clinical subjects.
- Common diagnostic correlates include borderline personality disorder and somatoform disorders.

ANX/ANT

- Unusual configuration of the clinical scales—somewhat of a contradiction in terms. Suggests a person who is impulsive and self-centered, yet experiencing considerable anxiety and tension. Because these two personality elements are so inversely correlated, if both are present the respondent probably fluctuates between these disparate elements, with periods of impulsive acting-out followed by worry and anxiety regarding the consequences of the respondent's impulsive behavior. These individuals may view themselves as incapable of controlling their reactions to stressful circumstances; however, this pattern of impulsivity will tend to be recurrent, ultimately leading others to doubt the sincerity of their concern and desire to alter their behavior.

- Treatment: Despite the likelihood of noteworthy impulse control problems in the clinical picture, the involvement of ANX in the profile may be a more favorable prognostic sign than if it were below average, which would represent a more purely antisocial condition.
- This pattern was never observed in the standardization clinical sample, which underscores its unusual nature.
- Pattern suggests consideration of diagnoses such as antisocial personality disorder or intermittent explosive disorder.

ANX/ALC

- Suggests a history of drinking problems accompanied by prominent anxiety. The anxiety and alcohol use may be related in a number of different ways; for example, alcohol use may be serving a functional role of tension reduction. It is also likely that the person is anxious and guilty about the impairment in social role performance that has resulted from drinking; the alcohol use is probably causing severe disruptions in relationships and work, with these difficulties serving as additional sources of stress and perhaps further aggravating the drinking problems.
- Secondary elevations on STR are often observed, which may be a reflection of the consequences of alcohol problems on current role function. In contrast, concomitant ARD-T elevations may suggest that the drinking may serve a stress-reduction role as an adaptation to historical stressors.
- Treatment: Role of anxiety as a withdrawal symptom should be examined, with consideration of need for possible alcohol detoxification.
- Relatively common profile pattern, observed in 1.0% of clinical subjects.
- Most typically associated with diagnoses of alcohol dependence, major depression, and dysthymic disorder.

ANX/DRG

- Configuration suggesting a history of substance abuse problems with concomitant anxiety. This anxiety and the substance use may be related in a number of different ways; for example, the drug use may be serving a functional role of tension reduction, or the impairments associated with the drug use may be heightening subjective distress. Such people also tend to be anxious and guilty about these impairments in social role performance, including relationships and work; these difficulties serve as additional sources of stress and perhaps further aggravate the tendency to abuse drugs.
- Secondary elevations on DEP and SUI are often observed; this pairing suggests marked pessimism and despair over the prospects for positive change and heightens concerns when the substance of choice has significant overdose potential. Also, it is not uncommon to see RXR in a range that suggests limited motivation for treatment.
- Treatment: There may be limited motivation for psychosocial interventions, associated with a historical reliance on drugs to solve one's problems. Also, the role of anxiety as a withdrawal symptom should be examined, with consideration of need for possible detoxification.
- Configuration observed in 1.0% of clinical subjects.
- Relatively uncommon in substance-abusing samples but is seen with some frequency in individuals with psychotic symptoms. In these patients, drugs such as hallucinogens or stimulants may be playing a role in precipitating or exacerbating psychotic processes.

ARD/DEP

- Suggests significant tension, unhappiness, and pessimism. Various stressors (both past and present) have probably adversely affected self-esteem. Such people tend to view themselves as ineffectual and powerless to change the direction of their lives. The disruptions in their lives have left them feeling uncertain about goals and priorities and fearful and pessimistic about what the future may hold. There are likely to be difficulties in concentrating and making decisions, and the combination of hopelessness, anxiety, and stress may present an increased risk for self-harm.

- Secondary elevations on ANX and SUI are often observed and heighten concerns for potential dangerousness to self when they are present.
- Treatment: Although there is considerable distress and an acute awareness of a need for help, a low energy level, tension, and withdrawal may hamper engagement in treatment. Psychopharmacological treatments may be warranted if there are prominent vegetative symptoms and may facilitate engagement in psychosocial interventions.
- A relatively common profile, observed in 2.5% of clinical subjects.
- Common diagnostic correlates include posttraumatic stress disorder and other anxiety disorders, major depression and dysthymic disorder, borderline personality disorder, and schizoaffective disorder.

ARD/MAN

- Unusual combination suggests a person who is fearful, irritable, and affectively labile. May see themselves as overextended and vulnerable, confronted with goals and expectations that are beyond their capacity, leaving them stretched thin and hindering their ability to perform any roles effectively. There may be an underlying rigidity (particularly if ARD-O is driving the ARD elevation) that is being taxed by the respondent's self-imposed demands; the resulting strain has probably left the person feeling intensely frustrated and overwhelmed by the obstacles to completing these demands. Close relationships may have suffered particular strain from the moody, impatient, and demanding presentation of the respondent.
- Treatment: Lack of perseverance and affective lability raise the likelihood of treatment dropout.
- Profile pattern is rare; it was never observed in the standardization clinical sample.

ARD/PAR

- Unusual configuration suggests prominent hostility and suspiciousness in a person who is acutely tense, fearful, and hypersensitive.

The heightened sensitivity in social interactions will serve as a formidable obstacle to the development of close relationships; those relationships that have been established are probably a source of ruminative worry. If ARD-T appears to be driving the ARD elevation, the intense mistrust may be associated with perceptions of exploitation (such as abuse) in historical relationships. Although the pattern hints at considerable anger and resentment, the degree of anxiety around social interaction may lessen the likelihood that this anger is directly expressed.

- Secondary elevations on BOR and NIM are often observed with this code type, raising the likelihood that the person views the world with profoundly negative expectations.
- Treatment: Configuration suggests that establishing trust in therapy will be a critical early step because such clients are likely to be skeptical of treatment providers. Exploring perceptions of previous treatment experiences may be particularly valuable.
- This profile is rare, observed in only 0.1% of clinical subjects.

ARD/SCZ

- Configuration suggests significant thinking and concentration problems accompanied by prominent distress and ruminative worry. The particular combination of elevations on ARD-T and SCZ-T points to possible disruptions of intrusive thoughts or images related to a traumatic event; other combinations may point to less specific fears or ruminations. In either case, the client is likely to be withdrawn and isolated, feeling estranged from others. As a result, there are probably few (if any) close interpersonal relationships because such people tend to become anxious and threatened by such relationships. Social judgment is likely to be fairly poor, and such individuals are often confused about their goals and pessimistic about what the future may hold.
- Secondary elevations on SUI are often observed with this code type, and the combination of marked anxiety and clouded judgment combined with marked suicidal preoccupations heightens concerns for self-harm.

- Treatment: Often motivated for treatment by distress, these individuals are likely to respond positively to structure and support early in treatment. Medication evaluation should be considered when SCZ is markedly elevated.
- Profile seen in 0.4% of clinical subjects.
- Common diagnostic correlates include posttraumatic stress disorder and bipolar disorder is also disproportionately represented.

ARD/BOR

- Suggests a person who is uncomfortable, impulsive, angry, and resentful. Such a person is likely to be presenting in a state of crisis and marked distress. Such crises are often associated with difficulties or rejection (perceived or actual) in intimate interpersonal relationships. Such individuals often feel betrayed or abandoned by those close to them, perhaps including previous therapists. This configuration probably reflects a more general pattern of anxious ambivalence in close relationships, marked by bitterness and resentment on one hand and dependency and anxiety about possible rejection on the other. Various stressors (both past and present) may have contributed to and maintained this pattern of interpersonal turmoil, and ARD-T and STR may yield information about the relative importance of recent (STR > ARD-T) as opposed to more distant (ARD-T > STR) stressors. Regardless of the temporal progression, the disruptions in their lives leave such people uncertain about goals and priorities and tense and cynical about future prospects.
- Concomitant elevations on DEP and SUI are often observed with this code type, and these secondary features are more likely to wax and wane as a function of the immediacy of the current crisis.
- Treatment: Initial motivation for treatment is likely to be strong but may wane rapidly, particularly with resolution of some current crisis; important goals may involve recognition of crisis as part of a recurrent pattern and forming an alliance toward bringing about enduring changes. Limited trust in the therapist may be manifested by repeated testing of the limits of the parameters of treatment (e.g., out-of-session contacts).

- Profile is relatively common, obtained in 1.6% of clinical subjects.
- Common diagnostic correlates of this configuration include borderline personality disorder, major depression, and dysthymic disorder.

ARD/ANT

- Unusual configuration suggests tension and rumination combined with impulsivity and acting-out potential. The respondent may alternate between these elements, with periods of impulsive acts followed by worry and rumination regarding the consequences of these behaviors. Such individuals may see themselves as hapless victims of their own impulsivity—as people who are incapable of controlling reactions to stressful circumstances. However, the recurrent nature of this pattern may lead others to view the respondent as irresponsible and ultimately as insincere or manipulative.
- Secondary elevations on MAN and PAR are common and reflect poor prognostic signs, suggesting that the potential inhibiting effects of anxiety or ideational rigidity represented by ARD are failing to control the impulses and hostility represented by ANT.
- Treatment: Response to treatment may be better when ANT-A and ARD-T are driving the observed elevations, suggesting that behavioral problems may be resulting from a poorly processed traumatic event. A combination such as ARD-O and ANT-E reflects a particularly poor prognosis for formation of any type of treatment alliance because such an individual is likely to reject personal responsibility for current problems.
- A rare profile, observed in 0.1% of clinical subjects.
- Diagnostic possibilities include antisocial personality disorder or posttraumatic stress disorder.

ARD/ALC

- Suggests a history of drinking problems accompanied by prominent stress and anxiety. Alcohol use could be serving a functional role of tension reduction; it may be seen as relieving the impact of stressors past (perhaps witnessed on ARD-T) or present (these stressors would most likely be evident on STR). If ARD-O is prominent in the ARD elevation, there is likely to be considerable rumination about life circumstances, and cravings and the urge to drink may be at the center of these ruminations. Part of the anxiety may result from impairments in social role performance that have resulted from drinking; alcohol is probably causing disruptions in relationships and work, with these difficulties serving as additional sources of stress and perhaps further aggravating drinking problems.

- Secondary elevations on BOR and DEP are common and may reflect episodes of impulsive binge drinking followed by periods of remorse and self-condemnation.
- Treatment: Efforts at relapse prevention may focus on the relationship of alcohol use to high-risk, anxiety-arousing situations.
- Profile observed in 0.6% of clinical subjects.
- Most commonly associated with a diagnosis of alcohol abuse or dependence.

ARD/DRG

- Configuration suggests a history of substance abuse problems accompanied by prominent stress and anxiety. Drug use may be viewed by the respondent as a coping strategy to relieve the impact of historical stressors. Such individuals ruminate about life circumstances, with drug cravings at the center of these ruminations. Anxiety is also likely to result from impairment in social role performance that arises from drug misuse.
- Secondary elevations on BOR and ANT are common and suggest characterological problems that may lead to externalizing of blame and responsibility for the drug misuse.
- Treatment: Motivation for change may be strong initially but may not be sustained as tension associated with presenting crisis dissipates. Involvement in group-based substance abuse treatment may be a helpful adjunct to any individual interventions.
- Relatively uncommon profile, observed in 0.2% of clinical subjects.
- Common diagnostic correlates include substance abuse, major depression, and acting-out personality disorders such as borderline and antisocial personality disorders.

DEP/MAN

- Unusual and somewhat contradictory configuration that suggests the experience of both elevated and depressed moods. There is likely to be severe distress, irritability, and unhappiness punctuated by periods of heightened activity and energy. When MAN is higher than DEP, hypomanic features may be masking a severe depression that may not be readily apparent from overt behaviors. Such people are likely to be preoccupied and self-absorbed by their mood state, regarded by others as irritable and self-centered.
- Individuals with marked mood swings tend not to obtain this profile; instead, the currently experienced mood state tends to dominate the profile configuration. In bipolar mood disorders, a history of symptoms associated with the other mood more typically leads to modest (e.g., around 60t) elevations on the accompanying scale, rather than having both scales elevated in excess of 70t.
- Treatment: Establishing treatment targets may be difficult because the presenting complaints may be unstable and variable in early stages of treatment.
- Very rare configuration; this pattern was never observed in the standardization clinical sample.

DEP/PAR

- Suggests prominent depression and hostility, likely to present as an embittered pessimism. Negative life circumstances are likely to be attributed to the shortcomings of others, with resulting despair about the ability to change these circumstances. A heightened sensitivity in social interactions has most likely led to significant withdrawal and probably serves as a formidable obstacle to the development of close and trusting relationships. Although such people harbor considerable anger and resentment, this anger is as much self-directed as it is directed at others.
- Secondary elevations are common, both for neurotic (ANX, SOM, ARD) and for more impaired features (SCZ, BOR, SUI). The strongly negative evaluation of both self and the external world tend to lead to a pathological coloration in the perception of events.

Thus, indications of negative profile distortion (particularly NIM) should be evaluated carefully. Elevations on NON are also observed with this code type and underscore the degree of resentment directed at significant others; with the NON elevation, the major sources of distress are particularly likely to be attributed externally.

- Treatment: Despite the level of distress, treatment can be challenging because mistrust of therapist may hamper alliance formation. Focusing early on depressive symptoms may be less threatening to the client than attempting to address interpersonal failures.
- Profile was observed in 0.9% of clinical subjects.
- Common diagnostic correlates of this configuration include schizoaffective disorder, major depression, and posttraumatic stress disorder.

DEP/SCZ

- Suggests severe distress and dysphoria accompanied by significant thinking and concentration problems. The respondent is likely to be demoralized, withdrawn, and isolated, feeling estranged from others. The configuration of hopelessness and pessimism combined with the likelihood of impaired judgment and interpersonal distancing may place such individuals at increased risk for self-harm—secondary elevations on SUI are often observed with this code type.
- To the extent that DEP-P exceeds SCZ-P, this configuration is more suggestive of a severe depressive episode rather than a focal psychotic disorder.
- Configuration is fairly common in clinical settings—observed in 2.4% of subjects in the clinical standardization sample.
- Treatment: Likelihood of severe apathy and depressive symptomatology may require early pharmacological intervention to engage the person successfully in psychosocial treatments.
- Common diagnostic correlates include schizoaffective disorder, posttraumatic stress disorder or other severe anxiety disorders, borderline personality disorder, major depression, and schizophrenia.

DEP/BOR

- Suggests unhappiness, emotional lability, and considerable anger that may be partially masked as depression. Typically accompanies marked distress seen during a state of crisis, often precipitated by difficulties or rejection (perceived or actual) in interpersonal relationships. Individuals with such profiles often feel betrayed or abandoned by those close to them, which compounds their feelings of helplessness and hopelessness. For the respondent, the current crisis may be part of a more general pattern of need-fear conflicts in close relationships, marked by bitterness and resentment on one hand and dependency and anxiety about possible betrayal on the other. The underlying anger may often cloud judgment and may cause these individuals to lash out impulsively at those closest to them. However, the anger can be as much self-directed as it is directed at others.
- The combination of hopelessness, resentment, and impulsivity may place such people at increased risk for self-harm; SUI and STR are commonly elevated with this code type and exacerbate these concerns.
- Treatment: Strong expressions of desire for change are likely (look for a low RXR), but treatment may be frequently disrupted by crises arising from impulsive or self-destructive behaviors.
- Relatively common profile, observed in 2.5% of clinical subjects.
- Common diagnostic correlates include borderline personality disorder, major depression, and adjustment disorders.

DEP/ANT

- Fairly unusual configuration suggests dysphoria and pessimism manifested in combination with impulsivity and acting-out behaviors. Clinical picture probably fluctuates between these elements, with periods of impulsive acts followed by worry and guilt regarding the consequences of these behaviors. Such people may see themselves as incapable of controlling their acting-out behavior, viewing it as a reaction to stressful external circumstances. However, this pattern of impulsivity tends to be recurrent, eventually leading others to doubt the sincerity of the professed remorse and of any stated desire to change.

- Secondary elevations from other neurotic elements are uncommon, suggesting that most of the distress arises from external rather than internal sources. More typical are elevations on PAR (indicating an outward projection of blame for current sources of stress) and on ALC or DRG (indicating that substance misuse may be part of the pattern of impulsive action).
- Treatment: Presenting distress may be situational; as the situation resolves, commitment to treatment and change is likely to ebb. The client's unreliability and failure to follow through on treatment plans are likely to be a source of frustration to the treating professional.
- Unusual profile type, observed in only 0.2% of clinical subjects.

DEP/ALC

- Configuration suggests unhappiness and pessimism coupled with a history of drinking problems. Depression could be primary, driving the alcohol use, or it could be a secondary consequence of the social disruption associated with alcohol use. In either case, alcohol problems have probably led to severe impairment, leading to significant alienation from others. Social role setbacks have probably led to significant self-blame and rumination about life circumstances.
- Secondary elevations on SUI are often observed with this code type, and (when present) they heighten concerns about possibility of self-harm, given the potential for disinhibition associated with alcohol use.
- Treatment: Prognosis for intervention may be mixed; the respondent is likely to feel desperate for help but cynical about prospects for change or improvement. May be a valuable window for treatment if DEP elevation reflects a crumbling of denial surrounding alcohol-related problems.
- Reasonably common profile, observed in 1.7% of clinical subjects.
- Commonly associated with diagnoses of alcohol dependence, major depression, and posttraumatic stress disorder.

DEP/DRG

- Configuration indicates a history of substance abuse problems in an individual who is unhappy and pessimistic. Depression is likely to be exacerbated by drug-related impairment in maintenance of social role expectations around relationships and employment. Impulsive, self-destructive behaviors may have alienated close relationships, and this may have led to considerable guilt and distress about current circumstances. The depression could be driving the use of drugs in an unsuccessful effort to avoid experience of negative affects.
- Secondary elevations on SUI are often observed, and suicidality should be monitored closely, given the potential for overdose or simply the disinhibition resulting from acute drug misuse. A secondary elevation on ANT increases the likelihood that the depression is a consequence of the disruption associated with substance abuse rather than a causal factor in the drug use.
- Treatment: Such clients may enter treatment pessimistic about their prospects for change or improvement, potentially because of a history of repeated relapse.
- Configuration is found in 1.0% of clinical subjects.
- Commonly associated with diagnoses of borderline personality disorder, major depression, and drug dependence.

MAN/PAR

- Rare combination suggests expansive mood and heightened activity accompanied by prominent hostility and irritability. Such people tend to see themselves as having had their plans thwarted by neglect or obstruction by others; however, these individuals are probably more impeded by an activity level that includes expectations for performance that are beyond their actual capacity. Sensitivity in social interactions, egocentricity, and unrealistic self-appraisal impede the development of close relationships. The combination of impulsivity, resentment, and high energy levels could cause such individuals to lash out impulsively at those who they believe have slighted them in some way, and any relationships that have been established are likely to have suffered as a result of this pattern.

- Secondary elevations on NON underscore externalization and projection of responsibility for problems; this pattern also points to the potentially unrealistic demands that such individuals place on supportive relationships.

- Treatment: Retaining such clients in treatment can be very difficult; clients are typically uninterested in treatment because they externalize responsibility for all problems onto others. Early treatment may need to concentrate on establishing goals for personal change rather than cataloging the many changes that are desired from others.

- An uncommon profile, observed in only 0.1% of clinical subjects.

MAN/SCZ

- Particularly serious combination of features suggests significant thinking and concentration problems accompanied by heightened activity levels and irritable and expansive mood. Such people are likely to be agitated and confused, feeling irritated with and alienated from the people around them. Their judgment is probably poor, particularly in social situations; those relationships that have been maintained are probably strained by the respondent's erratic and disorganized style of relating to others.

- Secondary elevations on STR are often seen with this code type, probably suggesting the impact of poor judgment on role functioning.

- Treatment: The combination of high energy and questionable judgment is a poor prognostic sign, and the presenting situation should be closely monitored. Individuals with this configuration may need a high level of structure in treatment, and psychopharmacological therapies should be considered.

- A relatively uncommon profile pattern, observed in only 0.1% of clinical subjects.

MAN/BOR

- Pattern suggests labile mood, impulsivity, and heightened activity levels, accompanied by prominent hostility and irritability. Relationships are likely to be fairly stormy, and any close relationships that have been maintained have most likely suffered particular strain from an impatient, unpredictable, and often demanding presentation. The combination of low frustration tolerance, resentment, and high energy levels could cause such people to overreact to minor events and to react impulsively to the actions of those around them, with little consideration for the consequences to the relationship. These same traits also place the respondent at increased risk for acting-out behaviors.
- Secondary elevations on NON are often observed with this code type, suggesting that many key social support contacts either have been driven away or are viewed with skepticism. DOM elevations are also common and can indicate strong needs for control in relationships that are not likely to be met.
- Treatment: May initially present with intense desperation and pleas for help, but there may be little follow-through by the client. When the respondent is presenting during a crisis, the overt level of distress may mask a surprising lack of insight.
- Observed in 0.5% of clinical subjects.
- This configuration appears to be more strongly related to bipolar disorder than to borderline personality disorder although the two disorders can coexist.

MAN/ANT

- Configuration suggests impulsivity, hostility, and difficulties with empathy. Relationships are likely to be conflictual and short-lived; any that are maintained are probably sustained by the perseverance of the other party in the relationship, who must be able to tolerate the client's impatient, self-centered, and often hostile presentation. There is likely to be little tolerance for frustration, with lingering resentment toward past sources of frustration. A driven energy level combined with limited consideration for the needs of others can cause such people to lash out impulsively at those around them when such individuals have been crossed. These same traits also place such people at increased risk for acting-out behaviors, and it is likely that these behaviors have led to impairment in their ability to maintain role expectations in both formal (e.g., work) and informal settings.

- Secondary elevations on STR are common, generally signifying a deterioration in social role performance that the respondent may minimize. Elevations on AGG are also frequent and in the context of this code type represent a particular concern because there may be potential for impulsive violence.
- Treatment: Motivation for treatment tends to be low; such clients typically do not present for treatment voluntarily unless there is some secondary gain perceived to be associated with it. Such clients may respond to group interventions with clients sharing similar characteristics; such interventions can serve a mirroring function that can help these clients gain some insight into their own behavior patterns.
- A fairly uncommon configuration, seen in 0.4% of clinical subjects.
- Observed with some frequency in patients with bipolar disorder, antisocial personality disorder, and drug abuse or dependence.

MAN/ALC

- Configuration suggests a history of drinking problems in a person who is emotionally labile and impulsive. Alcohol problems are probably part of a pattern of more general recklessness, which has probably led to fairly severe impairment in their ability to maintain social role expectations and has probably alienated friends and family. Such people are likely to be particularly disinhibited under the influence of alcohol and display exceptionally poor judgment and demonstrate other acting-out behaviors while intoxicated. It is also doubtful that there is much lasting remorse associated with any such

behaviors. Such people have limited insight into the extent and
severity of their drinking, and this denial of problems probably per-
sists into other life areas.

- Secondary elevations on STR often reflect impaired global functioning, and AGG elevations are also a frequent accompaniment, high-
lighting probable anger control problems while drinking.
- Treatment: Denial is likely to be prominent, and motivation for
treatment is probably low. Such denial may be effectively confronted
in group interventions with other clients who have alcohol-related
problems.
- A relatively rare profile, observed in 0.1% of clinical subjects.
- It is unusual to find this profile in the absence of alcohol dependence.

MAN/DRG

- Configuration suggests emotional lability and impulsivity accompanied by (and perhaps related to) substance abuse problems. Drug-
related problems have likely led to fairly severe impairment in
maintaining social role expectations, and a generally reckless and
directionless approach to life has probably driven away most friends
and family. These respondents are likely to be particularly disinhibited under the influence of drugs and may display markedly poor
judgment and demonstrate other acting-out behaviors while intoxicated.
- Secondary elevations on ANT and NON are often observed with
this code type and (when present) indicate the externalization and
projection of blame for the person's current difficulties.
- Treatment: Motivation for treatment is probably low and there is
probably limited insight into the extent to which drug use has
caused life disruptions. Confrontation of denial within a group substance abuse intervention may be particularly important for such
clients.
- This profile type is uncommon, observed in 0.1% of clinical subjects.

PAR/SCZ

- Configuration suggests an isolated individual with significant thinking and concentration problems. There is likely to be prominent hostility, resentment, and suspiciousness. Very sensitive in social interactions, such people are likely to be cautious, withdrawn, and feeling estranged from and mistreated by the people around them. There tend to be few (if any) close relationships, which exacerbates a potentially idiosyncratic worldview and resulting problems in judgment. The respondent is likely to be chronically tense and apprehensive about what the future may hold.
- Secondary elevations on NIM are often observed with this code type; when this pattern is present, it raises the possibility that symptom exaggeration or a highly negative worldview may be driving up the scores on PAR and SCZ. With secondary elevations on DRG, the possibility of drug-induced paranoid ideation should be evaluated.
- Treatment: Such individuals are not likely to pursue psychological treatment of their own accord; if such a person presents for treatment, establishing a therapeutic relationship will be challenging because such people are likely to become apprehensive and threatened by the offer of a close interpersonal relationship.
- A relatively common profile in inpatient settings, observed in 2.4% of subjects in the clinical standardization sample.
- Common diagnostic correlates include schizophrenia, schizoaffective disorder, antisocial personality disorder, and drug dependence.

PAR/BOR

- Configuration reflects considerable anger, resentment, impulsivity, and emotional instability. Such people are likely to be extremely sensitive in social interactions and very quick to perceive rejection (real or imagined) by others. A pattern of perceived betrayals by people once close to them may emerge upon inquiry. This is likely to be part of a general style of chronic maladjustment in social relationships—one marked by anxious ambivalence arising from bitterness, resentment, and expectancies of possible exploitation on one hand

and strong needs for social contact and understanding on the other. The bitterness is likely to surface readily, and these clients may react impulsively when they believe that others have slighted them in some way. The combination of impulsivity, anger, and dysphoria could place the respondent at increased risk for self-harm or acting-out behaviors.

- Treatment: Although an initial crisis situation may lead to apparent incentives to change, ultimately motivation for treatment may prove to be limited. The pattern of externalizing responsibility for life crises onto exploitative others may lead treatment progress to stagnate. Treatment behaviors may be disruptive and provocative as part of a pattern of testing the trustworthiness of the therapist. Individual therapy with these clients is likely to be stressful and will probably need to be long-term in nature.

- Secondary elevations on AGG and DEP are often observed with this code type; when it is present, this combination may indicate that angry outbursts tend to be followed by rumination over the interpersonal consequences of these outbursts.

- This profile, observed in 0.4% of clinical subjects, is observed in antisocial personality disorder as well as in borderline personality disorder.

PAR/ANT

- Configuration suggests impulsivity, hostility, bitterness, and problems in empathic relatedness. Interpersonal relationships are likely to be few; they are probably short-lived and conflictual when they do exist. Any sustained relationships will require the other participant to weather the respondent's irritable and self-centered style. Such people tend to be egocentric in their worldview and can lash out angrily at those who are perceived as having impeded them in some way. These same traits also place them at increased risk for acting-out behaviors, but responsibility for these actions will invariably be projected outwards. This pattern tends to lead to marked impairment in the capacity to work effectively with others, and there is likely to be a history of occupational failures.

- Secondary elevations on AGG and SUI are often observed with this code type, and this configuration presents heightened concerns about managing these individuals in treatment.
- Treatment: Motivation for change is likely to be low; there is often little recognition of their involvement in bringing about life circumstances and little idea of how to behave differently. Establishing a trusting relationship with the therapist will be particularly challenging, and acting-out behaviors may frequently disrupt treatment.
- This profile is seen in 0.4% of clinical subjects.
- Found with relative frequency among individuals with antisocial personality disorder.

PAR/ALC

- Configuration indicates a history of drinking problems in a person who is embittered and angry. Sensitivity and hostility in social interactions are likely exacerbated by alcohol use, which may be playing a functional role as an obstacle to the development of trusting relationships. Alcohol may serve to reduce the anxiety and threat that relationships pose but also increases alienation, withdrawal, and isolation. Such individuals probably ruminate about their adverse life circumstances, but they are likely to deny the severity of their drinking problem and its role in these circumstances. Although apparent impairment in social role performance has probably resulted from drinking, such people are more likely to attribute these problems to external factors than they are to admit its relation to their drinking.
- Secondary elevations on ANT or BOR suggest that the observed pattern is part of a more enduring, chronic pattern of adaptation. In contrast, an elevation on STR with both ANT and BOR in the average ranges suggests a problematic response to more focused situational stressors.
- Treatment: Engaging such individuals in typical alcoholism treatment programs that have an emphasis on group confrontation and disclosure may be a particular challenge. Such treatment should be accompanied by an individual intervention that will provide the opportunity to establish a trusting relationship.

- A relatively rare profile configuration, observed in 0.2% of clinical subjects.
- Commonly seen with diagnoses of substance abuse and antisocial personality disorder.

PAR/DRG

- Pattern indicates a history of substance abuse problems accompanied by considerable anger, bitterness, and suspicion. Use of drugs may be playing a functional role in helping such clients withdraw from close relationships or in reducing the anxiety and threat that relationships pose, but the drugs (both pharmacological effects and lifestyle impact) are also likely to be contributing to the suspicion and mistrust with which others are viewed. The respondent probably ruminates about life circumstances, and the urge and craving for drugs may be at the center of many of these ruminations. It is likely that significant impairment in social role performance has resulted from the substance abuse; however, respondents are more likely to attribute such problems to external factors (such as a string of bad luck) than they are to admit these problems' relation to drug use.
- Secondary elevations on BOR, ANT, and STR are often observed with this code type, and their relative positioning may be informative; the former pair suggests that the drug use may be part of enduring impulse control problems, whereas the latter may suggest a prominent situational crisis in need of resolution.
- Treatment: Prospects for group-based interventions for clients with illicit drug problems who display this pattern may be more favorable than are prospects for clients with alcohol problems because the suspiciousness that is manifested as part of a lifestyle focused on illegal activities may be attenuated in a group of similar individuals. Nonetheless, some opportunity should be provided that would allow the client to form a trusting relationship with a particular staff member.
- Pattern is found in 0.3% of clinical patients and is most commonly associated with substance abuse diagnoses.

SCZ/BOR

- Configuration suggests considerable confusion, emotional lability, and anger. With the combination of marked interpersonal dysfunction and significant thinking and concentration problems, it is possible that constant relationship preoccupations and bitterness impair the respondent's ability to think clearly. Clients with these profiles are typically presenting in a state of crisis and marked distress, often related to disruptions in important relationships. During such crisis periods, the respondent may experience brief episodes during which judgment and reality testing deteriorate markedly.
- Secondary elevations on DEP and AGG are often observed with this code type, and their relative positioning may reveal whether anger will be directed outward or inward.
- Treatment: Because of their unhappiness, resentment, impulsivity, and poor judgment, these individuals may be at increased risk for self-harm or acting-out behaviors. Initial stages of treatment should be highly structured, with clear contingencies for managing treatment-disruptive behaviors. Psychopharmacological treatments may be a useful adjunct (with perhaps an antipsychotic rather than antidepressant focus), but risk of noncompliance is probably high.
- Profile observed in 0.6% of clinical subjects.
- Configuration displays particularly strong associations with diagnoses of bipolar disorder and posttraumatic stress disorder.

SCZ/ANT

- Very unusual combination suggests significant thinking and concentration problems, accompanied by impulsivity and the potential for acting-out behaviors. Given such a pattern, social judgment is probably poor, and the few social relationships that have been maintained are probably strained by an unempathic and self-centered approach to relationships. The combination of impulsivity and poor judgment contributes to a propensity for antisocial behaviors; such people may view themselves as incapable of controlling these behaviors, viewing them as reactions to external circumstances. The client's level of psychopathology may be obscured by the more visible behavioral disruptiveness.

- Treatment: Establishing a trusting relationship with a therapist is likely to be a slow and difficult process because insight and motivation for treatment are probably low. Initial stages of treatment should be highly structured, with particular emphasis on contingency management.
- Very rare configuration—no patients in the clinical standardization demonstrated this pattern.

SCZ/ALC

- Configuration suggests a confused and socially isolated person with a history of drinking problems. General discomfort in social interactions probably serves as a formidable obstacle to the development of close relationships; thus, such people are likely to be withdrawn and isolated and are also likely to feel estranged from the people around them. Alcohol may be playing a functional role in helping them distance themselves from such relationships or in reducing the anxiety and threat that close relationships pose. Their judgment is probably fairly poor, and they are generally apprehensive about what the future may hold and cynical about the prospects for change. Inquiry should be made about possible hallucinatory experiences related to acute intoxication or detoxification.
- Secondary elevations on NIM are often observed with this code type, raising the possibility that symptom exaggeration may be contributing to the SCZ elevation. However, it is also possible that SCZ and other elements of profile elevation may be due to acute effects of detoxification; if the test was administered during the detoxification process, a follow-up administration should be considered.
- Treatment: The pattern of detachment in social relationships suggests that these individuals may display limited participation in typical group-based alcohol treatment programs, and some opportunity for development of an individual helping relationship should be provided. Close medical management of detoxification should be

provided if the SCZ elevations represent symptoms of delirium
tremens.
- This code type is not uncommon; it is seen in 1.0% of clinical subjects.
- Alcohol dependence is the most common diagnostic correlate of
this pattern.

SCZ/DRG

- Configuration suggests a history of substance abuse problems accompanied by confusion and social isolation. Drugs may be playing a
functional role in easing discomfort in social interactions or in reducing interpersonal anxiety or threat, but the mistrust and exploitative-
ness that characterize this lifestyle are likely to simply exacerbate such
problems. In most areas their judgment is probably fairly poor, and
they are sufficiently estranged from the people around them that
they are unable to make good use of corrective feedback from others.
- Secondary elevations on BOR and SUI are often observed with this
code type; when they are present, these elevations heighten concerns about the individual's capacity for self-destructive behaviors.
- Treatment: Such individuals tend to be pessimistic and cynical about
long-term plans for change, and risk of premature termination is relatively high. Treatment contacts may need to be highly structured
and relatively frequent to keep such clients engaged; clear contingencies surrounding expectations for participation in treatment may
need to be established early.
- Profile observed in 0.6% of clinical subjects.
- Seen with relative frequency in individuals with drug dependence as
well as in those with antisocial personality disorder.

BOR/ANT

- Configuration suggests prominent impulsivity, emotional lability,
and problems in the capacity for empathy. Interpersonal relationships are likely to be short-lived, are often characterized by marked
conflict, and may appear superficial to the outside observer, al-

though they are not necessarily experienced this way by the respondent. Any close relationships that have been maintained will have most likely suffered strain from the hostile, self-centered, and perhaps manipulative style of the respondent. The combination of egocentricity and poor self-control could cause such individuals to lash out impulsively at those who they believe have slighted them in some way. These same traits also place them at increased risk for acting-out behaviors, and it is likely that these behaviors have led to severe impairment in their ability to maintain employment. They may view themselves as incapable of controlling such acting-out behavior, viewing themselves as victims of unfair and stressful circumstances. However, this pattern of impulsivity will tend to be recurrent, leading others to view them as irresponsible or unreliable and to doubt the sincerity of any stated remorse or desire to change.

- Secondary elevations on AGG and SUI are often observed with this code type; when they are present, these elevations may point to a worrisome situational exacerbation of the characterological issues.

- Treatment: The ingrained nature of the problems and the likelihood of repeated treatment disruptions both point to an extremely difficult treatment course. It will be important to establish clear contingencies and limits early in treatment, and these limits are likely to be tested repeatedly. Such clients typically anticipate rejection by the therapist and may periodically attempt to provoke such rejection, leading to significant countertransference strain on the therapist.

- This profile is observed in 0.9% of clinical subjects.

- Particularly common in borderline personality disorder but is also seen with antisocial personality disorder.

BOR/ALC

- Configuration suggests marked impulsiveness and affective lability, with drinking problems a prominent part of a more general pattern of self-destructive behavior. Interpersonal relationships are likely to be volatile and characterized by marked conflict. Although alcohol-related problems may serve as a flash point for such conflicts, these relationships are likely to have suffered more from the immature and unpredictable nature of the respondent. Such people are likely to be particularly disinhibited under the influence of alcohol, and they may display remarkably poor judgment and demonstrate other acting-out behaviors while they are intoxicated, perhaps blaming the alcohol as an excuse for their own unacceptable behavior.

- Secondary elevations on STR are often observed with this code type, but this pattern typically reflects a consequence of the person's behavior rather than a contributing factor to it. Very low scores on RXR are sometimes observed; when this pattern is present, it suggests a possible collapse of the denial surrounding drinking and desperate recognition of the need for help.
- Treatment: Such individuals may present with strong initial motivation for treatment that can dissipate as current situational crises resolve—particularly those involving relationship struggles.
- This profile is relatively common, observed in 1.3% of clinical subjects.
- Common diagnostic correlates include alcohol dependence and antisocial as well as borderline personality disorders.

BOR/DRG

- Configuration suggests a person with a history of substance abuse problems who is impulsive and affectively labile. The drug use is likely to be part of a more general pattern of self-destructive behavior and probably exacerbates an already erratic approach to life. An unpredictable and hostile style of interaction has probably strained most relationships, and these relationships will likely have deteriorated even further as a consequence of the drug abuse. Such people are likely to be particularly disinhibited under the influence of drugs, and they will tend to display particularly poor judgment and reckless disregard for consequences while they are intoxicated.
- Secondary elevations on AGG are often observed with this code type; such clients may lash out angrily at those who are perceived as having wronged them in some way.
- Treatment: It will be important for treatment staff to recognize the substance misuse as part of a more general pattern of recklessness

and self-destruction rather than as the sole focus of treatment. Motivation for treatment is likely to be fleeting and situationally related; aggressive follow-through with such patients will be necessary to keep them engaged in treatment. In order to help prevent relapse, some exploration of the potential role of the abused substances in deadening a pattern of emotional overresponsiveness might be merited, along with an examination of the situations in which such responses are precipitated.

- This profile is observed in 1.1% of clinical subjects.
- Most commonly associated with diagnoses of drug dependence and borderline personality disorder.

ANT/ALC

- Configuration suggests a history of acting-out behavior—most notably in the area of alcohol abuse but probably involving other behaviors as well. Impulsivity and drinking problems have probably led to severe impairment in these individuals' ability to maintain social role expectations, and their reckless approach to life has probably alienated most of the people who were once close to them. Such persons are generally uninhibited and thrill-seeking, and the alcohol use probably further impairs their already suspect judgment. Interpersonal relationships are likely to be volatile and short-lived; even those relationships that have been maintained will have suffered some strain from the respondent's egocentricity and from the consequences of his or her drinking.
- Secondary elevations on DRG are often observed with this code type, and very low raw scores on this scale may reflect denial.
- Treatment: Motivation for treatment is often questionable; such respondents tend to downplay the severity of drinking problems and deny their responsibility for bringing about current life stressors. Group-based interventions with similar types of participants are often used to confront such issues and break down efforts at denial.
- This profile was observed in 0.7% of clinical subjects in the standardization sample.
- Observed frequently among polysubstance abusers.

ANT/DRG

- The configuration of the clinical scales suggests a person with a history of acting-out behavior, most notably in the area of substance abuse but probably involving other behaviors as well. Their impulsivity and drug use have probably led to severe impairment in their ability to maintain stable employment, and their recklessness has probably alienated most of their family and friends. Such persons are generally impulsive and thrill-seeking, and the use of drugs will likely further impair already suspect judgment. Interpersonal relationships are likely to be superficial, volatile, and short-lived; even those relationships that have been maintained will have suffered some strain from the respondent's egocentricity and from the consequences of drug use.

- Secondary elevations on AGG are often observed with this code type; when such elevations are present, they suggest that aggression or assaultive behaviors are possible results of the disinhibition associated with drug use.

- Treatment: Motivation for treatment is often dubious, and the level of denial in such clients tends to be high. Younger clients in particular may not follow through with treatment, whereas older clients may begin to recognize the self-defeating life pattern that has emerged. Group-based substance abuse interventions with similar types of participants are often used to confront such issues and break down efforts at denial.

- This profile is relatively common; it was observed in 2.1% of clinical subjects and is particularly common in correctional settings.

- This pattern is common in groups with diagnoses of drug dependence and in those with borderline personality disorder.

ALC/DRG

- Pattern suggests a history of polysubstance abuse, including alcohol as well as other drugs. When the respondent is disinhibited by the substance use, other acting-out behaviors may become apparent as well. The substance abuse is probably causing severe disruptions in social relationships and work performance, with these difficulties serving as additional sources of stress and perhaps further aggravating the tendency to drink and use drugs.

- Secondary elevations on STR are often observed with this code type and typically reflect social role disruptions as a consequence of the substance misuse.
- Treatment: In the absence of other prominent profile elevations, this profile is a good indication for a focused substance abuse treatment program. As other profile elevations are noted, the likelihood of comorbid psychiatric diagnoses increases, and treatment will probably be more complex and have multiple treatment targets.
- This profile pattern is common, observed in 9.0% of clinical subjects, and it characterizes roughly a quarter of individuals in alcohol or drug treatment.
- Aside from substance abuse diagnoses, other diagnostic correlates include antisocial personality disorder and bipolar disorder.

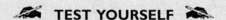

TEST YOURSELF

1. **The PAI two-point code refers to**
   (a) elevations on the two highest PAI scales.
   (b) elevations of at least 70t on the two highest clinical scales.
   (c) two-point discrepancies between different scales.
   (d) the highest clinical scale and the highest treatment consideration scale.

2. **A two-point code type may be indeterminate unless the two scales exceed the third highest elevation by**
   (a) 2 points.
   (b) 5 points.
   (c) 10 points.
   (d) 15 points.

(continued)

3. **Which of the following code types reflects an uncommon combination of PAI scale elevations?**
   (a) SOM/DEP
   (b) ANX/BOR
   (c) ANX/ANT
   (d) ANT/DRG

4. **Individuals with the same two-point code type may be quite different as a result of different subscale configurations for the two scales in consideration. True or False?**

5. **How many possible PAI clinical code types are there?**

Answers: 1. b; 2. b; 3. c; 4. True; 5. 55

Eight

STRENGTHS AND WEAKNESSES OF THE PAI

The strengths and weaknesses of the PAI will vary to a certain extent as a function of the application for which the test is being used. Even in a particular setting, the PAI may have different utility for addressing different questions. Consider, for example, the use of the PAI in consultation settings in which neuropsychological assessments are routinely performed. The test results will probably have very limited ability to assist in localizing brain damage, but they may be very useful for identifying concomitant affective or psychiatric conditions for differential diagnosis purposes.

The following sections describe a few of the central strengths and weaknesses of the PAI when it is used within its typical range of application, such as in mental health settings. These points are summarized in Rapid Reference 8.1.

STRENGTHS

Relevance Across Diagnostic Groups

The PAI contains numerous scales relevant to a wide variety of clinical conditions, and use of the test can provide information about client difficulties and assets in several critical areas. For diagnostic purposes, the utility of the test will vary across different target populations; for example, little information about eating disorders or neuropsychological impairment can be gleaned from the instrument. However, the broad range of symptomatology tapped by the PAI would still provide useful information in the clinical assessment of such groups. This information could assist in (a) identifying potentially associated problems in such groups, such as depression, anxiety, or anger; and (b) allowing for increased homogeneity for classification in such groups, such as

≡*Rapid Reference 8.1*

Strengths and Weaknesses of the PAI

Strengths	Weaknesses
• Relevance across many clinical contexts	• Susceptibility to impression management efforts and the limits of psychological insight
• Ease of administration and scoring	
• Availability of different normative referents	• Limited content coverage of various clinical syndromes, such as dissociative disorders or eating disorders
• Established reliability and validity	
• Cost-effectiveness	
• Ease of profile interpretation	• Needs for additional research for new applications and needs for cross-validation of existing strategies
• Availability of multiple assessments of protocol validity	
• Compatibility with contemporary theory and practice	

differentiating within such groups according to levels of depression, psychotic features, substance abuse, personality problems, and so forth.

From its inception, the PAI was designed to have wide applicability. As a pretreatment measure, the instrument provides a comprehensive assessment of different functional areas and provides information critical in making diagnostic and treatment decisions. The treatment consideration scales provide extradiagnostic information specifically relevant to determining treatment intensity (e.g., inpatient vs. outpatient treatment) by providing an assessment of potential for immediate crisis (such as suicide or assaultive behavior) as well as the client's motivation for treatment and likelihood of compliance with treatment. Also, scales such as those measuring environmental stress and social support levels provide valuable data for specifying environmental contributions to the presenting difficulties and for determining the risk of relapse of problems following treatment.

Simplicity in Administration and Scoring

The implementation of the PAI is simple in most settings. The test is self-administered in a paper-and-pencil format and also can be administered by computer. The required fourth-grade reading level for clients appears to involve the lowest reading levels among instruments of this type (Schinka & Borum, 1993). Hand scoring the test requires no templates and the test can be hand scored by clerical personnel in 10 min, although optically scanned computer scoring is also available. It is commercially available for use by both English- and Spanish-speaking clients, and it has been translated into a number of different languages.

Objective Standardization Referents

The PAI provides numerous referents against which the clinician can compare a given client. The t scores are referenced against a census-matched community sample; additional transformations are available in the test manual (Morey, 1991) based on norms for clinical subjects, college students, African Americans, and older adults. A large database of profiles obtained from individuals applying for public safety positions is also available (Roberts et al., 2000). In addition, mean profile data for many different diagnostic or evaluation groups are presented in the interpretive guide (Morey, 1996) and in the test manual (Morey, 1991).

Psychometric Adequacy

The psychometric characteristics of the PAI reflect one of the primary strengths of the instrument. The reliability of the instrument is very good, leading to standard errors of measurement that are sufficiently small to reliably detect even small changes that might be associated with treatment. The validity of the instrument has been documented with respect to widely used measures of treatment-associated changes, including self-administered (e.g., Beck Depression Inventory, State-Trait Anxiety Inventory) and clinician-rated (e.g., Hamilton Rating Scale for Depression, Brief Psychiatric Rating Scale) instruments as well as various experimental procedures such as simulation studies.

Cost-Effectiveness

The costs associated with the administration of the PAI are relatively minor. As a self-report instrument, it requires little professional time to administer or score. Scoring can be accomplished by hand in 10 min; alternatively, an unlimited-use computer scoring and interpretation program is available at a one-time cost. In addition, as discussed in chapter 9, the PAI has a separate screener, the Personality Assessment Screener (PAS; Morey, 1997) that can be administered in less than 5 min. The PAS provides an estimate of the likelihood that problems of various types will be identified in an administration of the full PAI. The combination of the PAS and the PAI makes it possible to provide a highly efficient sequential assessment that makes optimum use of both clinician and client time.

Ease of Interpretation

Most professionals easily understand the scale names and scaling procedures used in the PAI. PAI scale names such as Depression or Anxiety are straightforward descriptions of the types of questions contained on these scales, and the concurrent validity data support the conclusion that the scales measure what their names imply that they measure. The linear t score is easily interpreted by professionals, and these scores can also be expressed as percentile scores referenced against a variety of different groups (e.g., census-matched community sample, clinical sample, or various demographic or diagnostic groups) for communication to nonprofessionals. Although the multiple dimensions assessed by the PAI often present a complex picture for a given client, the use of profiles in presenting these data often render them comprehensible even to the client.

In particular, the focus on discriminant validity in the construction of the PAI serves to facilitate interpretation. Many of the difficulties in interpreting measures of psychopathology stem from inadequate discriminant validity, resulting in part from questionable psychometric practices such as allowing substantial item overlap among scales measuring supposedly distinct constructs. It can be challenging to interpret a scale that was intended to measure schizophrenia if there are dozens of other factors that can lead to scale elevations. Thus, interpreting the PAI is more straightforward than interpreting other instruments with lower discriminant validity. In addition, the computer interpretive report and accompanying graphical display of detailed profile information also assists in assuring reliable interpretations of PAI results.

Assessment of Protocol Validity

The PAI includes a number of strategies for determining the quality of the information provided by the client. These indicators can help the clinician determine the respondent's ability to read and understand the questions, the respondent's capacity to provide useful information, and information about distorting influences that may result in a portrayal of the client in either an overly positive or overly negative manner. The combination of conceptual and actuarial approaches, each of which have received support in validity studies, provides configural information that can help the clinician unpack the nature of any distorting influences on the test that may be present.

Compatibility With Clinical Theory and Practice

The development of the individual PAI scales was based on a systematic review of the extant theories and supportive empirical research surrounding each construct measured. Key theoretical elements that have received research support were included in scale construction; these elements included aspects from many different theories. Examples include cognitive mechanisms in depression (DEP-C), identity disturbance in borderline personality disorder (BOR-I), or sensation seeking in antisocial personality disorder (ANT-S). Thus, rather than adopting one theoretical approach and applying it to several different disorders, the PAI was constructed to tap specific theoretical elements that have received empirical support as they pertain to specific disorders. This grounding serves to provide a theoretical base from which treatment plans can be formulated. For example, in treating depression with cognitive therapy, it is assumed that alterations in the attribution system of the client will produce effects on other types of depressive symptoms. This theoretically anticipated pattern of change could be mapped by repeated administrations of the DEP scale; initial changes on DEP-C should be observed, with changes on DEP-A and DEP-P occurring later in the treatment process. Similarly, efforts at establishing interpersonal trust that might be leading to personal distress could be mapped by comparing the temporal pattern of changes observed on PAR and ANX.

WEAKNESSES

Limitations of Self-Report Questionnaires

Many of the central weaknesses of the PAI stem from the inherent limitations of self-report questionnaires. For example, self-report techniques have been criticized for decades for their vulnerability to impression management. The development of the PAI, which placed considerable emphasis on item content, led to the inclusion of many items that are unambiguous indicators of psychopathology. Although this strategy clarifies the meaning of elevations on particular scales, it also means that these items are sufficiently transparent to be intentionally manipulated, and numerous simulation studies demonstrate that manipulation incentives will have large effects on scores for the PAI clinical scales. Although the PAI includes many indicators that have established accuracy in these studies as effective in detecting such manipulations, the test is obviously limited in its ability to determine what may lie behind these manipulations. When evidence of such manipulation is present, the interpreter must seek additional data (e.g., the reports of family members or relatives) that may be less susceptible to such efforts.

Limits of Content Coverage

Another set of weaknesses of the PAI involves limits to the coverage of different clinical syndromes on the instrument. For example, little information about the identification of eating disorders, sexual dysfunction, or dissociative disorders can be gleaned from the instrument. Also, as mentioned in chapter 9, the PAI is primarily a clinical instrument, and as such its coverage of normal personality constructs tends to be limited. Finally, the test is aimed at the manifestations of clinical syndromes as they present in adults; use of the test with individuals under the age of 18 is constrained by the lack of normative data and by the orientation of some questions to adult experiences.

Research to Be Done

The development of a psychological test is an ongoing process that does not cease with the publication of the instrument or the manual. In many respects, publication is only the beginning of the development process. Many of the strengths of the PAI stem from research that has been conducted since the test was developed. In psychological assessment terms, the PAI appears to be in its adolescent years; clear signs of its potential have been demonstrated, but it has many more years of growth to come. There is still a need for additional research to cross-validate many of the scales, indexes, and interpretive statements that have emerged in the PAI literature, including many offered in this book. For example, there is a need for continuing refinement of the differential diagnosis of psychotic disorders using PAI data because there have been very few studies of the test in samples of patients who were not well into medication regimens at the time of testing.

 TEST YOURSELF

1. **Which of the following is not a strength of the PAI?**
   (a) cost-effectiveness
   (b) objective referents for comparison
   (c) compatibility with clinical theory and research
   (d) differential diagnosis of dissociative disorders

2. **Which of the following is most accurate?**
   (a) The PAI has little clinical utility for patients with eating disorders.
   (b) The PAI has little utility for diagnosing eating disorders.
   (c) The PAI includes an eating disorders scale.
   (d) The PAI can diagnose binge eating but not anorexia.

3. **An emphasis on discriminant validity helps make the PAI relatively easy to interpret as compared to instruments with lower discriminant validity.** True or False?

4. **The content basis of PAI items makes it relatively simple for respondents to manipulate their presentation of mental health.** True or False?

5. **The PAI manual includes norms for adolescents ages 13 to 17.** True or False?

6. **Is the PAI a measure of normal personality?**

Answers: 1. d; 2. b; 3. True; 4. True; 5. False; 6. Although it has relationships to some normal personality constructs, it is primarily a clinical measure.

Nine

CLINICAL APPLICATIONS OF THE PAI

The PAI has numerous potential applications for assessing clinical and personality constructs within the general population as well as in specific assessment contexts. It is commonly used in the clinical assessment of individuals presenting for mental health services in both inpatient and outpatient settings. However, the test is also used in many other settings. It is a widely used procedure for screening individuals during the hiring process for sensitive occupations, such as for law enforcement officers (Roberts et al., 2000). The PAI is also popular in forensic settings (Edens et al., 2001), including correctional applications, competency evaluations, personal injury claims, and issues of criminal responsibility. Furthermore, the PAI is also used to evaluate personality and clinical issues in neuropsychological and general medical decision making (e.g., Haley, Kurt, & Hom, 1997). A detailed discussion of these different topics lies outside of the realm of this volume. However, many of the fundamental issues presenting to users of the instrument are similar in these different applications. The following sections highlight essential information for six applications of the PAI:

- Clinical Screening
- Diagnosis
- Normal Personality Traits
- Suicide
- Violence
- Treatment Planning

CLINICAL SCREENING

The PAI has been applied effectively in a variety of contexts for the purpose of screening for emotional or psychological problems. Because it can be administered and scored with minimal professional supervision, it can be a very cost-effective strategy for providing a reasonably detailed amount of clinical information in a relatively brief period of time. However, in some instances there may be a need for a more rapid screening of mental health issues. For example, if the evaluator is involved in a setting where large numbers of participants need to be screened but the base rate of mental health problems is likely to be relatively low, a sequential screening strategy can greatly increase the efficiency of assessment. In this strategy, a very brief, sensitive, broad-band screening instrument can be administered, and positive results on this screener can be followed by a more in-depth assessment of clinical issues. In a large-volume, low-base-rate setting (e.g., patients in a general medical practice or an employee assistance program), this strategy can serve to eliminate large numbers of individuals who are not likely to require a thorough mental health assessment.

To provide a tool for such a strategy, Morey (1997) developed the PAS (see Rapid Reference 9.1). The PAS is a subset of 22 PAI items designed to pro-

☰Rapid Reference 9.1

Personality Assessment Screener (PAS)

Author: Leslie C. Morey

Publication date: 1997

Copyright holder: Psychological Assessment Resources

What the test measures: Brief screen for mental health problems

Age range: 18 years and older

Administration time: 3–5 minutes

Qualifications of examiners: A degree from an accredited 4-year college or university in psychology, counseling, or a closely related field *plus* satisfactory completion of coursework in psychological assessment or a closely related area; *or* license or certification from an agency that requires appropriate training and experience in the ethical and competent use of psychological tests

Publisher: Psychological Assessment Resources (PAR)
16204 N. Florida Avenue
Lutz, FL 33549
(800) 331-8378

vide a rapid screening for a broad range of different clinical issues. The 22 PAS items are organized hierarchically into a total score and 10 different elements representing 10 distinct domains of clinical problems. A brief description of these elements is provided in Rapid Reference 9.2. The development of the PAS utilized a framework that sought to identify items that were maximally sensitive to the broad range of clinical issues measured by the parent PAI. The approach placed a strong emphasis on item sensitivity and on breadth of content coverage. The 10 elements of the PAS were selected on the basis of the results of factor analyses of the parent instrument. These 10 elements provided a representation of the major domains of issues covered on the PAI, and they could be reliably identified across different factor analytic methods,

≡ Rapid Reference 9.2

Brief Description of PAS Scores

Total score: Assesses potential for emotional and behavioral problems of clinical significance and need for follow-up evaluation.

Negative Affect (NA) element: Suggests personal distress and the experience of unhappiness and apprehension.

Acting-Out (AO) element: Suggests behavior problems associated with impulsivity, sensation seeking, and drug use.

Health Problems (HP) element: Suggests somatic complaints and health concerns.

Psychotic Features (PF) element: Suggests risk for persecutory thinking and other psychotic phenomena.

Social Withdrawal (SW) element: Suggests social detachment and discomfort in close relationships.

Hostile Control (HC) element: Suggests an interpersonal style characterized by needs for control and inflated self-image.

Suicidal Thinking (ST) element: Suggests thoughts of death or suicide.

Alienation (AN) element: Suggests failures of supportive relationships and a distrust or disinterest in such relationships.

Alcohol Problems (AP) element: Suggests negative consequences related to alcohol use and abuse.

Anger Control (AC) element: Suggests difficulties in the management of anger.

across different samples, and at both item- and scale-level analyses of the PAI. Each element has clear connections to important constructs in mental disorder and considerable significance in contemporary clinical practice.

Unlike the PAI, which uses the normatively referenced t score, scores on the PAS and its elements are presented in the form of a novel transformation known as a p score. The p score is a probability estimate reflecting the likelihood that a given person completing the PAS would obtain a problematic protocol if he or she were to take the parent PAI. A PAS p score of $50p$ is that score on the PAS on which one half of the standardization sample obtaining that score had problematic PAI profiles, whereas the remaining one half of the sample obtained PAI profiles that were within normal limits. As a result, it is important to recognize that a p score of 50 does *not* reflect an average score in the general population; rather, it is the point at which there is a 50-50 chance that the person in question manifests some type of clinical difficulty as defined by the PAI. Thus, any PAS score greater than $50p$ indicates that it is more likely than not that the person is experiencing some type of clinically significant problem. These scores were derived from analyses of a sample of 2,631 individuals, reflecting the combination of the PAI clinical and community standardization samples.

On the PAS, when the respondent's score is elevated, he or she is reporting the experience of various indicators of clinical problems at a frequency or intensity beyond that of most people. Interpretation of PAS scores is based on a determination of whether the reported intensity of features is more consistent with individuals manifesting a PAI profile that is within normal limits or one that indicates problems of clinical significance. In general, a PAS score is considered to be elevated when it is more likely to reflect an elevated PAI profile than it is to reflect one that is within normal limits, which corresponds to a p score of 50% or a total raw score that is slightly above 19. Morey (1997) found that this cutting score correctly identified 84.7% of subjects who had at least one elevated scale on the PAI (i.e., sensitivity) and correctly identified 78.7% of subjects with no such elevations (i.e., specificity). When PAS results suggest that such difficulties are likely, the specific nature of the difficulties can then be ascertained with follow-up assessments.

Total PAS scores of 45 and above correspond to a p score of $99.88p$. In this range, the potential for reported emotional and behavioral problems is extremely high, substantially greater than is typical for clinical patients. Follow-up self-report assessments are nearly certain to identify significant problems; given the degree of symptomatology described, the follow-up assessment should include a careful evaluation of malingering. Scores of 24–44 ($75p$–$99.81p$) suggest that the potential for reported emotional and behavioral problems is substantially greater than what is typical for community adults; follow-up assessments for scores in this range are very likely to identify significant problems. This range can provide useful screening in research settings in which the goal might be to identify individuals with a certain type of problem without subjecting a large group of participants to an extensive evaluation. One can screen out 95% of individuals with nonproblematic profiles with a PAS raw score cutoff of 24 or above, although roughly a third of problematic protocols will also be excluded using this strategy.

PAS scores in the range from 19 to 23 ($50p$–$74p$) suggest potential emotional and behavioral problems of clinical significance, and more extensive follow-up assessment is recommended. Scores of 19 or above suggest that at least one PAI scale will display an elevated score; therefore, this *p* score can often serve as a useful cutting score. However, the efficiency and utility of any cutting score will vary in different applications. In a screening context, it is often advisable to make efforts to maximize sensitivity—maximizing the ability of a screening device to identify potential problems where they exist; this is particularly the case in settings where false negative decisions (concluding that there are no problems when in fact there are problems) represent costly mistakes. If it is desired to ensure that at least 90% of all potentially problematic protocols will receive a more thorough assessment, then the PAS cutting score of 16 or above will provide this degree of confidence while still screening out a majority (61.3%) of individuals with nonproblematic profiles. PAS scores in the range from 13 to 15 ($15p$–$29p$) suggest that follow-up assessments are likely to yield few reported problems. When scores are 12 or below, the likelihood of identifying problems is substantially below what is typical for community adults. Any follow-up assessments for scores in this range should include a careful evaluation of positive impression management.

Along with the total PAS score, the PAS provides scores for 10 elements. The individual PAS elements are each comprised of two to three items tapping different potential problem areas in mental health. Because of their brevity, the elements are designed to serve only as rough guidelines for subsequent assessment. In this capacity, they can be used to select assessment instruments that focus on particular content targets as supplements to the PAI. For example, the PAS Psychotic Features (PF) element involves indicators of persecutory thinking and other psychotic phenomena. If the PF element is elevated, the evaluator may wish to include follow-up assessments that provide a thorough evaluation of the respondent's thought processes and content.

ASSESSMENT OF SUICIDALITY

The assessment of suicide potential is a critical evaluation task in many clinical settings. The beginning point in the assessment of suicidality is the Suicidal Ideation (SUI) scale. As described in chapter 6, the content of the SUI items is directly related to thoughts of suicide and related behaviors, and this scale can alert the clinician to the need for further evaluation and intervention for suicidality. However, SUI elevations tend to be common in clinical settings because thoughts about suicide are nearly ubiquitous among individuals presenting for mental health treatment. Because SUI is a suicidal *ideation* scale rather than a suicide *prediction* scale, it is particularly critical to use supplemental information when making decisions regarding suicide risk.

To assist in the assessment of suicidality, Morey (1996) developed the Suicide Potential index (SPI; see Rapid Reference 9.3) as a supplement to the interpretation of SUI elevations. The SPI consists of 20 features of the PAI profile that tap what are described as key risk factors for completed suicide in the suicidality literature. Such factors include severe psychic anxiety, poor impulse control, hopelessness, and worthlessness. The specific rules for each of the 20 features are described in Morey (1996); the index score is computed by counting the number of positive endorsements on these 20 indicators. Morey (1996) reported that a factor analysis of these indicators yielded four factors that help describe the scales relevant in the computation of this index. Factor 1 appeared to represent a negative affect factor associated with marked anxiety and depression (e.g., DEP, ANX, ARD); Factor 2 involved moodiness, hostility, and interpersonal disruption (BOR, PAR, STR); Factor 3 was

≡ Rapid Reference 9.3

Suicide Potential index

Source: Morey, 1996.

Content: Twenty configural features of the PAI profile involving information from 21 different scales and subscales related to suicide risk factors.

Descriptive statistics: Community sample mean of 3.14 features ($SD = 3.22$); clinical sample mean of 7.74 ($SD = 5.30$).

Correlates: Index correlates highly with BOR, DEP, ANX, and other markers of depression and demoralization, and it correlates strongly with overall profile elevation. Also correlates highly with NIM and can thus be influenced by negative profile distortion.

Interpretation: Scores of 13 or above suggest the presence of numerous risk factors for suicidality; scores of 18 or above represent an extreme configuration of risk factors.

marked by poor impulse control and substance misuse (ANT, ALC, DRG); and Factor 4 involved listlessness, apathy, and withdrawal (low MAN, low WRM).

The SPI has been shown to correlate highly with a variety of other indicators of suicidal ideation (Morey, 1996), including current suicide risk status and self-report measures of suicidal ideation. Along similar lines, Wang et al. (1997) examined the correlations of the PAI clinical and treatment scales with the number of suicide risk assessments completed on inmates in a correctional setting. Although a number of PAI profile elements were significantly correlated with these markers, the largest correlations were found between the number of suicide risk assessments and SUI ($r = .45$), BOR ($r = .32$), DEP ($r = .29$), and the SPI ($r = .28$), and additional analyses found that SPI scores were related to a number of different types of risk categories.

An SPI score of 13 (i.e., 13 indicators scored positive) represents a score that is 1 standard deviation above the mean of the PAI clinical standardization sample and 3 standard deviations above the mean of community norms. Scores in this range suggest that the individual has a number of life circumstances that may exacerbate his or her risk for suicidal behavior, and careful assessment and monitoring are recommended. Morey (1996) notes that the relationship between SPI and SUI appears to be moderated by the NIM score, suggesting that an SPI elevation obtained with NIM scores that fall within normal limits merits particular attention.

ASSESSMENT OF DANGEROUSNESS

Decisions about aggressive potential, anger, and hostility are commonplace in many settings, and the PAI can be a useful part of risk appraisal in this area. The obvious starting point for the assessment of aggression with the PAI is the AGG scale, although studies have also suggested that ANT and BOR may be useful in this regard as well. For example, Wang et al. (1997) investigated the utility of the PAI in assessing aggressive behaviors among individuals in a corrections-based inpatient psychiatric hospital. The authors examined the relationship between the Overt Aggression Scale (OAS; Yudofsky, Silver, Jackson, Endicott, & Williams, 1986) and the PAI scales, subscales, and the Violence Potential index (VPI; see Rapid Reference 9.4). Significant correlations were found between the OAS total score and subscales from BOR, ANT, and AGG. In addition, individuals were grouped according to their VPI scores into either low or moderate-marked categories. Findings revealed that individuals in the low-VPI group had significantly lower OAS total scores compared to individ-

---

≡Rapid Reference 9.4

Violence Potential index

Source: Morey, 1996.

Content: Twenty configural features of the PAI profile involving information from 24 different scales and subscales related to risk factors for violence.

Descriptive statistics: Community sample mean of 1.58 features ($SD = 2.18$); clinical sample mean of 4.40 ($SD = 3.98$).

Correlates: Highest correlates are BOR, ANT, AGG-P, and other markers of antisocial behavior and attitudes. Correlates strongly with overall profile elevation and also correlates with NIM; the index can thus be influenced by negative profile distortion.

Interpretation: Scores of 9 or above suggest the presence of numerous risk factors for dangerousness; scores of 17 or above represent an extreme configuration of risk factors.

uals in the moderate-marked group. In a follow-up investigation, Wang and Diamond (1999) found that the three subscales of ANT could help in predicting institutional aggression within the first 2 months of hospitalization among mentally ill offenders. Profiles of individuals with a history of violence, presented in Morey (1991), have other distinguishing features as well. For example, such individuals tend to have scores on SUI that are lower than scores on AGG; this configuration is unusual in most clinical settings and suggests that anger is more likely to be directed outward than inward. A similar downward slope is seen in the relationship between DOM and WRM; these individuals seek to control relationships through hostile means. Scores on MAN-G tend to be above the mean—an unusual finding in clinical groups. Patterns of failure and discomfort in social relationships (BOR-N, SCZ-S) and a history of victimization (ARD-T) are also highlights of these configurations.

To supplement the use of individual scales in the difficult process of assessing dangerousness, Morey (1996) developed the VPI. This index consists of 20 PAI features that represent a variety of risk factors for violence that have been found to be useful for the prediction of dangerousness. Examples of such risk factors include explosive expression of anger, sensation seeking, substance abuse, and impulsivity. The specific rules for each of the 20 features are described in Morey (1996); like the SPI, the VPI is computed by counting the number of positive endorsements on these 20 indicators. Morey (1996) found the mean number of positive index items in patients presenting with issues that raise concerns of dangerousness are all elevated in comparison to community subjects as well as clinical subjects as a whole. The VPI has been shown to correlate with indicators of hostility and poor judgment on the MMPI, with Hare's (1985) self-report measure of psychopathic features, and with a diagnosis of antisocial personality disorder arrived at through structured interview (Morey, 1996; Edens, Hart, Johnson, Johnson, & Olver, 2000). Wang et al. (1997) grouped inmates according to their VPI scores into either low or moderate-marked categories, and found that individuals in the low-VPI group had significantly lower OAS total scores compared to individuals in the moderate-marked group.

A VPI score of 9 (i.e., nine indicators scored positive) represents a score that is 1 standard deviation above the mean of the PAI clinical standardization sample, and a score of 17 falls 2 standard deviations above the clinical mean. Scores in these ranges would suggest moderate and marked risk of violent behavior, respectively. Such scores, particularly in combination with elevated scores on AGG, should alert the clinician to both historical and personality factors related to dangerousness, and further evaluation of the potential for assault is warranted.

ASSESSING CLINICAL SYNDROMES

As described in chapter 5, there are a variety of ways to combine information about the PAI for use in making decisions, including deriving diagnostic hypotheses. The following sections provide a brief overview of scales relevant to the identification of a variety of diagnostic categories. The use of specific procedures to combine this scale information is presented in more detail in Morey (1996).

Depression and Related Disorders

The most specific measure of depressive symptoms on the PAI is the DEP scale; a diagnosis of depression in the absence of some elevation on DEP is unlikely unless defensiveness is distorting the profile. Other PAI scales are also useful in assessing associated symptoms and distinguishing between different depressive variants. When depression represents the affective component of an adjustment reaction, the STR scale often is the prominent scale in the profile, often accompanied by elevations on DEP, ANX, or ARD. In such profiles, MAN-G is often close to 50t, suggesting that self-esteem has remained intact in the face of environmental setbacks. In more chronic types of depression (such as dysthymic disorder), DEP plays a more prominent role than does STR in the profile. SUI and BOR elevations also tend to present in the same range as the DEP scale. However, such patients may not meet criteria for a major depressive episode, often lacking the physiological symptoms of depression that would be reflected by the DEP-P subscale. The patient in a major depressive episode typically has elevations on all three DEP subscales, and SUI is typically elevated as well. In these patients there also tends to be evidence of social withdrawal and apathy (SCZ-S) as well as cognitive inefficiency (SCZ-T), often leading the SCZ full scale to be an important secondary elevation. Finally, low scores (i.e., below 40t) on MAN-G and MAN-A are common among patients in a severe depressive episode.

Anxiety Disorders

Although anxiety disorders represent a major class of mental disorders, nearly all clinical disorders share anxiety as a feature. Among the individual PAI scales, ANX and ARD provide particularly critical information about these conditions. ANX is generally a nonspecific, global measure of anxiety that could be prominent in a number of different diagnostic groups. In contrast, ARD presents specific behavioral information that is more closely tied to specific anxiety conditions. Additional scales can also be helpful, depending on the specific anxiety disorder in question. For phobias, ARD-P inquires directly about phobic avoidance behaviors, and the associated distress associated with this condition is likely to be seen on ANX-A or ANX-C. Where the disorder involves a social phobia, low scores on WRM and high scores on SCZ-S may also be observed. If the anxiety disorder involves panic attacks, marked elevations on ANX-P are typically found because this scale inquires directly about a number of physiological symptoms often experienced during these attacks. Some panic patients interpret the attacks as evidence of a serious, undiagnosed illness, such as a heart condition or a seizure disorder. These beliefs often will lead to elevations on SOM-H. Because such individuals avoid novelty and unpredictability in their lives, scores on ANT-S that are considerably below average are typical. PAI profiles for patients with obsessive-compulsive disorder most characteristically display ARD-O elevations, but because the symptoms are a source of marked distress, the ANX scale is typically elevated as well. Among the ANX subscales, ANX-C is the most characteristic of the disorder because it captures the rumination and uneasiness of the obsessional individual. SOM and DEP elevations may also be observed in these patients.

The diagnosis of posttraumatic stress disorder (PTSD) is often associated with marked elevations on ARD-T, which makes direct inquiries about the existence of traumatic stressors. Although many clinical groups demonstrate ARD-T scores above 70t, PTSD subjects will typically score at least 80t on this scale. However, the diagnosis of PTSD should not be based solely upon an ARD-T elevation, because the syndrome includes other characteristic symptomatology that can be assessed with the PAI. All three DEP subscales may display elevations as a function of painful guilt feelings (DEP-C), recurrent distressing dreams leading to sleep disturbance (DEP-P), and diminished interest in significant activities (DEP-A). Other symptoms of PTSD include physiological anxiety reactivity, reflected on ANX-P; feelings of detachment or estrangement from others, manifested on SCZ-S and low WRM; hypervigilance, evidenced in PAR-H elevations; and irritability, which can be gauged using MAN-I. Difficulty in concentration and focus often leads to prominent SCZ-T elevations. Finally, outbursts of anger are also common, reflected in AGG elevations (with AGG-A and AGG-P typically elevated to a greater extent than AGG-V).

Somatoform Disorders

Somatoform disorders involve the presence of physical symptoms that suggest some type of medical problem not fully explained by any diagnosable medical condition. It should be noted that no self-report test is effective at distinguishing between functional and organic foundations of somatic complaints; rather, instruments such as the PAI are best at describing the involvement of somatic complaints in the clinical presentation. Such somatic problems are reflected primarily on SOM, and secondary elevations on ANX-P and DEP-P are common as indications of a physiological pattern of stress reactivity. Other prominent profile features tend to vary with the specific somatic disorder. Individuals with the vague and diverse somatic symptoms of somatization disorder typically present with prominent SOM-S elevations as well as considerable subjective distress evident on DEP-A and ANX-A. Because this pattern is often chronic, conflict with family or friends can develop, leading to elevations on BOR-N and NON. The characteristic sensory and motor disturbances in conversion disorder result in SOM-C elevations. The stereotyped indifference of conversion patients may be manifested in a DEP-A score considerably below the level of health concerns indicated by SOM-H. A certain degree of dependency may also be apparent in low scores on DOM and AGG with moderate to high scores on WRM.

Psychotic Disorders

A variety of different disorders can present with symptoms of psychosis such as delusions, hallucinations, gross distortions in reality testing, or disorganized behavior. During an active phase of schizophrenia, elevations on all three SCZ subscales may be found. In addition, specific elevations on other scales can arise, depending on the content of unusual beliefs, such as paranoid delusions (evident on PAR-P) or somatic delusions (often resulting in SOM-C elevations). During less acute phases of the disorder, the profile will probably be considerably less elevated, and of the three SCZ subscales, SCZ-P is most likely to return to normal limits during such phases. However, SCZ-T and particularly SCZ-S may remain elevated during this residual phase, and a SCZ-S elevation in the absence of elevations on DEP or ANX is particularly consistent with a schizoidal withdrawal. The more circumscribed symptoms of delusional disorder may also lead to some elevation on SCZ-P, typically accompanied by elevations on other scales that would give some indication of the nature of the preoccupation; for example, PAR-P for persecutory beliefs, MAN-G for delusional grandiosity, or SOM-C or SOM-H for somatic delusions. In the diagnosis, SCZ-T and SCZ-S can be within normal limits because this disorder does not involve affective responsiveness or cognitive function.

The diagnostic features of mania are represented on the MAN scale, including pressured speech, flight of ideas, and overinvolvement in activities (MAN-A), grandiosity and expansiveness (MAN-G), and mood instability with abrupt irritability (MAN-I). Secondary elevations on BOR-S and ANT-S are associated with the lack of inhibition in these patients, and PAR-P can capture their experiences of being obstructed (although without the resentment that would be found on PAR-R). On the interpersonal scales, DOM and WRM tend to be above average, and these individuals' lack of insight leads RXR to be higher than what is typically found in clinical patients (50*t* or even higher). Low DEP-C scores are also observed as an indicator of unwarranted optimism, although on occasion there may be mild elevations on DEP that reflect the patient's past symptoms rather than his or her current mood.

Personality Disorders

Although the traits subsumed under the broad category of personality disorder tend to be diverse, the extensive comorbidity among these disorders demonstrates that they have much in common. Among the common characteristics is an overall immaturity in the personality that leads to difficulties in establishing empathic relationships with others. Perhaps the closest operationalization of this general dimension of personality immaturity on the PAI is the BOR full scale; the greater the elevation on BOR, the more likely it is that personality problems are playing a role in the person's presenting complaints. Although the BOR scale tends to be elevated in most personality disorders, it invariably is a prominent part of the profile in borderline personality disorder. Marked elevations on DEP (more DEP-C and DEP-A than DEP-P) and SUI are also common in patients with this disorder. Other features of these patients that lead to characteristic scale elevations include a past history of reported trauma (ARD-T), marked anxiety (ANX), impulsive substance abuse (ALC and DRG); very low self-esteem (low MAN-G), and a broadly negative evaluative set that can elevate scores on NIM. Finally, desperation and unrealistic expectations for rapid improvement can often lead to extremely low scores on RXR.

For antisocial personality disorder, the most direct assessment of a pattern of antisocial behaviors is provided by the ANT-A subscale, although AGG-P also captures the aggressiveness and history of physical confrontation that are represented in the diagnostic criteria. The concept of psychopathy includes additional features such as lack of empathy and recklessness that are captured by ANT-E and ANT-S, respectively. Substance misuse, reflected in DRG elevation, is also common among these individuals. A downward slope of the interpersonal scales (with DOM considerably higher than WRM), representing a hostile-control interpersonal style, is also typical. Finally, often telling is the absence of neurotic symptoms, even in situations in which such symptoms might be anticipated; thus, the profile for antisocial personality disorder invariably is more elevated on the right-hand side of the clinical scales (BOR, ANT, ALC, DRG) than on the left-hand side (SOM, ANX, ARD, DEP).

Although the remaining personality disorders do not have specific scales on the PAI, a variety of indications are available. The inflated but often fragile self-esteem of the individual with narcissistic personality disorder can be reflected in elevations on MAN-G, MAN-I, and ANT-E; DOM scores also tend to be above average, reflecting the discomfort that narcissists feel surrounding positions of interpersonal inferiority. In histrionic personality disorder, BOR-A and ANT-E elevations capture the superficial emotions and egocentricity of this pattern; other features include a need for interpersonal interaction (high WRM) and inhibition of aggression in such interactions (low AGG-V). Paranoid personality disorder can be identified by elevations on PAR-H and PAR-R; typically PAR-P will be considerably below scores on those subscales. Additional elevations on SCZ-S and AGG-A are common, and WRM scores are generally below average.

Persons with schizoid personality disorder display social detachment and affective constriction directly captured by SCZ-S, and WRM is likely to be low. Relatively low scores on BOR-A, ANX, and DEP—consistent with affective constriction—can help to distinguish the disorder from many other personality disorders characterized by prominent social isolation. Individuals with schizotypal personality disorder display PAI scores that are similar to those for the residual phase of schizophrenia—elevations on SCZ-S, SCZ-T, and PAR-P but a SCZ-P score that (although it is above average) falls within normal limits. The social awkwardness and anxiety of the individual with this disorder would be lead to suppressed scores on WRM and secondary elevations on ANX and ARD-P (driven by the social anxiety items). Similarly, avoidant personality disorder will tend to lead to elevations on ARD-P and below-average scores on WRM. However, this group also tends to display low DOM and low scores on ANT-S because of their desire to avoid novelty or the scrutiny of others. For obsessive-compulsive personality disorder, ARD-O directly captures these personality elements, whereas affective constriction may prevent marked distress of the type that typically appears on ANX and DEP aside from a moderate elevation on ANX-C. BOR-A may also be low as a further indicator of this emotional constriction. Dependent personality disorder is best typified by very low scores on DOM, and WRM scores will invariably be higher than DOM scores because interpersonal relationships are of such importance. Low scores on MAN-G and AGG-V are also typical, reflecting poor self-esteem and lack of assertiveness. Finally, the passive-aggressive personality, although it is relegated to an appendix in the diagnostic system, does have a characteristic PAI pattern of elevated PAR-R, signifying hostility and resentment, combined with low scores on DOM, indicative of the passivity element of the disorder. Scores on WRM also tend to be below average because interpersonal relationships are typically unsuccessful. An elevation on AGG-P would be inconsistent with this disorder because it suggests that anger and resentment are likely to be expressed in a direct and overt manner.

Substance Abuse Disorders

The obvious beginning points on the PAI for considering a substance abuse diagnosis are the ALC and DRG scales. Generally, the distinction between substance abuse and substance dependence is accomplished through the elevations of these scales, with dependent individuals often presenting with substance abuse scales scores that exceed 80–85*t*. A few interpretive caveats about assessment in this population merit mention. First, because both ALC and DRG items directly address substance use, the scales are susceptible to denial, and chapter 5 describes the issue of assessing substance abuse denial in greater detail. If these indicators suggest that there may be marked denial of substance abuse, supplementing the PAI with the use of information from collateral informants (such as a spouse or family member) is recommended. Also, as described in chapter 6, some of the information gathered on these scales is historical, meaning that the scales can be elevated in people who have had a substance abuse problem in the past but are not currently drinking or using drugs. Because substance abuse diagnoses are based heavily on historical life event information rather than present mental status, it is necessary to establish that the difficulties have occurred within the past 12 months in order to assign a diagnosis. Elevations on scales such as DEP and STR can be a good sign that substance use is having current consequences for the client; ANT elevations can also suggest illicit activities associated with obtaining and using illegal drugs. Finally, NIM elevations have been reported in inpatient samples of substance abusers (e.g., Alterman et al., 1995; Boyle & Lennon, 1994), which may result from having the test completed during detoxification; this possibility should be considered when interpreting profiles with NIM elevations in substance abuse settings.

ASSESSMENT OF SELF-CONCEPT

The view that people have of themselves can play a critical role in determining their behavior. On the PAI, three clinical subscales are central in assessing three important facets of the self-concept. One facet, *self-esteem,* reflects the evaluative component of the self-perception—the feeling that one has worth and merits respect from the self and from others. The most direct measure of this self-facet on the PAI is the MAN-G subscale. A second facet, *self-efficacy,* reflects a sense of personal competence and perceived control (Bandura, 1977). The DEP-C scale provides information relevant to the person's perceived effectiveness; low scorers display a sense of competence, whereas high scorers feel ineffective and helpless in controlling the environment. The third facet involves the *stability* of the self-concept, which may be either fixed and enduring or (alternatively) unstable and reactive to environmental events. For example, two people who each have high self-esteem may differ substantially in the secureness of this esteem; one person may be capable of maintaining high self-esteem in the face of considerable evidence to the contrary, whereas the other's self-esteem may be vulnerable to even the slightest blow to the ego. BOR-I provides a measure of the stability of the self, with high scorers having the more variable and reactive self-concepts.

The different configurations of these three scales have different implications for the self-concept. MAN-G and DEP-C tend to be inversely related; thus, the typical configuration of these two scales is MAN-G low and DEP-C high (indicating feelings of helplessness and worthlessness) or MAN-G high and DEP-C low (indicating inflated self-esteem and overvalued competencies). When both scales are elevated, the person may feel ineffective in dealing with the world but is likely to ultimately project the responsibility for this ineffectiveness onto the external world. When both scales are low, the person may appear competent to others but may have inner self-doubts. Adding the BOR-I scale to this configuration provides information about the likely stability of this pattern. Thus, for example, if all three scales are elevated, the self-perception may vary from periods of very poor self-esteem and severe self-doubt to times of exaggerated confidence and overvalued accomplishments. On the other hand, if MAN-G and BOR-I are both low and DEP-C is high, this may suggest a fixed and harshly critical self-image. Such people are likely to dwell on past failures and lost opportunities. This self-view is relatively impervious to environmental events; such people are likely to attribute blame for any setbacks internally, and any successes are dismissed either as good fortune or as the result of actions by others more competent than the respondents themselves.

NORMAL PERSONALITY TRAITS

The PAI was designed to be used with clinical populations, and as such many of the scales it includes would be considered to provide an assessment of psychopathological rather than normative personality constructs under this criterion (Morey & Glutting, 1994). For example, most of the PAI scales and subscales demonstrate a pronounced positive skew in a community sample, and the average scores on many of the scales differ dramatically between clinical and community samples. However, there do seem to be some PAI scales that tap constructs falling within the normal range of personality according to criteria such as skewness and mean differences. For example, the interpersonal scales DOM and WRM demonstrate distributions that are similar in both community and clinical samples and are nearly normal. Furthermore, some of the clinical scales demonstrate rather small distributional differences across populations; for example, MAN (particularly MAN-G) and PAR (for both PAR-R and PAR-H) have fairly similar skewness values in the two populations. These results suggest that there are important elements of normal personality measured by these two constructs—perhaps self-esteem and interpersonal wariness, respectively. Thus, constellations of scores on these scales can be used to describe personality differences that are clearly meaningful within the normal range, without necessarily having implications of maladjustment or psychopathology.

The PAI has also been shown to demonstrate sizable correlations with measures of normal personality traits. For example, one of the most widely used and empirically tested schemes for representing normal personality traits has been the five-factor model (FFM) of personality. Historically based in studies of natural language trait terms and factor analyses of personality questionnaires, the FFM proposes that personality consists of five broad dimensions: Neuroticism (N), Extraversion (E), Openness to Experience (O), Agreeableness (A), and Conscientiousness (C). One widely used measure of this personality model, the NEO Personality Inventory–Revised (NEO-PI-R; Costa & McCrae, 1992b), has consistently demonstrated significant correlations with the PAI across different studies (Costa & McCrae, 1992a; Morey, 1991). *Neuroticism,* or the tendency to experience psychological distress, displays sizable positive correlations with ANX (particularly ANX-A), DEP (primarily DEP-A and DEP-C), BOR (mainly BOR-A and BOR-I), and ARD (including ARD-P and ARD-T), and it has a large inverse relationship with RXR. *Extraversion*—including sociability as well as the tendency to experience positive emotions—is associated with high scores on both DOM and WRM, elevations on MAN-G and ANT-S, and low scores on DEP, SCZ-S, and ARD-P. *Openness to Experience,* indicative of imaginativeness and intellectual curiosity, has relatively few correlates on the PAI; it is most associated with higher scores on MAN and ANT-S and lower scores on RXR. *Agreeableness,* indicating a trusting and sympathetic nature, is associated with high scores on WRM and low scores on PAR and AGG. Finally, *Conscientiousness* involves being scrupulous and well-organized; it is most associated with higher scores on ARD-O and RXR.

TREATMENT PLANNING

Another important clinical use of PAI is the evaluation of treatment amenability and progress (Morey, 1999; Morey & Henry, 1994). The PAI contains a number of useful features for refining treatment-related decision making; it provides important information relevant for determining prognosis, identifying treatment targets and obstacles, and considering different intervention strategies. The following sections provide some guidelines for the prediction of treatment process, identification of targets for treatment, differential treatment selection, and the use of the PAI in evaluating treatment outcome.

Predicting Treatment Process

Two primary measures relevant to treatment planning are the RXR scale and the Treatment Process index (TPI). The RXR scale, which is described in detail in chapter 6, includes items designed to assess treatment motivation applicable across different therapeutic modalities. The scaling of RXR is such that low scores reflect high motivation for treatment, whereas elevations indicate little motivation for treatment. Because PAI *t* scores are based on a community sample—a sample in which motivation for psychological treatment is generally low—a seemingly average *t* score of 50*t* indicates a remarkable lack of treatment motivation in an individual with significant emotional difficulties. Average scores on RXR among individuals presenting for treatment typically range between 30*t* and 40*t* in various studies (Alterman et al., 1995; Boyle & Lennon, 1994; Cherepon & Prinzehorn, 1994).

Although motivation for treatment is an important factor in determining whether a person will be willing to commit to treatment, it is certainly not sufficient by itself to ensure that the treatment will be successful. Although different types of patients will respond differently to different forms of treatments, there are a number of patient features that suggest a difficult treatment process, regardless of the type of treatment offered. To try to represent these features on the PAI, Morey (1996) devised the TPI (see Rapid Reference 9.5), a cumulative index of 12 features from the PAI profile that correspond to treatment amenability factors described in the psychotherapy literature. These items provide an indication of the level of disruptions that may be involved in the treatment process; examples of items include hostility, poor motivation, low psychological-mindedness, ego-syntonic defensive style, and limited social supports. The specific rules for each of the 12 features are described in Morey (1996); the total TPI score is computed by counting the number of positive endorsements on these 12 indicators. Among the PAI scales, the TPI score correlates most highly with BOR, ANT, and PAR; ARD (particularly ARD-T), AGG, STR, and SCZ also display sizable correlations. Thus, an approximation of this index can be achieved by examining elevations on these scales. With respect to external indicators, the TPI has been found to correlate highly with various indicators of character pathology and of an alienated, hostile detachment and withdrawal from others (Morey, 1996). The average patient in the clinical standardization sample presented with four of these features; thus, scores below 4 indicate the presence of numerous personal assets that may assist the treatment process. Scores between 7 and 10 lie more than 1 standard deviation above the mean of clinical patients and sug-

⩶Rapid Reference 9.5

Treatment Process index

Source: Morey, 1996.

Content: Twelve configural features of the PAI profile involving information from 22 different scales and subscales related to poor treatment prognosis.

Descriptive statistics: Community sample mean of 1.12 features (SD = 1.90); clinical sample mean of 3.86 (SD = 3.22).

Correlates: Highest correlates are BOR, ANT, PAR, and other markers of externalizing attitudes and behaviors. Correlates with overall profile elevation and also correlates with NIM; the index can thus be influenced by negative profile distortion.

Interpretation: Scores of 7 or above suggest a difficult treatment process; scores of 11–12 or above represent very difficult treatment and high risk of noncompliance.

gest there may be many and varied obstacles to a smooth treatment process; scores of 11 or 12 are more than 2 standard deviations above average for patients and suggest a very difficult and challenging treatment process. When scores fall in the higher ranges on the TPI, problems will tend to be complex and long-standing, and considerable effort will need to be devoted to establishing the therapeutic alliance needed to maintain the person in treatment.

Specifying Therapeutic Targets

The PAI can also be a useful source of data for isolating specific targets for therapeutic work. These targets can cut across different diagnostic categories and may provide some order to the priorities for intervention.

Poor Impulse Control

Failures of impulse control can reflect an important priority for intervention. Elevations on ALC, DRG, MAN, BOR (particularly BOR-A and BOR-S), ANT (particularly ANT-S), and AGG are all associated with poor impulse control; when many of these indicators are elevated, the problem is greater and the prognosis is poorer. In such instances, treatment will need to be carefully structured to address the risks posed by the impulsiveness. Treatment may involve medical management (as in the case of a manic episode) or may require direct limit-setting. Other structured techniques that may be necessary include therapeutic contracts (conditions under which therapy will or will not proceed), or anger management training.

Anger Inhibition

Some patients experience problems with overinhibition of impulses, such as an inability to appropriately express angry feelings, resulting in maladaptive strategies to contain anger. Such problems may be due to a fear of rejection, fear of loss of control, the unacceptability of angry feelings, and so forth. Repressed anger may express itself as timidity and lack of assertiveness (very low AGG, particularly AGG-V), as compulsive rigidity (elevated ARD-O and perhaps RXR), or as physical symptoms (SOM elevations). Patients with a history of abuse (observed on ARD-T) may also have difficulty expressing anger directly or in a moderated way, even though there may be deep underlying anger. In these cases, learning to acknowledge anger and encouraging a more direct and appropriate expression of anger may be useful as a first step.

Dependency

Excessive dependency may lead to a rapid initial commitment to treatment but a reluctance to carry the work of treatment into everyday life. A basic dependency pattern is evident from the combination of the interpersonal scales; above-average emphasis on attachment relationships (high WRM) combined with marked submissiveness (low DOM) suggests dependency issues. When BOR is elevated (BOR-I in particular), the yearning for acceptance can be pathological; such patients are at particular risk for exploitation—for example, they may be unable to leave abusive relationships, or will sacrifice their own needs to meet those of others.

Mistrust

Problems related to the ability to trust others can present a considerable obstacle in the early stages of treatment. The PAR scale is the most obvious indicator of such distrust, but there are many other indicators that can be related to a self-protective distancing in relationships, often based on anticipated rejection or exploitation by others. Elevations on ARD (particularly ARD-T but also ARD-P), SCZ-S, BOR (particularly BOR-N), ANT, AGG-A, or NON all raise the possibility that establishing trust should be considered a treatment goal as well as a treatment obstacle.

Constriction and Rigidity

A rigid, perfectionistic, or constricted style may create problems in living for clients as well as obstacles for treatment. Such a style can lead to difficulties adapting to unexpected events and change in routine, including those precipitated by therapeutic progress. Fears of loss of control may precipitate resistance or termination of treatment at critical therapeutic junctures. PAI indicators of these targets include an elevation on ARD-O and DOM, accompanied by an RXR score that is above average for patients in treatment (i.e., above 40t).

Lack of Self-Confidence and Low Self-Esteem

When low self-esteem presents in the absence of a complex clinical picture, it presents a target that is amenable to a variety of therapeutic interventions. Indicators include elevations on DEP-C and ARD-P, with suppression on scales such as AGG, DOM, or MAN-G. The isolation of this feature as a therapeutic target is most effective when there is a relative lack of elevations on other scales; otherwise the self-esteem issues tend to be part of a broader clinical constellation.

Cognitive Distortions

Addressing cognitive distortions that involve extremely negative evaluations of self, others, and situations is a focus of the cognitive treatment of many disorders. The PAI contains a number of indicators that suggest that such distortions represent a prominent part of the clinical picture. Within the realm of negative affect, ANX-C and DEP-C both provide a picture of cognitive involvement in these affects. ANX-C elevations indicate that such patients are prone to experience considerable tension and worry over events they cannot control but feel that they should be able to control; the DEP-C scale (when elevated) suggests unrealistic feelings of worthlessness, failure, self-blame, and hopelessness. A high NIM score indicates that an individual tends to think in extreme and categorical terms. Substantial NIM elevations in the absence of malingering (e.g., accompanied by low scores on the Rogers discriminant function) indicate that such patients are reporting a very negatively colored evaluation of themselves and their lives. Finally, scales such as PAR, BOR-N, or NON can indicate a fixed belief system involving distorted views and expectations of others. Such people may distort their experience in order to attribute their misfortunes to the actions (or inaction) of others.

Differential Treatment Planning

In recent years there has been increasing emphasis on the importance of matching the proper types of clients to the proper types of treatments, in an effort both to optimize outcome and to maximize use of mental health treatment resources. Although there is limited empirical evidence to suggest that a specific treatment is unequivocally indicated for a particular type of client, there are a number of areas in which treatment guidelines are beginning to emerge, and the PAI can provide information relevant to these decisions. The following sections describe information addressing decisions about treatment intensity, format, and approach.

Treatment Intensity

Treatment can take place in a variety of settings, ranging from less intensive (e.g., self-help groups) to more intensive (e.g., hospital-based inpatient treatment). A variety of factors can lead to the necessity for more intensive treatment settings. Marked *functional impairment* may render the person unable to meet major social role responsibilities. Such impairment is often found in individuals with noteworthy elevations on MAN, PAR (particularly PAR-P), and SCZ (particularly SCZ-P). However, even extreme scores on DEP or ANX—particularly in the absence of significant negative profile distortion—may suggest compromised functional capacity requiring intensive treatment. The patient's *potential for self-harm* is another factor that can necessitate intensive treatments such as hospitalization. Elevations on the SUI scale and the Suicide Potential index obviously raise concerns about suicidality. However, other self-damaging behaviors may arise out of impulsivity and poor judgment; elevations on MAN, BOR-S, and ANT-S can all suggest an increased risk for reckless and self-destructive behavior. Similarly, dangerousness to others merits close monitoring, and the AGG scale (particularly AGG-P), the ANT scale, and the Violence Potential index can each provide relevant information in this regard. Finally, *substance dependency* can involve high-intensity treatments if such patients require detoxification, if they pose a danger to themselves or others, or if they are unable to control their use in less intensive treatments. Marked elevations on ALC or DRG—particularly when they are accompanied by other indicators of severe impairment—raise the likelihood that intensive interventions will be required.

Another aspect of treatment intensity involves the *length of treatment* required to address certain problems. The duration of mental health treatments is often influenced by many factors, such as availability of treatment resources, type of treatment approach, and patient compliance issues. However, mental health utilization data makes it clear that some types of problems are likely to require longer periods of treatments. One global guide to such issues is the Treatment Process index, which will be elevated in individuals with refractory problems that will require treatments of greater intensity. Persons presenting with elevations on this index are unlikely to receive lasting benefit from brief interventions, which may effectively address a current crisis but would probably not alter what is likely to be an enduring pattern of recurrent crises.

Treatment Format

The format of treatment often involves individual contacts with a client, but it can also involve group and family-marital interventions provided in combination with or as an alternative to individual treatment. Although most difficulties represented by the PAI can benefit from individual treatment, some profile patterns suggest that these other formats may be particularly beneficial. A number of PAI scales are global indicators of social ineffectiveness of the type that might be amenable to *group intervention,* including low scores on WRM and high scores on SCZ-S and ARD-P. Other indicators of problems that may be helped with group-based treatments include marked distrust evident on PAR, high control needs indicated by high DOM, or the failures in empathy evidenced by ANT-E elevations. Group therapy may be helpful in diffusing the problems with resistance or hostility toward the therapist that are often associated with elevations on these latter scales. *Family and marital therapy* are particularly effective in ameliorating issues that lie primarily within a family system. On the PAI, marital and family issues are particularly evident on NON; scores on NON that are 10*t* points above scores on any of the clinical scales are an indication that the respondent views the primary concerns as existing within the marriage or the family. In considering these treatments, the clinician should pay particular attention to elevations on PAR and on BOR, which may indicate a generalized pattern of interpersonal bitterness of which the reported family difficulties are merely an instance.

Differential Treatment Approach

Although the research literature provides limited evidence to support the selection of specific therapies for specific problems, numerous such guidelines have been offered in theoretical writings. Morey (1996) provides a description of the operationalization of selective patient variables for various strategies. The *exploratory* approach focuses upon insight, understanding, and resolution of internal conflict, taking a developmental approach in understanding the individual's present difficulties. This approach is particularly suited for individuals with difficulties that are developmental in nature; hence, the issue of conflicts in past relationships (suggested by ARD-T, BOR-N, and BOR-I) is especially salient. However, use of this approach requires the individual to be reasonably psychologically minded (lower RXR), have the capacity for trust (lower AGG and PAR), and be able to handle the impulses resulting from a confrontation of their defenses (lower BOR-S). Individuals with more focused interpersonal problems or social deficits (e.g., high SCZ-S, low WRM)—particularly those pertaining to present-day relationships—might be better treated with an *interpersonal* approach. The *cognitive* approach is particularly suited to individuals with negative distortions of the self (high DEP-C or ANX-C, high NIM), and perhaps less useful for individuals with impulsive acting-out behaviors (lower ANT-A, AGG-P, and BOR-S). *Supportive* treatments are particularly important when there is evidence that the patient is extremely overwhelmed (extreme ANX and DEP, extremely low RXR), has highly disorganized thought processes (high SCZ-T), or is vulnerable due to traumatic stress reactions (extreme ARD-T, STR, and ANX). *Behavioral* or environmental manipulation procedures may be optimal for difficulties involving circumscribed phobias (ARD-P), somatization (SOM-S or SOM-H), assertiveness (low DOM), lack of impulse control (BOR-S, ANT-A), or need for relaxation training (ANX-P). As noted earlier, conjoint *family or marital therapy* should be considered in cases of extreme functional impairment or when the patient reports a marked lack of support by others, as suggested by elevated scores on NON.

Various PAI elevations can also suggest the need to consider *somatic* treatments. Antidepressant treatment may be indicated in the presence of marked vegetative signs (DEP-P), motor retardation (suppressed MAN-A), loss of control over thinking (SCZ-T), and obsessive rumination (ARD-O, ANX-C). With respect to antianxiety medications, the ANX and ARD scales are particularly informative, and marked elevations on STR may also reflect a degree of turmoil that may benefit from a combination of medical and psychosocial treatment. The need to consider antipsychotic medications is suggested by marked elevations on PAR (particularly PAR-P), SCZ (particularly SCZ-P but also SCZ-T), and possibly extreme elevations on BOR. Finally, marked elevations on MAN are unusual even in clinical samples and raise the possibility that medication for a manic episode should be considered.

Evaluating Treatment Outcome

The PAI has a number of characteristics that make it well suited for the evaluation of treatment efficacy. The breadth of content coverage and the scale and subscale structure make it particularly useful for charting patient changes. For example, in the treatment of depression, the relative changes in the affective, cognitive, and physiological components can be measured separately with a readministration of the test in order to better clarify the specific effects of treatment. Also, a readministration of the instrument during treatment can help the clinician to judge patient progress and gauge the need for updating the treatment plan. For example, for clients presenting with pretreatment RXR scores suggestive of treatment rejection, it would be anticipated that initial efforts in treatment might need to be directed at potential resistance. Alternatively, clients receiving an interpersonally based treatment might be expected to show changes on the interpersonal scales as a prerequisite to addressing distress that would be evident from the clinical scales. Similarly, clients receiving cognitive therapy for depression might be expected to show the most rapid improvements on the DEP-C subscale, with improvements in somatic and affective aspects of the syndrome contingent on this change. If anticipated changes are not observed, revisions in treatment intensity or treatment approach might be needed.

In general, a successful intervention should have the effect of moving the client's PAI scores in the direction of the norm for a community sample (i.e., $50t$). For most scales, this improvement would be reflected by reductions in scores, although there are exceptions to this rule. For example, MAN-G is often abnormally low in clinical samples, revealing very poor self-esteem; thus, increases on MAN-G would be desirable if the score fell substantially below $50t$. Increases on RXR would also be expected over the course of a successful treatment because many of the motivating sources for treatment (such as distress or interpersonal difficulties) would be gradually ameliorated.

PAI scores have been found to be stable over 1-month periods in nontreatment samples (Morey, 1991); the reliability of the instrument would be expected to be even higher over shorter intervals. Determining the significance of changes in PAI scores can be accomplished using the standard error of measurement (SEM) estimates calculated from this reliability information. The SEM provides an index of variability in measurement that would be expected strictly from score unreliability. Changes in scores that are less than 1 SEM cannot be interpreted as reflecting true change with any confidence. For each of the PAI full scales, the SEM is 3–4 t-score points, meaning that the 95% confidence interval for these scale scores is typically 5–7 points. As a result, changes in t scores that are 2 SEMs (i.e., 6–8t-score points) in magnitude can serve as a conservative threshold for detecting statistically reliable change in a given client.

The PAI can profitably be used to detect changes that might occur from week to week during treatment. Various studies have demonstrated that most if not all PAI scales do tend to show improvement with treatment (Friedman, 1995; Men Exploring New Directional Strategies [MENDS], 2002; Saper, Blank, & Chapman, 1995). Friedman (cited in Morey, 1996) performed a pre-post administration of the PAI with 25 patients during outpatient psychotherapy that had a median duration of 3 months. Friedman reported that 19 of the 21 scales of the PAI (excluding ICN) demonstrated statistically significant changes and found that the largest impact of psychotherapy could be observed in reduction of negative affect (ANX, DEP, ARD), improvement of self-esteem (PIM, RXR, BOR), and reduction of interpersonal and environmental turmoil (STR, BOR). The only PAI scale (other than INF, which would not be expected to change with treatment) that did not demonstrate a treatment effect was the full scale of MAN, but significant changes on MAN subscales did take place; MAN-G increased while MAN-I decreased, and the opposing changes in these two subscales canceled each other at the full-scale level.

Similar results were obtained in the MENDS (2002) study, which constitutes one of the largest-scale uses of the PAI as an outcome evaluation. This group studied an intervention developed by the MENDS group to address men's acute needs in the period following a divorce or separation. In an outcome study of 488 participants in this group, all PAI scales (again with the exception of INF and MAN) demonstrated highly significant improvement at posttreatment evaluation. The largest effects in this study appeared once again to involve reduction of negative affect (DEP, ANX, ARD), improved self-esteem (RXR, BOR), greater clarity of thought (SCZ, BOR), and reduction of interpersonal and environmental turmoil (STR, BOR, NON).

One interesting application of the PAI as an outcome measure was reported by Saper et al. (1995), who used the PAI to study treatment-related changes in a particular patient presenting with visual and auditory hallucinations that were refractory to conventional pharmacotherapy. The authors described a treatment that combined an imaginal exposure (implosion) treatment for the posttraumatic stress symptoms with fluphenazine medication. Saper et al. (1995) used the 11 clinical scales of the PAI and two treatment scales, SUI and AGG, as outcome measures. They reported two measures of treatment success: number of clinical scales reduced below 70t and number of scales that decreased following treatment. Significance testing was conducted in this case study by examining the binomial probability of the occurrence of each of these events. In their study, 12 of the 13 scales examined displayed decreased scores, and none of the seven scales that had been elevated before treatment were elevated above 70t following the intervention. The binomial probability that either of these outcomes will occur by chance was less than .01. These PAI changes were corroborated by mental status examination and staff observations at discharge. This use of the PAI is a valuable demonstration of how decisions about outcome and improvement can be made using a solid empirical foundation, even in the context of a case study.

🐟 TEST YOURSELF 🐟

1. **The PAS is a 160-item short form of the PAI.** True or False?

2. **The PAS p score**
   (a) has a mean of 50.
   (b) reflects the probability of at least one elevated scale on the PAI.
   (c) ranges from 1 to 10 elements.
   (d) can be interpreted as a percentile score.

3. **Conceptual indexes have been developed for all of the following except**
   (a) suicide potential.
   (b) violence potential.
   (c) adult attention deficit problems.
   (d) treatment process difficulties.

4. **The prediction of a difficult treatment is best made from**
   (a) RXR.
   (b) SOM.
   (c) NON.
   (d) TPI.

5. **The three scales most useful for understanding self-concept on the PAI include**
   (a) DOM, AGG, SUI.
   (b) NIM, PIM, BOR.
   (c) NON, PAR, ANT-E.
   (d) DEP-C, MAN-G, BOR-I.

6. **The PAI displays numerous correlations with most of the five-factor traits of normal personality, with the exception of**

   (a) Neuroticism.

   (b) Extroversion.

   (c) Openness to Experience.

   (d) Agreeableness.

7. **At the full-scale level, which clinical scale is least likely to display pre-post changes in treatment for most diagnostic groups?**

8. **What important profile element should be taken into account when interpreting indexes such as TPI, SPI, and VPI that involve scores from many different scales?**

9. **Why wouldn't a clinician administer the PAS and the PAI in the same sitting?**

Answers: 1. False; 2. b; 3. c; 4. d; 5. d; 6. c; 7. The MAN scale; 8. Degree of elevation on NIM; 9. All PAS items are included on the PAI.

Ten

ILLUSTRATIVE CASE REPORT

The construction of a case report for assessments involving the PAI requires the synthesis of the interpretive information provided in the preceding chapters with all available sources of information on the client. Although in some circumstances it may be possible to evaluate the PAI profile isolated from any other information about the case, it is typically not optimal to do so. The PAI is not intended to constitute the sole basis of any clinical decision and should always be considered to be one of numerous sources of hypotheses for professionals making decisions regarding screening, diagnoses, or treatments.

Although the structure of test reports may vary as a function of the nature of the assessment setting, they typically follow the following outline: First, some background information on the client is provided, including basic demographic information. Next, the referral question and pertinent history are provided. This section should include contextual aspects of the referral (e.g., Is this assessment court-mandated, and why? Is this a preemployment screening, and for what type of position?). This section should also present the reason for assessment from the client's perspective; chapter 2 discusses the therapeutic assessment strategy that encourages respondents to articulate their own goals for the assessment. The next section often provides behavioral observations of the client, including his or her overt approach to the evaluation and mental status during the assessment.

The next sections of the report address the testing, results, and interpretation. First, a section listing the relevant tests and procedures is provided. If different interpretive reports for the PAI are involved (for example, the standard clinical report and the public safety report), these reports should each be noted. Following this information, the interpretation of the test results is provided. Generally, it is best to integrate test results rather than present them serially; in this manner the convergence or divergence among different data can be more clearly described and reconciled. Although practices vary, this author prefers not to provide complete empirical results (e.g., listing all PAI scale *t* scores) in the report because the evaluating clinician should be responsible for interpreting the data, and typically the recipient of such reports is not qualified to make such interpretations. On occasion, it may be useful to reference a particular scale elevation, but it is typically more helpful to describe any result in terms of percentile ranks rather than *t* scores. In some instances describing the response to a particular item (such as a critical item) may also be helpful as an example, but the report should make clear that the interpretation does not hinge upon the response to any single item.

For presenting PAI information, the following outline often works well (see Rapid Reference 10.1): First, the validity of the test results is described to provide a context from which other interpretive statements must be considered. Second, the clinical features of the data are described, beginning with the most prominent but covering all features that appear to be clinically significant. Following this description are sections describing clients' perceptions of themselves and of the world around them. These sections are followed by a statement of the relevant diagnostic hypotheses (if any are applicable), using standard diagnostic codes. The final section provides treatment considerations and recommendations based on the formulation of the case.

The following case is presented to illustrate how PAI results can be presented in the format described in Rapid Reference 10.1. The test is interpreted in relative isolation from other clinical material to provide a clear focus for the basis of various interpretive statements; in routine clinical practice, these statements would also involve the synthesis of other test results and clinical data. Examples of other descriptions of PAI cases can be found in Morey and Henry (1994) and in Morey and Quigley (2002).

=== *Rapid Reference 10.1*

Sample Outline for PAI Report

I. Validity of test results

II. Clinical features and symptoms

III. View of the self and the external world

IV. Diagnostic hypotheses

V. Treatment considerations

THE CASE OF STEVE

Case Description

Steve was a 42-year-old married Caucasian man who presented to an inpatient substance abuse treatment program located at a veteran's hospital, seeking help with "problems with drinking and drugs." Steve was a Vietnam-era veteran who had seen substantial combat experience. He received a diagnosis of polysubstance abuse at intake, and a provisional diagnosis of antisocial personality disorder was also assigned. By his report, his level of functioning was adequate, but his occupational history was notable for its lack of success and his third marriage had significantly deteriorated in recent months.

Within the first few days of treatment, it became clear that Steve did not appear to be physiologically dependent on alcohol or other substances. In meetings, he tended not to be a very active participant. When pressed, he reported that he thought that his problems dated to his combat experiences, that he had not "felt right" since Vietnam and that he thought alcohol and drugs were mainly a way to dull his feelings about his experiences. The treatment staff were skeptical of Steve's description of his symptoms, and there was some suspicion—consistent with the antisocial personality disorder diagnosis—that Steve might be seeking combat-related disability pay. The substance abuse treatment staff thus requested a referral from psychological services to evaluate the possibility of a posttraumatic stress disorder diagnosis. This evaluation was conducted near the end of the first week of treatment, but shortly after the assessment (and before the consultation report was complete) Steve requested and was granted a discharge from the inpatient program with the recommendation that he pursue outpatient substance abuse treatment. At the time of feedback, the consulting psychologist noted that the testing revealed a number of significant concerns, but the treatment staff felt that discharge was justified because the level of substance involvement was not sufficient to keep Steve hospitalized against his will.

Approximately 1 week after his discharge, Steve was admitted to the inpatient psychiatric unit of the same hospital following a suicide attempt in which he had cut his wrists. This attempt had been precipitated by his wife's leaving him. This decision followed an argument in which Steve had returned to their home intoxicated, at which point the wife had confronted him about this behavior that occurred so soon after his being in treatment for substance problems. During this argument, he described losing his temper and hitting his wife a number of times, leading her to announce that she was moving out of the house and seeking a divorce. The suicide attempt followed shortly thereafter, after which Steve telephoned for an ambulance. During treatment in the psychiatric program, it came to light that his wife had insisted on the prior substance abuse treatment as a condition to remaining in the marriage because he often became abusive when he had been drinking or using drugs. During this treatment he also acknowledged that the physical abuse had been a recurrent pattern and that both previous marriages had ended due to his abusive and violent behavior.

The following sections follow the outline for presenting PAI results described in Rapid Reference 10.1. Steve's PAI full-scale profile is presented in Figure 10.1, the subscales are plotted in Figure 10.2, and supplemental profile indexes are listed in Table 10.1. The report is parenthetically annotated with references to scales that provide supportive evidence for the interpretive statements that are offered.

Validity of Test Results

The testing results provide a number of validity indicators that are designed to identify factors that could distort the results of testing. For example, the extent to which the respondent attended appropriately and responded consistently to the content of test items is evaluated. The respondent's scores suggest that he did attend appropriately to item content (INF) and responded in a consistent fashion to similar items (ICN).

The degree to which response styles may have affected or distorted the report of symptomatology on the inventory is also assessed. The score for these indicators fall in the normal range, suggesting that the respondent answered in a reasonably forthright manner and did not attempt to present an unrealistic or inaccurate impression that was either more negative (NIM, Rogers discriminant function, Malingering index) or more positive (PIM, Cashel discriminant function, Defensiveness index) than the clinical picture would warrant. The absence of any evidence suggesting malingering is particularly relevant, given the referral questions about the veracity of reported symptoms of posttraumatic stress. Also, it does not appear that he is likely to be underreporting his level of substance involvement (ALC and DRG estimates are very close to those observed).

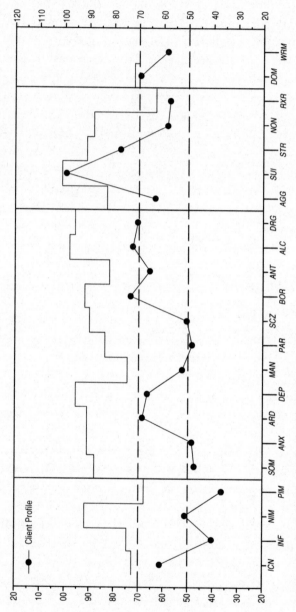

Figure 10.1 PAI Full-Scale Profile for Case Study

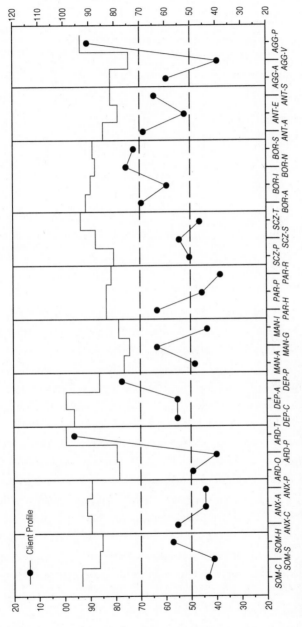

Figure 10.2 PAI Subscale Profile for Case Study

Table 10.1. Supplemental Profile Indexes for Case Study

Supplemental index	Value	*t* score
Defensiveness index	3	51
Cashel discriminant function	138.67	50
Malingering index	0	44
Rogers discriminant function	−1.44	46
Suicide Potential index	1.0	71
Violence Potential index	8	79
Treatment Process index	7	81
ALC estimated score	71	(1*t* lower than ALC)
DRG estimated score	72	(2*t* higher than DRG)

Clinical Features

A broad range of significant clinical features and the possibility of multiple diagnoses (three clinical scales above 70*t*) mark Steve's clinical profile. The configuration of the clinical scales suggests a person with a history of drinking problems who is impulsive and affectively labile (BOR/ALC profile code type). His drinking may be part of a more general pattern of self-destructive behavior (concurrent elevations on BOR-S, SUI). His interpersonal relationships are likely to be volatile and characterized by marked conflict (BOR-N), and even the close relationships that have been maintained will have suffered some strain from his controlling and hostile (DOM, AGG) style of interaction; these relationships will likely have deteriorated even further as a consequence of his drinking (ALC). He is likely to be particularly disinhibited under the influence of alcohol (ANT-S), and he may display particularly poor judgment and demonstrate other acting-out (ANT-A, AGG-P) behaviors while he is intoxicated.

Steve describes a number of problematic personality traits. It is likely that he has a history of involvement in intense and volatile relationships and tends to be preoccupied with consistent fears of being abandoned or rejected by those around him (BOR, BOR-N). He is also impulsive and prone to behaviors that are likely to be self-harmful or self-destructive, such as those involving spending, sex, or substance abuse (BOR-S, ALC, DRG). This pattern of impulsivity and volatile relationships may place him at increased risk for self-mutilation or suicidal behavior, particularly during times of marked conflict in relationships (BOR-S, SUI). Steve also reports that his use of alcohol and drugs has had a negative impact on his life. Problems related to substance abuse are likely, including difficulties in interpersonal relationships, difficulties on the job, and possible health complications (ALC, DRG).

Steve reports that he has experienced disturbing traumatic events in the past—events that continue to distress him and that produce recurrent episodes of anxiety (ARD-T). He describes a variety of symptoms that may be a part of a stress reaction pattern, including possible disturbances in sleep pattern (DEP-P), heightened vigilance and stress reactivity (STR, PAR-H), and problems with anger control (AGG-P, AGG-A).

Self-Concept

Steve's self-concept appears to involve a self-evaluation that has both positive and negative aspects (MAN-G and DEP-C both above average). His attitudes about himself may vary from states of pessimism and self-doubt to periods of relative self-confidence and self-satisfaction. Fluctuations in self-esteem are likely to be observed in reaction to his current circumstances, to a degree greater than that experienced by most adults (BOR), and relationship stressors are particularly likely to have an impact on his self-concept (BOR-N). During such stressful times, he is likely to be self-critical and uncertain of his future directions (BOR).

Interpersonal and Social Environment

Steve's interpersonal style seems best characterized as involving very strong needs for attention and affiliation (high DOM, above-average WRM). He is likely to be perceived by others as having strong needs for control (DOM); these needs may be particularly salient in social interactions, which he may seek to control to meet his own needs (DOM, BOR-N). Although this control may be intended as helpful by the respondent (WRM), he may also attempt to control others through intimidation (AGG-P, Violence Potential index) or exploitation (ANT-A), and it is likely that his controlling behavior is not viewed positively by those around him.

Steve's responses concerning his social environment indicate that he is likely to be experiencing notable stress and turmoil in a number of major life areas (STR). A review of his current employment situation, financial status, and in particular family and close relationships (BOR-N) will clarify the importance of these in the overall clinical picture. At the moment, he reports that he has supportive relationships that may serve as some buffer against the effects of this stress (NON within normal limits, although this score preceded the separation).

DSM-IV Diagnostic Possibilities

Axis I Diagnostic Considerations:

309.81	Posttraumatic stress disorder
305.00	Alcohol abuse
312.34	Intermittent explosive disorder
305.90	Psychoactive substance abuse
300.4	Dysthymic disorder

Axis I Rule Out:

296.20	Major depressive disorder, single episode, unspecified

Axis II Diagnostic Considerations:

301.7	Antisocial personality disorder
301.83	Borderline personality disorder

Treatment Considerations and Recommendations

Steve's test results suggest a number of significant aspects of the clinical picture that can complicate treatment efforts. Most notable is that Steve reports experiencing intense and recurrent suicidal thoughts at a level typical of individuals placed on suicide precautions (SUI). His potential for suicide should be evaluated immediately, and appropriate interventions should be implemented without delay. A careful follow-up regarding the details of his suicidal thoughts and the potential for suicidal behavior is warranted, as is an evaluation of his life circumstances and available support systems as potential mediating factors (Suicide Potential index).

Also, Steve describes himself as prone to more extreme displays of anger, including damage to property and threats to assault others (AGG-P, Violence Potential index). These outbursts may be unexpected and take others by surprise (AGG-P above average, AGG-V below average). Given his report of conflictual close relationships (BOR-N) and his strong needs for control (DOM), a careful follow-up of his potential for violent behavior is recommended. It is likely that those closest to him are particularly likely to be intimidated by his temper and by his potential for violence.

It is important to note that Steve's interest in and motivation for treatment is well below what is typical of individuals being seen in treatment settings (RXR). His responses suggest that he is generally satisfied with himself as he is (MAN-G, relatively low DEP and ANX) and that he sees little need for changes in his behavior, despite his recognition that a number of areas of his life are not going well at this time; this is of particular concern, given his marked suicidal ideation (SUI), because he may be unlikely to alert or seek help from caregivers (RXR) during times of particular crisis.

The nature of Steve's problems suggests that treatment will be challenging, with a difficult treatment process and the probability of frequent reversals (Treatment Process index). Particular areas of attention or concern in the early stages of treatment may involve a defensive resistance because he may be reluctant to discuss or acknowledge his involvement in his problems; therefore, he may be at risk for early termination (RXR). Furthermore, he may have initial difficulty in placing trust in a treating professional as part of his more general problems in close relationships (BOR-N, PAR-H).

★ TEST YOURSELF ★

1. **It is a good idea to include all PAI t scores in the report to assist the referral sources in understanding test results.** True or False?

2. **Beginning a description of test results with a comment on test-taking attitudes and validity helps provide a context for the rest of the results.** True or False?

3. **Specific PAI results should be described separately from results obtained using other tests or sources of information.** True or False?

Answers: 1. False; 2. True; 3. False

References

Ackerman, S. J., Hilsenroth, M. J., Baity, M. R., & Blagys, M. D. (2000). Interaction of therapeutic process and alliance during psychological assessment. *Journal of Personality Assessment, 75,* 82–109.

Akiskal, H. S., Yerevanian, B. I., & Davis, G. C. (1985). The nosological status of borderline personality: Clinical and polysomnographic study. *American Journal of Psychiatry, 142,* 192–198.

Alcoholics Anonymous. (1937). *Alcoholics anonymous.* New York: Author.

Alterman, A. I., Zaballero, A. R., Lin, M. M., Siddiqui, N., Brown, L. S., Rutherford, M. J., et al. (1995). Personality Assessment Inventory (PAI) scores of lower-socioeconomic African American and Latino methadone maintenance patients. *Assessment, 2,* 91–100.

Andraesen, N. C. (1985). Positive vs. negative symptoms: A critical evaluation. *Schizophrenia Bulletin, 11,* 380–389.

Angrist, B., Rotrosen, J., & Gershon, S. (1980). Differential effects of amphetamine and neuroleptics on negative vs. positive symptoms in schizophrenia. *Psychopharmacology, 72,* 17–19.

Baer, R. A., & Wetter, M. W. (1997). Effects of information about validity scales on underreporting of symptoms on the Personality Assessment Inventory. *Journal of Personality Assessment, 68,* 402–413.

Bagby, R. M., Nicholson, R. A., Bacchiochi, J. R., Ryder, A. G., & Bury, A. S. (2002). The predictive capacity of the MMPI-2 and PAI validity scales and indexes to detect coached and uncoached feigning. *Journal of Personality Assessment, 78,* 69–86.

Ban, T. A. (1982). Chronic schizophrenias: A guide to Leonhard's classification. *Comprehensive Psychiatry, 23,* 155–169.

Bandura, A. (1977). Self-efficacy: Toward a unifying theory of behavioral change. *Psychological Review, 84,* 191–215.

Beck, A. T., & Emery, G. (1979). *Cognitive therapy of anxiety and phobic disorders.* New York: Guilford.

Bell-Pringle, V. J., Pate, J. L., & Brown, R. C. (1997). Assessment of borderline personality disorder using the MMPI-2 and the Personality Assessment Inventory. *Assessment, 4,* 131–139.

Belter, R. W., & Piotrowski, C. (2001). Current status of doctoral-level training in psychological testing. *Journal of Clinical Psychology, 57,* 717–726.

Boccaccini, M. T., & Brodsky, S. L. (1999). Diagnostic test usage by forensic psychologists in emotional injury cases. *Professional Psychology: Research and Practice, 30,* 253–259.

Boyle, G. J., & Lennon, T. J. (1994). Examination of the reliability and validity of the Personality Assessment Inventory. *Journal of Psychopathology and Behavior Assessment, 16,* 173–188.

Byrne, D. (1961). The repression-sensitization scale: Rationale, reliability, and validity. *Journal of Personality, 29,* 334–349.

Cashel, M. L., Rogers, R., Sewell, K., & Martin-Cannici, C. (1995). The Personality Assessment Inventory and the detection of defensiveness. *Assessment, 2*, 333–342.

Cherepon, J. A., & Prinzhorn, B. (1994). The Personality Assessment Inventory (PAI) profiles of adult female abuse survivors. *Assessment, 1*, 393–400.

Cleckley, H. (1941). *The mask of sanity.* St. Louis, MO: Mosby.

Costa, P. T., & McCrae, R. R. (1992a). Normal personality in clinical practice: The NEO Personality Inventory. *Psychological Assessment, 4*, 5–13.

Costa, P. T., & McCrae, R. R. (1992b). *Professional manual: Revised NEO Personality Inventory (NEO-PI-R) and NEO Five-Factor Inventory (NEO-FFI).* Odessa, FL: Psychological Assessment Resources.

Cronbach, L. J., & Meehl, P. E. (1955). Construct validity in psychological tests. *Psychological Bulletin, 52*, 281–302.

Crowne, D. P., & Marlowe, D. (1960). A new scale of social desirability independent of psychopathology. *Journal of Consulting Psychology, 24*, 349–354.

Deffenbacher, J. L. (1992). Trait anger: Theory, findings, and implications. In C. D. Spielberger & J. N. Butcher (Eds.), *Advances in personality assessment* (Vol. 9, pp. 177–201). Hillsdale, NJ: Erlbaum.

Domken, M., Scott, J., & Kelly, P. (1994). What factors predict discrepancies between self and observer ratings of depression? *Journal of Affective Disorders, 31*, 253–259.

Edens, J. F., Cruise, K. R., & Buffington-Vollum, J. K. (2001). Forensic and correctional applications of the Personality Assessment Inventory. *Behavioral Sciences and the Law, 19*, 519–543.

Edens, J. F., Hart, S. D., Johnson, D. W., Johnson, J., & Olver, M. E. (2000). Use of the PAI to assess psychopathy in offender populations. *Psychological Assessment, 12*, 132–139.

Fals-Stewart, W. (1996). The ability of individuals with psychoactive substance use disorders to escape detection by the Personality Assessment Inventory. *Psychological Assessment, 8*, 60–68.

Fals-Stewart, W., & Lucente, S. (1997). Identifying positive dissimulation substance-abusing individuals on the Personality Assessment Inventory: A cross-validation study. *Journal of Personality Assessment, 68*, 455–469.

Fantoni-Salvador, P., & Rogers, R. (1997). Spanish versions of the MMPI-2 and PAI: An investigation of concurrent validity with Hispanic patients. *Assessment, 4*, 29–39.

Finger, M. S., & Ones, D. S. (1999). Psychometric equivalence of the computer and booklet forms of the MMPI: A meta-analysis. *Psychological Assessment, 11*, 58–66.

Finn, S. E., & Tonsager, M. E. (1992). Therapeutic effects of providing MMPI-2 test feedback to college students awaiting therapy. *Psychological Assessment, 4*, 278–287.

Finn, S. E., & Tonsager, M. E. (1997). Information-gathering and therapeutic models of assessment: Complementary paradigms. *Psychological Assessment, 9*, 374–385.

Finn, S. P. (1996). *Manual for using the MMPI-2 as a therapeutic intervention.* Minneapolis: University of Minnesota Press.

Fischer, C. T. (1994). *Individualizing psychological assessment.* Hillsdale, NJ: Erlbaum.

Friedman, P. H. (1995). *Change in psychotherapy: Foundation for Well-Being research bulletin 106.* Plymouth Meeting, PA: Foundation for Well Being.

Gaies, L. A. (1993). Malingering of depression on the Personality Assessment Inventory. (Doctoral dissertation, University of South Florida, 1993). *Dissertation Abstracts International, 55*, 6711.

Grinker, R. R., Werble, B., & Drye, R. C. (1968). *The borderline syndrome*. New York: Basic Books.

Goodwin, F. K., & Jamison, K. R. (1990). *Manic-depressive illness*. New York: Oxford University Press.

Haley, R. W., Kurt, T. L., & Hom, J. (1997). Is there a Gulf War syndrome? Searching for syndromes by factor analysis of symptoms. *Journal of the American Medical Association, 277,* 215–222.

Hare, R. D. (1985). Comparison of procedures for the assessment of psychopathy. *Journal of Consulting and Clinical Psychology, 53,* 7–16.

Hare, R. D., Harpur, T. J., Hakstian, A. R., Forth, Hart, & Newman. (1990). The revised Psychopathy Checklist: Reliability and factor structure. *Psychological Assessment, 2,* 338–341.

Hart, S. D., Cox, D. N., & Hare, R. D. (1995). *Psychopathy Checklist: Screening version*. Toronto, Ontario, Canada: Multi-Health Systems.

Hart, S. D., & Hare, R. D. (1989). Discriminant validity of the Psychopathy Checklist in a forensic psychiatric population. *Psychological Assessment, 1,* 211–218.

Hart, S. D., Kropp, P. R., & Hare, R. D. (1988). Performance of male psychopaths following conditional release from prison. *Journal of Consulting and Clinical Psychology, 56,* 227–232.

Helmes, E. (1993). A modern instrument for evaluating psychopathology: The Personality Assessment Inventory professional manual. *Journal of Personality Assessment, 61,* 414–417.

Herman, J. L., Perry, J. C., & Van der Kolk, B. A. (1989). Childhood trauma in borderline personality disorder. *American Journal of Psychiatry, 146,* 490–495.

Hurt, S. W., & Clarkin, J. F. (1990). Borderline personality disorder: Prototypic typology and the development of treatment manuals. *Psychiatric Annals, 20,* 13–18.

Jackson, D. N. (1971). The dynamics of structured personality tests. *Psychological Review, 78,* 229–248.

Kernberg, O. F. (1975). *Borderline conditions and pathological narcissism*. New York: Jason Aronson.

Koksal, F., & Power, K. G. (1990). Four systems anxiety questionnaire (FSAQ): A self-report measure of somatic, cognitive, behavioral, and feeling components. *Journal of Personality Assessment, 54,* 534–545.

Lang, P. J. (1971). The application of psychophysiological methods. In S. Garfield & A. Bergin (Eds.), *Handbook of psychotherapy and behavior change* (pp. 75–125). New York: Wiley.

Leary, T. (1957). *Interpersonal diagnosis of personality*. New York: Ronald.

Loevinger, J. (1957). Objective tests as instruments of psychological theory. *Psychological Reports, 3,* 635–694.

Loranger, A. W., Susman, V. L., Oldham, J. M., & Russakoff, L. M. (1987). The Personality Disorder Examination: A preliminary report. *Journal of Personality Disorders, 1,* 1–13.

Meehl, P. E., & Rosen, A. (1955). Antecedent probability and the efficiency of psychometric signs, patterns, or cutting scores. *Psychological Bulletin, 52,* 194–216.

Men Exploring New Directional Strategies. (2002). *Assessment outcomes of MENDS clients*. Brisbane, Australia: Author.

Moran, P. W., & Lambert, M. J. (1983). A review of current assessment tools for monitoring change in depression. In M. J. Lambert, E. R. Christensen, & S. S. DeJulio (Eds.), *The measurement of psychotherapy outcome in research and evaluation* (pp. 263–303). New York: Wiley.

Morey, L. C. (1989, August). *Borderline personality: Search for core elements of the concept.* Paper presented at the meetings of the American Psychological Association, New Orleans, LA.

Morey, L. C. (1991). *The Personality Assessment Inventory professional manual.* Odessa, FL: Psychological Assessment Resources.

Morey, L. C. (1995). Critical issues in construct validation. *Journal of Psychopathology and Behavioral Assessment, 17,* 393–402.

Morey, L. C. (1996). *An interpretive guide to the Personality Assessment Inventory.* Odessa, FL: Psychological Assessment Resources.

Morey, L. C. (1997). *The Personality Assessment Screener: Professional manual.* Odessa, FL: Psychological Assessment Resources.

Morey, L. C. (1999). The Personality Assessment Inventory. In M. Maruish (Ed.), *Psychological testing: Treatment planning and outcome assessment* (2nd ed.). Hillsdale, NJ: Erlbaum.

Morey, L. C. (2000). *PAI software portfolio manual.* Odessa, FL: Psychological Assessment Resources.

Morey, L. C., & Glutting, J. H. (1994). The Personality Assessment Inventory: Correlates with normal and abnormal personality. In S. Strack & M. Lorr (Eds.), *Differentiating normal and abnormal personality* (pp. 402–420). New York: Springer.

Morey, L. C., & Henry, W. (1994). Personality Assessment Inventory. In M. Maruish (Ed.), *The use of psychological testing for treatment planning and outcome assessment* (pp. 185–216). Hillsdale, NJ: Erlbaum.

Morey, L. C., & Lanier, V. W. (1998). Operating characteristics for six response distortion indicators for the Personality Assessment Inventory. *Assessment, 5,* 203–214.

Morey, L. C., & Quigley, B. D. (2002). The use of the Personality Assessment Inventory (PAI) to assess offenders. *International Journal of Offender Therapy and Comparative Criminology, 46,* 333–349.

Newman, M., & Greenway, P. (1997). Therapeutic effects of providing MMPI-2 test feedback to clients at a university counseling service: A collaborative approach. *Psychological Assessment, 9,* 122–131.

Osborne, D. (1994, April). *Use of the Personality Assessment Inventory with a medical population.* Paper presented at the meetings of the Rocky Mountain Psychological Association, Denver, CO.

Peebles, J., & Moore, R. J. (1998). Detecting socially desirable responding with the Personality Assessment Inventory: The Positive Impression Management scale and the Defensiveness index. *Journal of Clinical Psychology, 54,* 621–628.

Piotrowski, C., & Belter, R. W. (1999). Internship training in psychological assessment: Has managed care had an impact? *Assessment, 6,* 381–389.

Riley, W. T., & Treiber, F. A. (1989). The validity of multidimensional self-report anger and hostility measures. *Journal of Clinical Psychology, 45,* 397–404.

Roberts, M. D., Thompson, J. A., & Johnson, M. (2000). *PAI law enforcement, corrections, and public safety selection report module.* Odessa, FL: Psychological Assessment Resources.

Rogers, R., Bagby, R. M., & Dickens, S. E. (1992). *Structured Interview of Reported Symptoms: Professional manual.* Odessa, FL: Psychological Assessment Resources.

Rogers, R., Flores, J., Ustad, K., & Sewell, K. W. (1995). Initial validation of the Personality Assessment Inventory–Spanish Version with clients from Mexican American communities. *Journal of Personality Assessment, 64,* 340–348.

Rogers, R., Ornduff, S. R., & Sewell, K. (1993). Feigning specific disorders: A study of the Personality Assessment Inventory (PAI). *Journal of Personality Assessment, 60,* 554–560.

Rogers, R., Sewell, K. W., Morey, L. C., & Ustad, K. L. (1996). Detection of feigned mental disorders on the Personality Assessment Inventory: A discriminant analysis. *Journal of Personality Assessment, 67,* 629–640.

Rogers, R., Ustad, K. L., & Salekin, R. T. (1998). Convergent validity of the personality assessment inventory: A study of emergency referrals in a correctional setting. *Assessment, 5,* 3–12.

Rush, A. J., Hiser, W., & Giles, D. E. (1987). A comparison of self-reported versus clinician-rated symptoms in depression. *Journal of Clinical Psychiatry, 48,* 246–248.

Salekin, R. T., Rogers, R., & Sewell, K. W. (1997). Construct validity of psychopathy in a female offender sample: A multitrait-multimethod evaluation. *Journal of Abnormal Psychology, 106,* 576–585.

Salekin, R. T., Rogers, R., Ustad, K. L., & Sewell, K. W. (1998). Psychopathy and recidivism among female inmates. *Law & Human Behavior, 22,* 109–128.

Saper, Z., Blank, M. K., & Chapman, L. (1995). Implosive therapy as an adjunctive treatment in a psychotic disorder: A case report. *Journal of Behavior Therapy and Experimental Psychiatry, 26,* 157–160.

Schinka, J. A., & Borum, R. (1993). Readability of adult psychopathology inventories. *Psychological Assessment, 5,* 384–386.

Schlosser, B. (1992). Computer assisted practice. *The Independent Practitioner, 12,* 12–15.

Schneidman, E. S. (1985). *Definitions of suicide.* New York: Wiley.

Scragg, P., Bor, R., & Mendham, M. C. (2000). Feigning post-traumatic stress disorder on the PAI. *Clinical Psychology and Psychotherapy, 7,* 155–160.

Serin, R., Peters, R. D., & Barbaree, H. E. (1990). Predictors of psychopathy and release outcome in a criminal population. *Psychological Assessment, 2,* 419–422.

Trull, T. J. (1995). Borderline personality disorder features in nonclinical young adults: 1. Identification and validation. *Psychological Assessment, 7,* 33–41.

Trull, T. J., Useda, J. D., Conforti, K., & Doan, B. T. (1997). Borderline personality disorder features in nonclinical young adults: 2. Two-year outcome. *Journal of Abnormal Psychology, 106,* 307–314.

Wang, E. W., & Diamond, P. M. (1999). Empirically identifying factors related to violence risk in corrections. *Behavioral Sciences & the Law, 17,* 377–389.

Wang, E. W., Rogers, R., Giles, C. L., Diamond, P. M., Herrington-Wang, L. E., & Taylor, E. R. (1997). A pilot study of the Personality Assessment Inventory (PAI) in corrections: Assessment of malingering, suicide risk, and aggression in male inmates. *Behavioral Sciences & the Law, 15,* 469–482.

Yudofsky, S. C., Silver, J. M., Jackson, W., Endicott, J., & Williams, D. (1986). The Overt Aggression Scale for the objective rating of verbal and physical aggression. *American Journal of Psychiatry, 143,* 35–39.

Zajonc, R. B. (1980). Feeling and thinking: Preferences need no inferences. *American Psychologist, 35,* 151–175.

Annotated Bibliography

Ackerman, S. J., Hilsenroth, M. J., Baity, M. R., & Blagys, M. D. (2000). Interaction of therapeutic process and alliance during psychological assessment. *Journal of Personality Assessment, 75,* 82–109.

This important paper highlights the therapeutic potential of PAI-based assessment. This study examined the interaction between therapeutic alliance and in-session process during the assessment phase of treatment utilizing a collaborative therapeutic assessment model that included the PAI. Two patient groups received different assessment strategies: a therapeutic assessment group (n = 38) versus a traditional information-gathering model (n = 90) of assessment. The results of this study indicated that the use of the therapeutic assessment model may decrease the number of patients who terminate treatment against medical advice. The therapeutic alliance developed during the assessment was also found to be related to alliance early in psychotherapy.

Cashel, M. L., Rogers, R., Sewell, K., & Martin-Cannici, C. (1995). The Personality Assessment Inventory and the detection of defensiveness. *Assessment, 2,* 333–342.

An important article that provided the rationale for and described the development of the equation known as the Cashel discriminant function. This paper examined the use of PAI validity scales to detect defensiveness in 45 male criminals and 38 male undergraduate psychology students who were provided with incentives to complete the PAI under two conditions—standard instructions and experimental instructions—to feign a specific, positive role. The study replicated the optimal cutting score for PIM that was originally presented in the test manual. The Cashel function involved a stepwise discriminant function analysis, which significantly predicted honest and feigning conditions with a hit rate of 84.1%. In Morey (1996), a cross-validation of this function yielded nearly identical results.

Edens, J. F., Cruise, K. R., & Buffington-Vollum, J. K. (2001). Forensic and correctional applications of the Personality Assessment Inventory. *Behavioral Sciences and the Law, 19,* 519–543.

One of the most popular applications of the PAI involves its use in clinical assessment in forensic and correctional contexts. This paper provides a comprehensive review of the psychometric properties of the PAI—specifically in reference to its ability to assess factors relevant to forensic decision-making as well as its utility to provide clinically relevant information about correctional populations in general.

Fals-Stewart, W. (1996). The ability of individuals with psychoactive substance use disorders to escape detection by the Personality Assessment Inventory. *Psychological Assessment, 8,* 60–68.

Fals-Stewart, W., & Lucente, S. (1997). Identifying positive dissimulation substance-abusing individuals on the Personality Assessment Inventory: A cross-validation study. *Journal of Personality Assessment, 68,* 455–469.

Fals-Stewart provided the first documentation of the ability of the PAI to detect substance abuse denial. Patients receiving treatment for drug abuse who were instructed to respond honestly (n = 59) had significantly higher scores on the PAI scales measuring problems with alcohol and other drug use than did (a) patients instructed to respond defensively (n = 59), (b) respondents suspected of abusing psychoactive substances who were referred for an evaluation by the criminal justice system and who had reasons to conceal their drug use (n = 59), and (c) respondents from a nonclinical control group (n =59). Although the PIM scale was able to identify more than 80% of the problematic responders, a discriminant function proved to provide somewhat better discrimination. However, in the follow-up 1997 investigation, the discriminant function displayed considerable shrinkage, while PIM performed similarly to the results in the 1996 study.

Morey, L. C. (1996). *An interpretive guide to the Personality Assessment Inventory.* Odessa, FL: Psychological Assessment Resources.

This book reflects a comprehensive guide to the interpretation of the PAI. The rationale and development of many of the supplemental indexes for the PAI—including the Defensiveness index, the Malingering index, the Treatment Process index, the Suicide and Violence Potential index, and the substance abuse estimation procedures—are described in this book.

Morey, L. C., & Lanier, V. W. (1998). Operating characteristics for six response distortion indicators for the Personality Assessment Inventory. *Assessment, 5,* 203–214.

This paper was the first to examine various PAI distortion indicators using receiver operating characteristic curve analyses. The characteristics of six different indicators of response distortion on the PAI were evaluated by having college students complete the PAI under positive impression management, malingering, and honest responding conditions. Protocols of students asked to malinger were compared with those of actual clinical patients, while protocols of students asked to manage their impression in a positive direction were compared with those of students asked to respond honestly. All six indicators demonstrated the ability to distinguish between actual and feigned responding. The Rogers discriminant function was particularly effective in identifying malingering. Although Cashel function displayed significant validity, it was less effective than were other measures in identifying positive impression management, although it appeared to also have promise as an indicator of malingering.

Piotrowski, C. (2000). How popular is the Personality Assessment Inventory in practice and training? *Psychological Reports, 86,* 65–66.

Piotrowski reviewed recent survey data and concludes that the PAI ranks among the most frequently used objective personality tests in practice and clinical training. He states that the future popularity of the instrument will largely be based on whether this personality test can offer a substantial improvement in clinical utility over alternative instruments, and on the deleterious effects of many managed health care policies toward personality assessment in general.

Rogers, R., Sewell, K. W., Morey, L. C., & Ustad, K. L. (1996). Detection of feigned mental disorders on the Personality Assessment Inventory: A discriminant analysis. *Journal of Personality Assessment, 67,* 629–640.

This important article describes the development of the equation known as the Rogers discriminant function. The paper investigated the effectiveness of the PAI in detecting participants feigning three specific disorders: schizophrenia, major depression, and generalized anxiety disorder. The authors tested the PAI validity scales on 166 naive and 80 sophisticated (doctoral psychology students with

1 week preparation) participants, comparing their results to those of persons with the designated disorders: schizophrenia (n = 45), major depression (n = 136), and generalized anxiety disorder (n = 40). Although the validity scales were effective, they proved to be better at identifying feigning in naive simulators than in their sophisticated counterparts. The authors then developed and cross-validated a discriminant analysis that yielded a hit rate of over 80% that was maintained in the cross-validation sample, regardless of the particular feigned disorder or the sophistication of the simulators.

Rogers, R., Ustad, K. L., & Salekin, R. T. (1998). Convergent validity of the Personality Assessment Inventory: A study of emergency referrals in a correctional setting. *Assessment, 5,* 3–12.

An important validity study involving clinician markers, this article examined the convergent validity of the PAI with a variety of measures and behaviors in 80 emergency referrals in a metropolitan correctional facility. Validating markers included the Schedule of Affective Disorders and Schizophrenia (SADS), the Structured Interview of Reported Symptoms (SIRS), and the Suicide Probability Scale (SPS). Overall, results indicated moderate to good convergent validity for screening for feigned profiles, establishing clinical correlates of common disorders, and evaluating the potential for suicidal ideation.

Wang, E. W., Rogers, R., Giles, C. L., Diamond, P. M., Herrington-Wang, L. E., & Taylor, E. R. (1997). A pilot study of the Personality Assessment Inventory (PAI) in corrections: Assessment of malingering, suicide risk, and aggression in male inmates. *Behavioral Sciences & the Law, 15,* 469–482.

One of the first studies to provide additional validity evidence for various PAI supplemental indexes. Wang et al. examined the usefulness of the PAI for assessing problematic behaviors in a corrections-based psychiatric hospital. Selected PAI scales and indexes were compared to evidence of malingering on the SIRS, occurrence of suicidal threats and gestures, and staff ratings of aggression on the Overt Aggression Scale (OAS). In general, results supported the use of the PAI for the assessment of these problematic behaviors.

Index

About the Author

Dr. Leslie C. Morey is professor of psychology at Texas A&M University. He received his doctorate in clinical psychology from the University of Florida and has served on the faculty at Vanderbilt University, Harvard Medical School, the Yale University School of Medicine, and the University of Tulsa. He has published more than 100 articles, books, and chapters on the assessment and diagnosis of mental disorders. He is the author of the Personality Assessment Inventory, the Personality Assessment Screener, and the *Interpretive Guide to the Personality Assessment Inventory;* serves as the associate editor of the journal *Assessment;* and has conducted numerous training seminars and workshops on the PAI for the past decade.

CPSIA information can be obtained at www.ICGtesting.com
Printed in the USA
BVOW02n0747060115

382004BV00012B/20/P